A TRACE OF DESERT WATERS

SARATOGA SPRINGS IN DEATH VALLEY
Habitat of the pupfish species *C. nevadensis nevadensis.*

A Trace of Desert Waters
THE GREAT BASIN STORY

by

SAMUEL G. HOUGHTON

*The beasts of the field shall honor me, the dragons and
the owls: because I give waters in the wilderness,
and rivers in the desert, to give drink to
my people, my chosen.*—Isaiah 43:20

Howe Brothers

SALT LAKE CITY   CHICAGO

published by
HOWE BROTHERS
Salt Lake City, Utah

Manufactured in the United States of America

First Howe Brothers printing 1986

This book was first published in 1976 by Arthur H. Clark Co.

LIBRARY OF CONGRESS CATALOGING-IN-PUBLICATION DATA
Houghton, Samuel G. (Samuel Gilbert), 1902-1975.
    A trace of desert waters.

    Reprint. Originally published: Glendale, Calif. : A.H.
Clark Co., 1976.
    Bibliography: p.
    Includes index.
    1. Lakes—Great Basin. 2. Rivers—Great Basin.
3. Great Basin—History. 4. Natural history—Great Basin.
5. Water-supply—Great Basin. I. Title.
[GB705.G72H68 1986] 979 86-21054
ISBN 0-935704-35-3 (pbk.)

Contents

Great Basin Portfolio

Black and White Illustrations

All photos by the author unless otherwise noted

Maps

All maps drawn by Susan Nichols

Foreword

A *Trace of Desert Waters* will probably become a western desert classic. It is devoted to explaining and describing the Great Basin, one of the American West's fascinating but little known anomalies. An enormous 7 percent of the land area of the United States, the Basin is an authentic desert. But it is important because it is unique: a huge area (parts of four western states) with no outlet to the sea. Within it there is a complex series of smaller basins where separate, quite discrete water systems (streams, lakes, ponds, marshes) are found. This book describes all these systems, covering the geology, hydrology, archaeology, history, and local climate of each area. Equal attention is given to natural history. The exploits of the men who explored, prospected for minerals, or studied wildlife are noted. But the central fact of the Basin is that water is scarce. Water dominates the book.

Many of us feel the same appreciation for the Great Basin and its wide physiographic and environmental diversity that Sam Houghton felt. Possibly, someone else could have written a comparable book, but no one else could have written this one, because Sam's book somehow manages to capture or reflect the essence of his great concern for the region. Sam was a responsible citizen, not merely of Nevada, where he lived, but of the Desert West. He was a man whose curiosity about the land and desire to conserve and enjoy it led to an intense environmental consciousness — a natural and inevitable consequence of his involvement. He was, moreover, an intelligent and lively conversationalist whose enthusiasms were strong and infectious. All of this shows in the book.

I met him during the period of research on *A Trace of Desert Waters* and came to appreciate the excitement a new insight or unexpected new data afforded him. So, since the book gave him so much pleasure in the writing (he never saw a printed copy) but especially because it is an honest, competent, well-organized collection of solid information, it richly deserves a second printing and a bigger audience. It has something for everyone who observes the outdoors or appreciates the richness and diversity of mountains and deserts. Those who read it and become acquainted with its wealth of Great Basin lore will soon come to appreciate the strength of Houghton's personality, as well as his dedication to the West.

It was my good fortune to provide a little help during the research. Sam doggedly worked his way through the monographs and articles I had recommended to help him understand the prehistory of the Great Basin and environs. For several years after we became acquainted, he visited Salt Lake City and observed the activity at the Utah Archeological Research Laboratory. As a result, he donated modest but regular amounts of money for me to divert to needy, deserving students. With those funds, I was able to assist eight or ten students; Sam steadfastly refused to allow me to reveal his generosity.

Small wonder that I respected Sam and feel a sense of real indebtedness to him. Naturally, I was honored by Edda Houghton's (now Morrison) invitation to write a short foreword to the second edition of her late husband's work and found it a pleasure to respond. I hope she approves of what I have written. I hope Sam would too.

JESSE D. JENNINGS
Professor of Anthropology
University of Utah
University of Oregon

Publisher's Preface

When Samuel Houghton completed *A Trace of Desert Waters: The Great Basin Story* in 1975, he, of course, could not foresee the events that would have a significant impact on the region in the following years. A decade later, we can only wish that he were here to bring the Great Basin story up to date. He is not; he passed away in October, 1975, before his book was released.

When Howe Brothers decided to reprint the book in a paperback edition, hoping that it would reach a wider audience, we considered asking someone to revise the text to bring it up to date. After all, the always remote and underpublicized Great Basin probably had been in the news more frequently in the decade since 1975 than during any previous decade other than the years of the Comstock Lode. On the one hand, a government that already seemed to consider the Basin one giant weapons test range decided to turn much of it into an enormous shell game with MX missiles, only to have its mind changed by an unlikely alliance among Indians, antinuclear activists, cowboys, conservationists, and the Mormon church. On the other hand, for a while those same Indians, Western Shoshones, seemed likely, based upon a century-and-a-quarter-old treaty, to legally reclaim a vast segment of the central Great Basin. Then, in 1983, the natural environment itself, not the people using and occupying it, created the biggest headlines when the wet cycle that Mr. Houghton had seen signs of in 1974 (see page 239) hit full stride. Record precipitation radically increased stream flow and the size of many lakes, notably the Great Salt Lake. It even restored such seemingly permanently dry lakes as Sevier Lake, and it caused major flooding, which included the spectacle of rivers running down main thoroughfares of Salt Lake City and other towns. Samuel Houghton emphasized the important role water had played in the Great Basin since the era when Pleistocene lakes first had such a lasting impact on the Great Basin's landscape. He might have enjoyed the vivid reminders during the years since 1983 of those ancient soggy days.

Time has brought elaboration and change to other things he discussed: for example, it brought the indemnification of Japanese-Americans who were uprooted and confined during World War II in two Great Basin camps, Manzanar and Topaz, and the passing, for the time being, of the energy crisis from the headlines, as evidenced by the coming and going of a minor regional geothermal boom. It now appears that, if not enough, at least much more of the Great Basin will be preserved as a result of the national wilderness review process. There is even a growing likelihood that a Great Basin National Park will be established around Wheeler Peak and Lehman Caves National Monument.

These are circumstances that, as some urged us, might have called for wholesale revision and updating of *A Trace of Desert Waters: The Great Basin Story*. But no book that purports to tell the story of an entire region can remain very long up-to-date. More importantly, Mr. Houghton's book remains a comprehensive and accurate account of the Great Basin from Pleistocene times to 1975, which is, after all, some 2 million years to balance against the last ten. Moreover, it is *his* account, one that amidst all the facts and detail remains very personal, a record of his love affair with a special region.

We have made two significant changes. Following the recommendation of Edda K. Morrison, who was married to Samuel Houghton, we returned to a series of articles he wrote for *Nevada* magazine. These, which led to his more thorough study of the Great Basin for this book, were illustrated with color photographs by the great nature photographer Philip Hyde. Here was an opportunity not only to enhance our edition of the book but to do it with illustrations the author had originally hoped to use. Therefore, we have included a selection of these photographs. We also added a short foreword by the eminent archaeologist Jesse D. Jennings, who can be considered the father of modern Great Basin archaeology and who knew Samuel Houghton, providing advice and encouragement when he was preparing his book.

And so, to those few who are already aware of *A Trace of Desert Waters*, we hereby offer you the chance to rediscover it. To the many who are not, we would like not only to introduce you to Samuel Houghton, but also to acquaint you, as no other book can, with the Great Basin.

Preface

This book is an extension of six articles written for the quarterly magazine *Nevada Highways and Parks*, which dealt with some of the ancient lakes in the Great Basin and their surviving remnants. It seemed logical and worthwhile to expand the material they presented so as to include the entire province and bring together in a single account the several kinds of history involving not only the lakes but also the rivers supplying them. The function of water as a geographic and ethnographic determinant must be evident upon any examination, however superficial, of this broad region.

Restless water, worrying the land, has left its marks. Supporting vegetation and wildlife, it has inevitably governed the distribution of human beings. It was deeply important to the aborigines, to explorers and to those who followed—the fur traders, settlers, miners, railroad-builders and stockmen. Water was a prime influence in establishing centers of population. Rival users battled for it, courts awarded rights to its use, legislatures apportioned it and almost always it has been in short supply.

The story is told of a group of Arabs who, when the League of Nations was formed, came to Geneva to represent one of the desert countries. They went sight-seeing in the strange capital but their serious preoccupation was not with tall buildings or the intricate mechanisms of a society never before encountered. Rather, they gathered at the River Rhone where the swift and sweeping waters leave the lake in never-ending flow. One said, after long and silent contemplation, "Allah is good to the Swiss."

Those who live in places favored by nature with ample rainfall are prone to take it for granted until the inevitable drought. But in the intermountain West drought is the normal condition. Therefore we give thought to the lifeblood concept of water and its impact on the behavior of people, from the earliest times we know of down to the present. Professor Walter Webb's view of the West as an oasis civilization is borne out by the continuing scarcity. We must also inquire: what of the future?

Water is essential not only to the domestic, industrial and agricultural sectors but to the development and conversion of energy. The present critical need for new sources and greater quantities of energy has focused much attention upon the West. Here may be found huge deposits of sulfur-free coal and oil shale, natural gas and petroleum prospects, geothermal steam and a climate conducive to the collection and storage of solar heat. The Great Basin carries much promise—one may confidently say expectation—of broad energy resource discoveries.

It seems appropriate to state at the outset what this book is not. No scholarly distinction is pretended since no original research has been conducted. Nor is it a textbook or a guidebook. It does not probe beyond the borders of the Great Basin or behind the past 75,000 years; thus we do not trespass upon adjacent areas, among them the vicinities of Boise, Phoenix, Las Vegas and Los Angeles; nor do we include mention of the dinosaurs and similar life forms that thrived and disappeared long before our selected time span.

It should be recognized by the reader that fresh discoveries of science in many fields, particularly those related to archeology, are so numerous and rapid that whatever is written is subject to change momentarily and can even become outdated by the time a book goes to press. Thus inevitably there will be inadequacies in this work, increasingly obvious as time goes on and new evidence appears or innovative techniques are developed. Theories change and fashions in thinking come and go as they do in medicine, the law and the arts. One may even conclude in cynical moments that truth itself is a fluid proposition and reality an illusion. Yet if one were to wait for perfection, nothing would ever be written or published.

The author cherishes a feeling that any place, unspoiled, can be worth knowing intimately. To paraphrase Will Rogers' assertion of faith, he never knew a place he didn't like. Involvement with nature requires no more than a basic inquisitiveness and an eye for telltale forms and qualities. It follows that the better one knows a place the more likely he is to accept it—perhaps even to love it—for the harshest environments on earth have their devotees, people who given a choice would live nowhere else. Others may acquaint themselves vicariously.

What we mainly present here is an idiosyncrasy: the choosing and assembling of various histories, organizing them with a particular point of view and setting them forth in a personal way. We proceed from a conviction that the need exists for a study which is serious of purpose but avoids the raptures of the intellectual deep.

The arid intermountain West, relatively uniform, has been favored in at least one respect advantageous to our purpose. The rate of erosion in dry regions is very slow and accordingly much evidence of the Wisconsin episode survives. Many of its geological features remain comparatively unaltered, and the language of the mountains and the deserts finds constant expression in these surroundings. Only a little familiarity with its vernacular is needed to apprehend the endless progression of terrestrial change. In such observation lies much delight, and that is the substance of the work presented here.

The author wishes to express his appreciation to Vincent P. Gianella, Carl L. Hubbs, Jesse D. Jennings and Charles T. Snyder, who read portions of the manuscript and offered valuable suggestions toward improving it; also to Donald L. Bowers, Max D. Crittenden, Jr., James W. Hulse, Philip Hyde and Vernon E. Scheid for advice and encouragement; and to James R. Firby, Don D. Fowler, Paul Gemmill, David J. Gray, John G. and Ruth M. Houghton, Robert S. Leighton, Edward C. Maw, Alvin McLane, Norma B. Mikkelsen, T. J. Trelease, Frits W. Went and Roland D. Westergard for sharing their specialized knowledge; also to many, many others who in one way or another have been of assistance to him in this writing project. Errors and omissions are of course his own responsibility.

SAMUEL G. HOUGHTON

Reno, Nevada, June 1975

Abbreviations and Explanations

B.L.M. . . . . Bureau of Land Management
G.P.O. . . . . Government Printing Office
N.P.S. . . . . National Park Service
U.S.D.A. . . . . U.S. Department of Agriculture
U.S.G.S. . . . . U.S. Geological Survey
A&P . . . . Atlantic and Pacific R.R.
B&G . . . . Bullfrog and Goldfield R.R.
C&C . . . . Carson and Colorado R.R.
CP . . . . Central Pacific R.R.
D&RGW . . . . Denver and Rio Grande Western R.R.
E&P . . . . Eureka and Palisade R.R.
NCO . . . . Nevada-California-Oregon R.R.
SP . . . . Southern Pacific R.R.
T&T . . . . Tonopah and Tidewater R.R.
UP . . . . Union Pacific R.R.
V&T . . . . Virginia and Truckee R.R.
WP . . . . Western Pacific R.R.
a.f. acre feet
a.s.l. . . . . above sea level (altitudes)
B.P. . . . . before present (earlier dates)
c.f.s. . . . . cubic feet per second
ORV . . . . off-road vehicle
p.p.m. . . . . parts per million
TCID . . . . Truckee-Carson Irrigation District

Citations: Where a statement is made that might need substantiation the source is given in parentheses, as: (Jennings, 1974). The work thus referred to will be found in the bibliography of this volume.

Dates: These are given in actual or estimated years ago, B.P. or A.D., see abbreviations explanation.

Altitudes: Figures are shown in feet above mean sea level (a.s.l.) for mountain summits, surfaces of lakes, etc.

Depths and areas set forth for the Pleistocene lakes represent maximum developments which may or may not have been long sustained.

Lakes: In general, the Pluvial lakes carry names preceded by the designation Lake (as Lake Bonneville), whereas living bodies have names followed by this term (Utah Lake, Pyramid Lake, etc.). A notable exception is the Great Basin feature, Lake Tahoe, which is very much alive today.

The Bonneville Salt Flats, west of the Great Salt Lake

A Great Basin Portfolio
Photographs by Philip Hyde

Pyramid Lake at its northern end. Strand lines at the
base of the mountains indicate former lake levels

The Truckee River on its way east out of the Sierra
Nevada, western boundary of the Great Basin

Tufa formation near the dry bed of Winnemucca Lake

Lake-bed deposits near Zabriskie Point, Death Valley
National Monument

Honey Lake, California remnant of Pleistocene-era
Lake Lahontan

Telescope Peak and the floor of Death Valley

Desert valley near the Utah-Nevada border

Bear River Migratory Bird Refuge; in 1986 this scene was
submerged under the Great Salt Lake

Mono Lake tufa

A Trace of Desert Waters

for EDDA

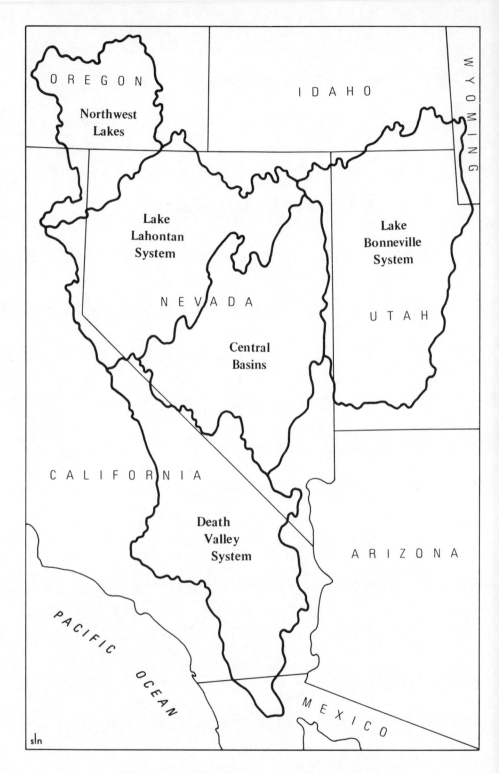

HYDROLOGIC REGIONS OF THE GREAT BASIN

CHAPTER I

Of Time and Place

This is the story of the Great Basin, a vast region of mountains and desert lying between the western ranges of the Rockies and the Sierra Nevada, south of the Columbia River system and northwest of the Colorado River. It was the last-discovered province of the United States and is today perhaps the least generally known and understood. Representing more than one-fifteenth the area of the nation, it is quite uniform in most of its principal characteristics and it can be defined and circumscribed quite precisely on the basis of drainage—the land we are examining has no outlet to the sea.

We shall be concerned with the history of this region from the beginning of the last major advance of glaciers, known as the Wisconsin age, down to the present. At least a million years ago the Pleistocene epoch, or Ice Age, succeeded the Pliocene and its closing phase—the Wisconsin—began about 75,000 years ago. This ended in turn when most of the ice sheets and widely scattered lakes disappeared about 10,000 B.P.[1] and the Holocene, sometimes called the Recent epoch, began. The Pleistocene and Holocene together comprise the Quaternary period.

The basic structure of the Great Basin was established long before the Pleistocene began. Evidence of crustal disturbance subsequent to the Tertiary is meager. Only a few dispersed volcanic eruptions have left cinder cones and lava beds here and there, and some dislocation of Ice Age features such as moraines indicates slow displacement of underlying blocks, but it is clear that the major tectonic changes occurred in much earlier times.

Although there were a number of ice ages before this one[2]—four or five at least—the glaciers that carved out features we recognize readily in our mountains today came into existence during the Pleistocene, so it is widely known as *the* Ice Age though others lasted much longer and covered more ground. The characteristic continental ice sheets, which in the West did not spread south of the Canadian border, disappeared long ago and only the persisting Greenland ice cap and the massive Antarctic layer remain. Whereas some of our inland water bodies such as the Great Lakes were formed after the continental ice retreated, the development of lakes and glaciers tended to be simultaneous. This was generally the case in the West where many lakes had no glaciers at all in their drainage areas.[3]

The same climatic elements brought about both lakes and glaciers. Colder temperatures and increased precipitation, with attendant persisting cloudiness that decreased the evaporation rate, produced these accumulations. The essential condition was consistently cooler and wetter weather, with seasonal gains exceeding seasonal losses regularly, causing the waters and bodies of moving ice to expand and deepen. But these processes—the formation and extension, also the later shrinking—were altogether very gradual, and we must keep in mind the time dimension; for we are dealing here with millennia. The Pleistocene lasted at least ten thousand centuries.

The Wisconsin age, as we have pointed out, is the name given to the period that lasted from about 75,000 to 10,000 B.P. At least two main glacial maxima developed in the West during this se-

[1] Morrison (1968) points out that authorities differ widely on the Pleistocene-Holocene boundary, some placing it as far back as 30,000 years ago in the mid-Wisconsin, some as recently as 4,000 to 5,000 B.P. in the last postglacial thermal maximum.

GEOLOGIC TIME SCALE

ERA	PERIOD	EPOCH	BEGINS YEARS B.P.
CENOZOIC	Quaternary	Holocene (Recent)	11,000
		Pleistocene (Glacial)	500,000 to 2,000,000
	Tertiary	Pliocene	13,000,000
		Miocene	25,000,000
		Oligocene	36,000,000
		Eocene	58,000,000
		Paleocene	63,000,000
MESOZOIC		Cretaceous	135,000,000
		Jurassic	180,000,000
		Triassic	230,000,000
PALEOZOIC		Permian	280,000,000
		Pennsylvanian (Upper Carboniferous)	310,000,000
		Mississippian (Lower Carboniferous)	345,000,000
		Devonian	405,000,000
		Silurian	425,000,000
		Ordovician	500,000,000
		Cambrian	600,000,000
PRECAMBRIAN			

[2] The earliest ice age we have positive knowledge of occurred in Huronian times about 1.6 billion years ago.

[3] The widespread notion that Pluvial lakes were created by melting glaciers has no foundation—the glaciers were coincidental, not tributary. Examples of drainage basins that never had glaciers include Fort Rock and Warner valleys in Oregon; Long Valley, Columbus and Teel's marshes, Diamond Valley, in Nevada (Gianella, correspondence). They all contained lakes.

quence and they coincided roughly with very high levels of the lakes. Blackwelder (1948) mentions that glacial episodes were much shorter than the intervening warmer times and that evidence shows they were maintained for only ten or twenty thousand years, thus they constituted only minor fractions of the entire epoch.

Climatic change had profound effect upon the distribution of living forms, both animal and vegetable.[4] Life zones moved hundreds of miles southward and far down mountainsides during the Pluvial extensions. We have proof of this in plant material found in caves, from species that must have once grown close at hand but are not now found below levels 2,000 feet higher. Fossil remains establish the fact that animals now long extinct walked the land during the late Pleistocene stages. The tar pool varieties, of which the Rancho La Brea examples comprise an especially diverse group, are believed to have flourished 10,000 to 20,000 years ago.[5] Whereas the sabre cats, ground sloths, tapirs, dire wolves, early forms of horse, and tall camels of that day chose moderate, warmer climates, in colder loftier places beasts like the musk ox, hairy mammoth, bison *latifrons*, mastodon and an extinct caribou thrived. Many of these last avoided the desert, thus we find that Pleistocene fossils, though plentiful in the Great Basin, are somewhat limited in variety.

We have particular knowledge of wide climatic swings that occurred during the last 10,000 years. These greatly altered both the flora and the fauna of the desert West. Antevs (1948) designated this period as the Neothermal—it is also called the Postglacial or Postpluvial—and he subdivided it into three phases. The first of these, the Anathermal, covered the years 9,000 to 7,000 B.P. and began with a subhumid climate rather like today's, but grew warmer; it led to the Altithermal, 7,000 to 4,500 B.P., which was distinctly warmer than at present, with arid conditions characterized by the total disappearance of most lakes and glaciers. (The Altithermal concept has been challenged by some scholars, particularly as to its aridity.[6]) Lastly, the Medithermal, carrying down to the present with a cooler and semiarid influence, has brought about a rebirth of many lakes and glaciers.

---

[4] Hubbs (1957) maintains that climatic conditions in the Pleistocene trended toward drier and less uniform sequences with enormous fluctuation through Postglacial time, that Wisconsin glaciation occurred in periods of intense cold. He thinks rigors of climate hastened the extinction of the great Pleistocene fauna.

[5] The La Jolla radiocarbon laboratory obtained a positive dating of 14,500 B.P. from Pleistocene mammal remains at La Brea tar pits (Carl L. Hubbs, in *Science*, vol. 134, no. 3488, Nov. 3, 1961).

[6] Controversy involving the Altithermal interlude is reflected by Aschmann (1958) who

Climatic conditions in the Great Basin were heavily influenced by the state of glaciation in Western Canada and the adjoining United States during the Quaternary. Storm tracks were pushed south of their modern courses and brought precipitation even in the warm seasons. Antevs has observed that glacials and interglacials in the north corresponded to pluvials (rainy, wet ages) and interpluvials in the Basin—changes that were typical of the entire Quaternary.

A definition of the term Pluvial (capitalized) might be useful here. It applies precisely to the span of time that includes the two or more stages of the Wisconsin when the western basins contained lakes. Earlier periods of very high humidity are simply called "early pluvials" and these have left no clearcut shore features. The period of desiccation following the last high stage of the lakes is referred to as the Postpluvial.

Conjecture exists as to whether our present situation may be just another glacial pause or is otherwise (postglacial). François Matthes (1947) observed that the glaciers in high western mountains attained their greatest extent of the past 10,000 years about 1850 A.D. and that the Great Basin lakes, low at the time, rose rapidly during the 1860s. He pointed out that Pyramid Lake's coating of white tufa marking the 1868 level of 3879 feet is the highest mark of its kind in that basin, from which he concluded the lake had not risen above that level for at least 100 years previously. Mono Lake's historic maximum occurred in 1919, and this he thought to be higher than any level achieved "since 1750 or earlier."

Matthes' keen observation and intuitive process contributed greatly to the science of glaciology. By 1941 he had concluded that most of the glaciers in the western United States were not remnants of Pleistocene bodies, as previously assumed, but instead were "modern" glaciers which became re-established as recently as 4,000 years ago or less. He called this the "Little Ice Age," and his view has become widely accepted by scholars (Fryxell, 1962).

Most current 20th century glacier studies and measurements tend to show that they are receding, and long-range climatic observations likewise indicate a general warming trend. The phenomenal retreat

asserts that the Antevs sequence has become a Procrustean bed into which some archeologists laboriously chop and fit their stratigraphic data. He finds no evidence that the Basin was uninhabitable from 7,000 to 4,000 B.P. But Cressman (1966) refutes him in part by saying that no responsible archeological opinion supports the theory of an uninhabitable province here. The position, he states, is that conditions for habitation were definitely less favorable than before or after that period, and occupation occurred but on a necessarily restricted basis. He points out further that there were regional climatic variations in different areas, both at the beginning and at the end of the Altithermal.

of glacial ice in Alaska's Glacier Bay, recorded during the past 200 years, shows to what an extent attrition has set in. But now and then some contrary evidence turns up.

The United States Geological Survey has been conducting a program of photography and actual measurement of many Sierra Nevada glaciers for the past 80 years or more, with Forest Service and National Park personnel cooperating, and a special ten-year study in conjunction with the International Hydrological Decade was started in 1965. McClure glacier and those of Mt. Lyell and Mt. Dana are centers of their interest. It was found that these bodies increased in area as a result of the record 1969 snowfall, revealing a short-term fluctuation counter to the general trend. How significant this may be remains to be seen. Long-term changes are very gradual indeed and conclusive establishment of a cycle might require observation by mankind over many generations.

The land we are examining stretches from Lake Tahoe in California to the Bear River in Wyoming, and from the Snake River country of Idaho down to Laguna Salada in Mexico. It covers over 220,000 square miles and portions of six states. It was named in 1844 by (then) Brevet Captain John C. Frémont, who was the first person to recognize its unique geophysical isolation. It is not a single large bowl but a gathering of many enclosed basins—well over 100—with high ridges between which suggests to this writer the patterns of snow cups found in summer on exposed ice fields, each cup with a small segregated pool.

Mountain ranges are quite regularly spaced throughout much of the Basin, trend generally north to northeast, vary for the most part from 40 to 80 miles in length, and have crests usually 8,000 to 10,000 feet high. There are at least 150 of them. They are mostly block-faulted and tilted, their valleys filled with sediments from minor ephemeral streams. The valley bottoms and basin floors, though low in relation to surrounding ranges, stand higher than much of the Appalachian chain. The region's altitude varies considerably, with its center higher than its borders and a broad slope dropping away to the south. The quality common to all of it is aridity, which results from a number of complicated factors that include the rain shadow of the Sierra Nevada, the distance from any ocean, and latitudes unfavorable to recurrent storm patterns.

The ratio of precipitation to potential evaporation regulates this aridity, and desert conditions prevail where the latter greatly exceeds the rainfall. Some authorities, among them Thornthwaite, put the steppe-desert boundary at the 7-inch isohyet. The valley areas of the Great Basin fall into the desert category as a rule, and their characteristic sagebrush or greasewood carries right down to the alkali flats (playas). Higher up, with rainfall increasing as much as an inch for every 200-foot rise, the vegetation becomes more substantial and varied. But although there are wooded slopes in most parts of the Basin, much of it designated National Forest, there is little marketable timber except at the outer borders, east and west.

This land of interior drainage is not all desert, by any means, in spite of its dryness. While there are classic examples of the Sonoran life zones, the biotic procession carries upward through the Canadian and Hudsonian levels to some occurrences of even the arctic-alpine above timberline. A notable incidence of this is on the long, exposed ridge that culminates in White Mountain Peak (14,246), highest point in the Great Basin, which exhibits typical alpine fell-fields. We will take a closer look at this part of California in Chapter IX.

Some authorities, notably the geographer Nevin M. Fenneman, exclude from the Basin that portion lying south of Death Valley, which is referred to by them as the Sonoran Desert section; it contains the Salton Sea. But by our standard of interior flow the region qualifies for inclusion and it will be discussed.[7]

Living rivers other than the Humboldt are peripheral and all of them, fluctuating seasonally, are utilized for human needs. No known sub-surface outflow of significant proportions leaves the Great Basin and none at all flows out at the surface (Thomas, 1964). Streams are born in the high snow storage and their normal courses lead to enclosed basins, few of which maintain any surface waters. They are brief in length and in spate. The only river system of magnitude is the Humboldt, which has many tributaries; but otherwise, the Truckee, Carson, Walker, Owens, Bear, Weber and Sevier Rivers are quite long and contain water at all times of the year. Each of them is totally managed and utilized, and rarely gets out of hand. Probably there had been no important change in the location or the flow of these watercourses since the diminishing of the Pluvial lakes until man began diverting them, for the land

[7] The boundaries of the Great Basin depend on which scientist is talking. The geologist, biologist, climatologist and archeologist each have a different concept. Jennings (1964) writes: "The Great Basin is a distinctive natural area only in the physiographic sense; in its biotic assemblage it is part of a larger province." The divergences stem from specialized criteria in each discipline.

itself has not undergone much alteration and the snows of winter continue to accumulate in the same high places.

To make order out of this wide jumble of drainage patterns and lake basins is no easy task and the solution of the puzzle has appeared to lie with separate treatment of each major modern river complex. In this way, most of the Great Basin can be divided and described. Four of the rivers contributed to Lake Lahontan, three to Lake Manly in Death Valley, and four to Lake Bonneville. Otherwise, there were three isolated regions containing lakes but without any river: in the northwest, at the center, and in the far south. Starting with Oregon, we shall swing around the Basin in counterclockwise direction, ending in the northeast.

We shall have much to say about the nature of the desert in the course of this work, but one point should be cleared up at the start: the deserts we are discussing bear little resemblance to the schoolroom version of endless Saharan wastes, with dunes piled high in a scorched and blazing emptiness, a property skull in one corner. There are indeed some impressive sandy places, among them an area 40 miles long by 8 or 10 miles wide north of Winnemucca, Nevada, averaging 35 feet in depth (Fenneman, 1931). Elsewhere there are sand dune accumulations: southeast of the Ruby Mountains, throughout the Sevier Desert, and alongside the Salton Sea, for example; and there are solitary mountains of sand near one end of Eightmile Flat in central Nevada and near Lathrop Wells in the southern part of that state. But these are atypical. Dunes do not occupy any considerable portion of the province, says Fenneman, "certainly not one per cent."

Rather, the surface of the land is broadly clothed with vegetation of many kinds. In the north common sagebrush is the dominant cover, while pinyon and juniper mark rather sparsely the adjoining hillsides. A diffuse and varied flora carpets the ground and softens the rocky line. In the hotter and low-lying southern regions greasewood, creosote bush and Joshua tree are types that flourish, decorating the desert.

Any catalogue of Great Basin features should include the geothermal springs dispersed quite consistently throughout it. Some 400 sites have been listed and mapped by the U.S. Geological Survey (Waring, 1965). They are important indicators of an energy potential that can be exploited without causing atmospheric or terrestrial pollution. With the dwindling of fossil fuel supplies attention has been focused on this resource, and the Great Basin could emerge in time as a center for clean power production. The technology and the economic climate appear at long last to be propitious.

The United States has lagged in developing this form of energy. Some modest use of geothermal steam has been made for domestic heating but only one source—at The Geysers, 90 miles north of San Francisco—has been developed commercially. In 1904 Italy began converting steam at Lardarello and since then nearly a dozen other nations have followed suit: notable among them Japan, Iceland, New Zealand and Mexico are putting it to work (though New Zealand is shifting emphasis to a huge new gas field). At the southern tip of the Great Basin near Laguna Salada the Mexican government has drilled wells and built a plant to produce initially 75 megawatts of power, this to be doubled shortly. Northward from this site at Cerro Prieto the Imperial Valley extends to the Salton Sea, where in the vicinities of Niland and El Centro a few producing wells have been put down; a prototype power plant is in the works and several major oil companies are interested. Local communities have contracted for the steam.

It is generally conceded that the Pleistocene was coextensive with human evolution. Man in the western hemisphere is assumed to be of Asiatic origin in view of the basically Mongoloid characteristics of the aboriginal population; but there remains some argument as to when he first arrived on the continent. Most scholars agree he must have crossed the Bering-Chukchi platform at a time when the giant ice sheets stored much water now returned to the oceans. This phenomenon, called glacioeustacy, is known to have taken place on a number of occasions.[8] With the sea level much lower than it is today, the shallow strait between the continents lay exposed, and the presumption has been that large animals came over this land bridge seeking food and were pursued by hunters; the various species including man himself then spread eastward and southward through gaps in the Wisconsin ice. Central and northwestern Alaska were never covered by ice (Jennings, 1968)

---

[8] For extended periods during the Wisconsin age the sea was 300 to 330 feet lower than today and immigration from the Old World to the New would have been possible during the period prior to 40,000—35,000 B.P.; then again from 28,000 or 25,000 until 23,000 B.P.; and finally, between 13,000 and 10,000 B.P. (Bandi, 1970). Alaska was mostly free of glaciers during the Ice Age and its lowlands were open and inhabited by a great variety of animals. The most important species were the mammoth, bison and caribou. Even today the minimal distance between Siberia and Alaska is no more than 50 miles and it may at times have measured much less. The Diomede Islands lie midway between, land is almost always visible in the straits, and ice is constantly moving here. The Eskimos are the only native population living on both continents.

though great sheets of it persisted across Canada and might have blocked migration for extended periods of time. But they withdrew at intervals sufficiently to permit the passage of man at a number of well-established lacunae.

Other possibilities are regarded skeptically: that man might have evolved independently in the West, or that he could have arrived by sea. There is no authentic evidence of any unique origination, nor any record of distant ocean travel prior to the Christian era. The compass was invented by the Chinese (or possibly the Arabs, the Etruscans or the Greeks—no one knows for certain) but its navigational use appears to date from as recently as 1297 A.D. In any case we still lack solid proof of actual transpacific contacts (Ekholm, 1964).

The question as to when the first migration took place is in considerable dispute. There were many opportunities, for the land bridge was often in being. Estimates of man's antiquity in the New World range from 12,000 to 35,000 years, but new indicators keep turning up. The late Dr. Louis S. B. Leakey described a find at Calico Hill in the Mojave Desert region northeast of Barstow, California, and proposed an even earlier human occupation, highly controversial. We shall have more to say about this discovery in Chapter XI when we discuss the Mojave and Lake Manix.

There are various sophisticated approaches to the problem of dating archeological evidence. Techniques of chronometry include the following: dendrochronology (tree-ring dating); radiometric and thermoluminescent dating; and newer, less common methods such as fission track and obsidian dating, paleomagnetic and archeomagnetic correlation, analysis of amino acid or fluorine content, and pollen study. Chronology may be absolute or relative. Tree-ring and radiometric methods are examples of absolute dating, whereas association of evidence with substances of a known age provides a relative dating. The stratigraphic principle setting forth that the deepest undisturbed layer is the earliest has been generally accepted, thus a lower or higher level already identified provides relative information about new material.

Obsidian, or volcanic glass, absorbs water at a constant rate, producing a cortical change. By measuring the cortex of an obsidian specimen one may estimate its age, especially if the piece has been chipped—such as a hunting point. However, this process is still experimental. The fluorine content of exhumed bones depends upon how long they have been buried and how high that element runs in the local water. Relative dates can be determined in some cases through chemical analysis and it is interesting to note that the famous Piltdown Man hoax, long-suspect and finally exposed in 1955, was confirmed as such through a fluorine test. Pollen studies reflect climatic conditions in earlier times and have been found useful at some American sites. Blanketing of artifacts by lava or tephra (ash-fall layers) has helped in some cases to set the ages of strata.

Later in this work we will look into the history and techniques of dendrochronology and radiometric dating, and as each area is discussed we will describe some of the important archeological sites within it. Their artifacts shed much light on the ancient lifeways. The desert waters broadly determined the distribution and the habits of aboriginal man, and his culture reflects their influence.

We have learned a great deal about the early American as he roamed the province during some ten millennia of prehistoric times. Much of the evidence has come from caves discovered and examined professionally before they could be vandalized by pot hunters. There is considerable truth in the cliche that these caverns are windows on the past, and at least they have remained free from the natural despoliation to which open sites are subjected; their fossils and artifacts have not been leached by rain or dispersed by the forces of erosion. Many parts of the Great Basin have their caves, from which we have obtained rich information.

Most of them faced a Pluvial lake and many were formed by wave action. None was excavated by man. Some were deep enclosures, others only open-faced shelters. The objects they contained shed light upon such matters as climate, the surrounding fauna, diet, foraging methods, food preparation and use of fire, even esthetic skills and interests. Some of the finds were extensive and extremely important while others merely confirmed what was already known, or proved negligible.

In the northwest there was Fort Rock Cave, by an Oregon lake once almost 600 square miles in area. Ten miles east of Las Vegas, Nevada, there was Gypsum Cave, just outside the Great Basin but strongly reflecting its culture. And a mile east of Wendover, Utah, the largest and most revealing inventory found anywhere in the province was excavated by Jennings, 1951–53, in Danger Cave. These will be treated in forthcoming chapters, for each is an extremely important focus of the Desert culture.

The Great Basin, spacious and undisturbed, was still completely unknown to any white man as recently as 1774. By contrast, Mexico suffered Hernando Cortez in 1519, Frobisher entered Hudson Strait

in 1578—the year Sir Francis Drake sailed up the northwest coast—
and Dutch merchants including the indefatigable Willem Barents
prowled northern Canada late in the 16th century. These ventures
preceded Jamestown, 1607, and the founding of Santa Fe by Oñate
in 1609. Vitus Bering passed through the straits named after him
in 1728. It was half a century after that when the first European
set foot inside the Great Basin and even so the circumstance was
modest, receiving no worldwide notice. In January two years before
the Declaration of Independence, 282 years after Columbus, Juan
Bautista de Anza and his men thrust across the southern tip of
it in their successful effort to reach and supply the coastal Spanish
missions. And then in 1776 came the first very limited attempt
to explore the region—Father Garcés' transit of the Mojave Desert.
(See chronology at the end of this chapter.)

Later that same year two other priests made an entry 500 miles
to the northeast. Fathers Domínguez and Escalante, bent also upon
the task of finding an overland route to the missions and wholly
unaware of the extent of their problem, camped by the shore of
Utah Lake, then passed some distance south along the Wasatch
Range before giving up and heading back. Technically, the white
man had arrived, but another 35 years were to elapse before the
first Anglo-Americans entered. Lewis and Clark, in 1804, had
avoided the Basin altogether, but seven years later five white trappers working for Astor blundered into the Bear River Valley, its
northeastern extension.

In the following decade came Peter Skene Ogden, bent upon
harvesting beaver. The son of a New York royalist who had fled
to Canada at the time of the Revolution, he first trapped the Great
Basin in 1825 and made a very significant penetration along the
Humboldt in 1828–30. He had worked streams in Oregon earlier,
as well as the Bear River. Jedediah Smith and the mountain men
followed; we mention them in this account though they were not
really explorers and certainly not geographers. No truly comprehensive appraisal of the Basin took place until Frémont came in the
1840s. Its existence was known mostly by rumor, up until 1837
and the publication that year of Washington Irving's *Adventures
of Captain Bonneville*. That work aroused widespread interest and
led to Frémont's being commissioned. He breached our province
late in August of 1843 at the Bear River, on the second of his
several expeditions, left it by way of Fort Hall, and then late in
the year re-entered through southeastern Oregon. He skirted the
western border of the Great Basin by way of the Truckee, Carson

and Walker river watersheds, crossed the Sierra Nevada, and after spending some months in California returned through the Mojave Desert in May 1844. Passing through the southern tip of Nevada and up the eastern flank of the Basin to Utah Lake, he thus completed the circuit and established the fact that no outlet existed. We shall encounter him in forthcoming chapters, as they treat the areas he explored. In 1845 Frémont, in great haste, crossed from east to west on this third expedition, accompanied by a force of men and imbued with military fervor; but his impetuosity brought him much trouble and this time he retraced his steps as a virtual prisoner facing court martial. His importance to us lies with his curiosity, drive and imagination; he stirred all who came in contact with him, for he was not a passive figure.

The first settlers were Mormons coming in the wake of trappers and early emigrants and preceding the trampling hordes of Forty-niners. Until then the Great Basin was mainly a bridge province, land to be traversed as quickly as possible in spite of distances and difficulties. Next came the surveys, the telegraph and the railroads; towns sprang up, though many were short-lived as the mining booms flared and flickered out. But permanent settlement gradually took hold and the cities, which were located mostly around the rim, began to grow. We will look into these matters in greater detail as we cover the separate regions.

The Basin's Indians will receive attention. Paiute and Shoshone tribal groups, living here when the Spanish Fathers came, suffered from white competition and soon dwindled, yet in this century they have recovered and progressed. It is not our purpose to examine sociological values here or to pass any judgments, but we will mention the contacts, events and statuses where it seems appropriate to do so.

East of a line drawn from about Mt. Whitney to Boise, Idaho, the land belonged to the Shoshone and west of it lived the Paviotso, or Northern Paiute. The Utes occupied the Utah plateaus and reached into the Basin at Sevier Lake. Southern Nevada and southwestern Utah provided a homeland for the Southern Paiute. These were the main divisions, with strong cultural links between them. Smaller tribes such as the Washo at Lake Tahoe and the Serrano of the Salton Trough lived at hand, as did the Panaiti, or Bannock, who roamed southern Idaho, and in the northwest the Modoc, Klamath, Tenino and Molalla Indians.

The Great Basin Indians were wanderers, poorly clothed, housed

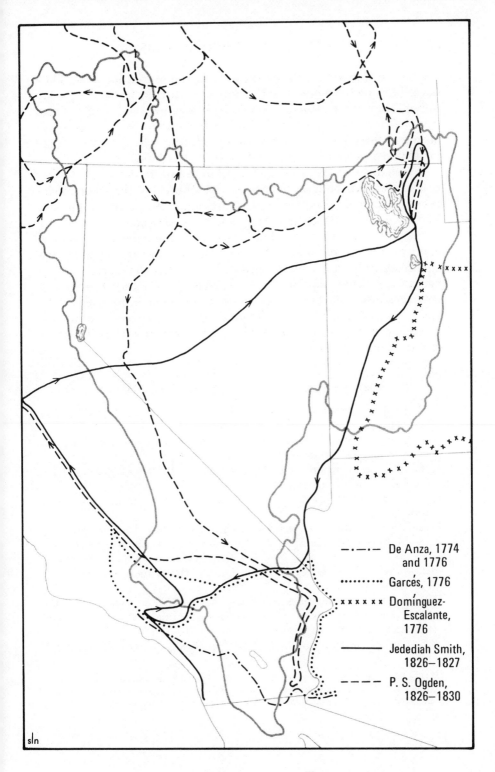

— · — · —	De Anza, 1774 and 1776
· · · · · · ·	Garcés, 1776
× × × × × ×	Domínguez-Escalante, 1776
————	Jedediah Smith, 1826–1827
– – – –	P. S. Ogden, 1826–1830

ROUTES OF EXPLORERS AND TRAPPERS

and fed, and involved almost entirely in the search for food. They never became horsemen like the Sioux or warriors like the Apache; rather, they were gentle, peaceable—and hungry. But the Basin was their country and they knew how to survive in it, which was no mean feat. Except for the overwhelming white invasion they might have persevered indefinitely in this fashion.

We shall be looking in considerable detail at the Pluvial lakes that influenced the lives of these early Americans and their predecessors, especially Bonneville, Lahontan and their living remnants. There were over 100 of these lakes and they occupied about one-fifth of the entire Basin area.[9] The paradox of these far-flung waters, many containing permanent fish populations, existing in places now almost entirely dry, is most beguiling. At peak development they marked a strongly aquatic design. How they were then distributed, how they rose and fell, disappeared or lingered in remnant state, how they influenced their surroundings and to some extent still touch the lives of the people—these are matters within the scope of this inquiry.

HISTORICAL CHRONOLOGY OF THE GREAT BASIN

1772—Fr. Juan Crespi and Capt. Pedro Fages discover the Sierra Nevada mountains.

1774—Juan Bautista de Anza crosses the Colorado Desert from Yuma to San Gabriel, first white entrants.

1776—Fr. Garcés explores the Mojave Desert; Fr. Domínguez and Fr. Escalante reach Utah Lake.

1811—Five white trappers working for Astor wander into the Bear River drainage.

1813—The Arze-García expedition reaches Utah Lake from Abiquiu.

1818—McKenzie's Snake River Brigade enters Bear Valley, the first British visitors.

1822—Gen. William Ashley and Maj. Andrew Henry found the American Fur Company.

1824—Jedediah Smith brings the Rocky Mountain Fur Company to the Great Basin; Peter Skene Ogden replaces Alexander Ross as leader of the Snake Country Expedition.

1825—Ogden traps in the Great Basin; Jim Bridger discovers Great Salt Lake.

---

[9] Many Pleistocene lakes developed in the western United States outside the Great Basin. Four or five large ones appeared in the drainage of the Columbia-Snake river system, others in Montana, southern Wyoming, Arizona, New Mexico and California's Central Valley (Feth, 1961.).

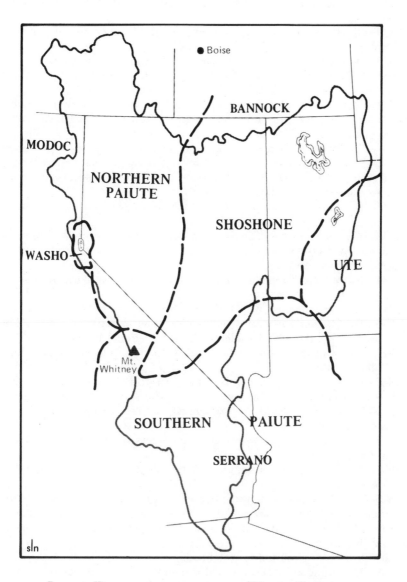

INDIAN DISTRIBUTION SINCE THE WHITE CONTACT

1826–27—Smith circles the Great Basin, makes first transit of the Sierra Nevada.

1828–30—Ogden discovers the Humboldt River and traps its length, exploring.

1829—Ogden journeys through the Owens River Valley to the Colorado River.

1829–30—Antonio Armijo begins the New Mexico-California trade.

1831—William Wolfskill and George C. Yount are the first to travel the entire Old Spanish Trail.

1832—Capt. Bonneville comes west to seek his fortune in the fur trade.

1833—Joseph R. Walker and company travel from Great Salt Lake Valley to California.

1837—Washington Irving's *Adventures of Captain Bonneville* is published.

1841—William Workman and John Rowland bring the first emigrant train over the Old Spanish Trail; Bartleson and Bidwell take first emigrant party across the northern Great Basin.

1843—The Chiles-Walker party bring the first wagons overland to California.

1843–44—John C. Frémont leads his Second Expedition from the Columbia River counter-clockwise around the Great Basin and establishes its hydrographic nature.

1844—The Stevens-Townsend-Murphy party are the first to use the Donner Pass route.

1845—Frémont conducts his Third Expedition westward to California.

1846—The Donner Party meet with catastrophe in the High Sierra; Congress accepts the 49th Parallel as the International Boundary.

1847—Under Brigham Young the first Mormons reach Great Salt Lake Valley in July.

1849—The Gold Rush attracts thousands of fortune-hunters to California.

1849–50—Capt. Howard Stansbury conducts his survey of Great Salt Lake.

1850—California is admitted to statehood; the first settlement in Nevada is founded at Genoa.

1853—Capt. John W. Gunnison and seven others are murdered by Indians in Utah.

1857—A party of Arkansas emigrants, 140 in all, are massacred at Mountain Meadows.

1859—The Comstock Lode is discovered; Capt. James H. Simpson locates route from Utah to Carson Valley; Oregon is admitted to statehood.

1860—The Pyramid Lake war between Paiute Indians and settlers breaks out in May.

1864—Nevada is admitted to statehood.

1868—The transcontinental railroad is completed; service begins by mid-year.

1877—Brigham Young dies.

1890—Idaho and Wyoming are admitted to statehood.

1896—Utah finally achieves statehood.

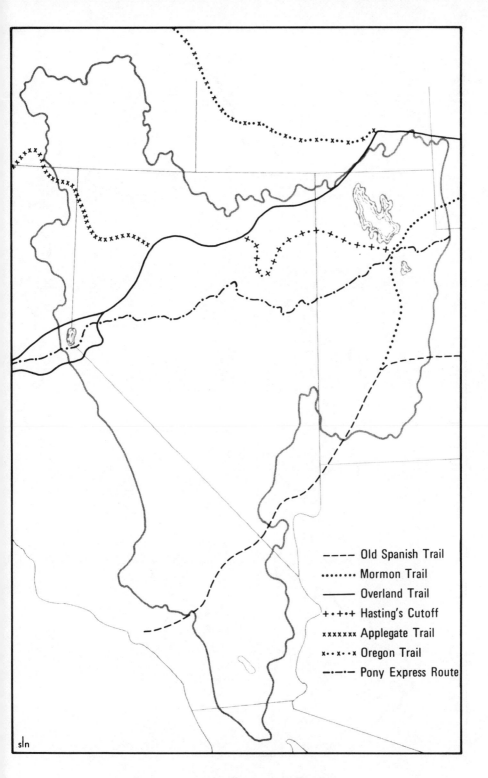

ROUTES OF THE EMIGRANT PARTIES

---- Old Spanish Trail
.... Mormon Trail
—— Overland Trail
+·+·+ Hasting's Cutoff
xxxxxxx Applegate Trail
x··x··x Oregon Trail
—·—·— Pony Express Route

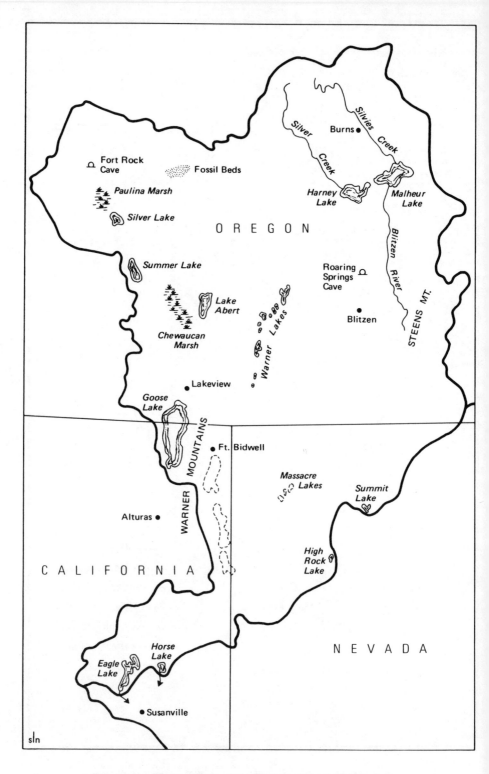

REMNANT WATERS IN THE NORTHWESTERN BASIN

CHAPTER II

The Northwest Lakes
In Oregon and Northern California

Having indicated that the Great Basin is easily defined, we should now qualify that statement. It may be bounded quite precisely by *today's* land of interior drainage, which is what we are examining, but such confinement has not always been maintained in some situations within the Wisconsin limit. For instance, Lake Bonneville spilled to the Snake River for many centuries, and parts of the Basin in southern Nevada discharged at one time to the Colorado River, as did the waters at the southern tip of the province.

A lake when filled may overflow to some drainage leading to the sea until evaporation or local physiographic change severs it from any outside connection. The hydrographic relationship of several Pluvial lakes in the northwest flange of the Great Basin illustrate such alteration. This extension protrudes deeply into Oregon, reaching to the South Cascade Mountains and the headwaters of the Deschutes, which is a branch of the Columbia River. It occupies approximately 16,000 square miles of that state. The Blue Mountains lie north, and small tributaries of the Snake River form beyond to the northeast. Eight separate troughs in this part of our province bear evidence of Pluvial lake formations. One of these spilled to the Snake, another by way of the Pit River to the Sacramento, both eventually to the Pacific Ocean. However, their basins have long been closed. In contrast, a ninth confinement where Pluvial Lake Klamath accumulated was captured by the Klamath-Trinity River system and has since remained outside our boundary.

Lake Malheur rose in Oregon's Harney basin and became the third largest of all the Great Basin's Pleistocene lakes. Main highways cross the wide sweep of Harney Valley, site of today's town of Burns, where this relatively shallow water (never more than 70 feet deep) once spread like a great evaporating pan. At one point in time it covered 920 square miles and during this peak it briefly poured into the Snake River by way of Crane Creek and the Malheur River's south fork. Its small remaining waters are Harney and the modern Malheur Lakes, which join and are terminal. Inflow comes from Silver Creek, the Blitzen River and Silvies Creek. Much of the land along the streams and beside the lakes is marshy wilderness, a favorable habitat for some 200 kinds of wildfowl and shore birds; the Malheur National Wildlife Refuge has been established here to protect them. Runoff is carried northward from the Steens Mountains, a range about 100 miles long, via a number of small creeks and the Blitzen River, whereas Silver and Silvies creeks flow southward from forested highlands beyond Burns. The region all about is now generally arid and quite empty of settlements.

About 50 miles west of Harney basin two more lakes half as large as Malheur gathered. One lay as much as 100 feet deep where Fort Rock, Silver and Christmas valleys cluster together but it has bequeathed an almost waterless estate. Playas, lava beds and volcanic buttes mark the depression, in which spring runoff quickly disappears except at Paulina Marsh and Silver Lake. Immediately to the south the other, called Lake Chewaucan, left a more plentiful heritage encountered at Abert Lake, the Chewaucan Marshes and Summer Lake. Here the waters had been once at least 300 feet deep. One of the most spectacular scenes in this part of Oregon is the massive Abert Rim below which the highway passes for 15 or 20 miles along the lakeshore. It is an abrupt and formidable palisade resulting from an earthquake fault that displaced it long before the Pleistocene began. The pleasant littoral with its clusters of waterbirds, the chain of hills and buttes beyond, and the morning shadows of the great rim provide a most agreeable interlude in the extended desert scene.

Alkali, Warner, Catlow and Alvord valleys all carried Pluvial lakes that ran in area from 200 to almost 500 square miles each, quite evenly spaced in this corner of Oregon. Lakes Warner and Alvord were long and narrow, reaching south across the Nevada border, and have left vestigial swamps and ponds. In the Warner Valley ten or a dozen strung together are known today as the Warner Lakes; behind them to the east the terrain is very rugged and here the Hart Mountain National Antelope Refuge has been set aside. The plateau drops off sharply in steep and colorful cliffs indented by small canyons and dotted with a thin forest. Since antelope compete with domestic cattle for forage—sagebrush community here—the refuge has not been popular with local ranchers, who have opposed its inclusion in the Wilderness system. The pronghorn, *Antilocapra americana,* is a purely North American mammal and not a true antelope. Unlike Old World varieties, it sheds the outer sheath of its horns each year; it reaches a height of about three

SUMMER LAKE, OREGON, WITH WINTER RIDGE AT LEFT
One of two remnant lakes, the other being Abert,
where Pleistocene Lake Chewaucan once rose.

THE ABERT RIM IN SOUTHERN OREGON
High escarpment along the eastern shore of Lake Abert.

feet and a weight of 100 to 125 pounds, is fairly common to many parts of the Great Basin and to the western plains. This gregarious animal is keen-eyed and graceful, capable of speeds up to 40 miles an hour, and widely hunted as a trophy species.

Many of the Oregon lakes had caves nearby where early man took shelter and left signs of his presence. The best-known and richest site was Fort Rock Cave, overlooking the valley so named and the one-time lake within it. A hearth found there has been dated about 13,200 B.P. (Bedwell, 1973) and charred bark sandals—between 75 and 100 of them—situated beneath a layer of volcanic debris were radiocarbon dated at over 10,000 B.P. (Jennings, 1968). Artifacts recovered in addition to the sandals included scrapers, drill points, projectile points, manos, a bone awl, an antler flaking tool, wooden items and a bit of basketry made from tule fibre (Antevs, 1948).

Ten miles northeast of the town of Blitzen in Catlow Valley another very important locality, Roaring Springs Cave, was excavated by Cressman, who worked many sites in the region between 1938 and 1942; here he found fire drills and two complete atlatl shafts. (The atlatl was a primitive throwing weapon used to hurl darts at game animals).

Caves of importance in addition to these two, all containing traits of the Desert culture, included Catlow, the several Paisley caves at Lake Chewaucan, and Plush by Lake Warner. Cougar Mountain Cave was discovered north of Fort Rock Lake not far from Newberry Crater and yielded hunting points presumably derived from Newberry volcanic material.

Layers of tephra (volcanic ash) make excellent time-stratigraphic markers. Readily identified pumice from the climactic explosion of Mount Mazama, which occurred about 7,000 B.P., has been found at several sites including Wikiup and Paisley Caves 60 miles north and 75 miles east, respectively, of Crater Lake where Mount Mazama once towered many thousand feet above the caldera remaining today. Newberry had several eruptions of characteristic material, the last taking place about 2,600 years ago, and these have been valuable in determining relative dates.

The Paleo-Indian of glacial and Anathermal age who occupied some of these shelters differed in a few vital respects from more recent peoples, generally classed as Protoarchaic. Hunting traditions changed as animals disappeared. At Paisley Cave worked obsidian, together with charcoal and ashes, lay in association with horse,

AN ABANDONED RANCH IN FORT ROCK VALLEY, SOUTH CENTRAL OREGON
Without water in dependable quantity, occupation becomes impractical.

FORT ROCK, WITH BEGGARHEEL, SITE OF FORT ROCK CAVE
SHOWING AT THE LEFT, A MILE DISTANT
Here rich remains of Desert Culture were excavated by Cressman and others.

camel and elephant bones—animals long extinct in North America (Camp, 1970). The presence of large game in this part of the Basin in some quantity is verified not only by the remains found in Paisley (and at least one other cave) but also by ossa from Fossil Lake. This is a dunes area 7 or 8 miles long in Christmas Valley where ancient bones emerge from time to time as the wind-blown sand shifts about.

Little is known concerning the early Americans who inhabited these parts between the disappearance of the archaic people and the arrival of tribes found here today. Students of prehistory assume a continuity of the Desert culture, that they were engaged in gathering and small-game hunting like the modern Numic tribes encountered by the first European entrants. These limited Oregon groups, never more than a few thousand members altogether, included the Yahuskin and the Walpapi, essentially Northern Paiute specializations (Forbes, 1967).

The Oregon basins we are describing were first penetrated by white men early in the 19th century when the fur trade was well under way. Donald McKenzie built Fort Nez Percé in 1818 on the Columbia half a mile from the mouth of the Walla Walla River, and it was from this point that Peter Skene Ogden launched several expeditions into the unexplored region lying to the south. On the third of these, 1826–27, he reached Malheur Lake and his associate, Antoine de Sylvaille, discovered the Silvies River (for whom, after a fashion, Ogden named it) in February 1826. His fifth expedition two years later took him to the Humboldt River and we will have more to say about this in Chapter VIII. In 1831 John Work explored and trapped along the streams of southwest Oregon.

Governmental jurisdiction in the northwest territory was non-existent and unasserted until 1818 when the United States and Great Britain agreed to a "joint occupation" but avoided any clearcut definition of the land covered by the agreement. In 1827 it was renewed without any stated time limit. After considerable oratory and sword-rattling the two countries came to a final concordat in 1846 with the present international boundary accepted. Oregon was admitted to statehood in 1859 and permanent settlement of the eastern valleys followed.

John C. Frémont probed south from Fort Vancouver near the mouth of the Columbia late in 1843, and with the professional help of Charles Preuss mapped his way through this lobe of the Great Basin, bestowing names along the way. He plotted Summer Lake (from Winter Ridge) and Lake Abert, which he named after his *Chef de Corps*. Christmas Lake was described on that holy day in 1843, but he was then looking at one of the Warner Lakes, and today that name is attached to a small playa remaining from the Fort Rock Pluvial predecessor far to the north. Frémont continued southward in Oregon to Klamath Marsh before turning to the east and thence to the Lahontan basin. We will pick up his trail in many places as this account proceeds.

Goose Lake straddles the California-Oregon state line south of Lakeview, north of Alturas, and provides us with another example of an altered drainage changing the Great Basin perimeter. It is classified as a disrupted portion of the Sacramento River system, which it once added to by overflowing into the Pit River. Yet for many thousands of years it has been quite self-contained. At one time 25 miles long and 170 feet deep, it wore down the rim at its southern end, then fell permanently below that level. Its shallow remnant, in area perhaps two-thirds of an ancient maximum of 368 square miles, is still quite substantial.

This cornering of California and northwestern Nevada is marked by many lava flows, some millions of years old, some quite recent, and it held several large Pluvial lakes. For example Surprise Valley, which extends down Modoc County along the state boundary, carried an unusually deep one—650 feet—and 70 miles long; its configuration was relatively narrow between desert ranges, and of a surface once 500 square miles in area only three small playas remain. These carry waters that fluctuate seasonally and are shown on the map as Upper, Middle and Lower Alkali Lakes. Fort Bidwell, Lake City, Cedarville and Eagleville are California settlements that lie at the foot of the Warner Mountains along the valley's western edge. Here erosion from somewhat heavier rainfall and relatively thick vegetation have largely obscured or obliterated signs of Pluvial Lake Surprise. But many of the eastern hills retain its strand lines and exhibit them quite prominently. Within Surprise Valley a number of steaming hot springs indicate the existence of a geothermal resource.

The Warner Mountains were named after Capt. William H. Warner of the Corps of Topographical Engineers, U.S. Army, who came to Goose Lake in September 1849, with a small survey party looking for new railroad routes into the Sacramento Valley. They reconnoitered southeastern Oregon but on returning to California were ambushed by Pit River Indians. Warner, who was then Chief

Topographical Engineer of the Corps, was killed along with two others and this incident became known as the Warner Massacre.

Fort Bidwell was established at the head of Upper Lake as an Army depot in 1866 together with Camp Alvord, east of the Steens Mountains, and "Old" Camp Warner north of Lakeview. There was a Camp Harney too, and all these came to be known as "Forts" in time. As such, they were perhaps more reassuring to worried pioneers when Indians rose up under Chief Paumina following the Battle of Pyramid Lake in 1860. Hostilities continued sporadically to 1868 and many outrages were perpetrated, including the Ward Massacre in southwest Idaho where an entire wagon train was destroyed (Murray, 1959). This, the Paiute War, gradually subsided though underlying problems remained unsolved. Fort Bidwell's military life was relatively brief and inactive, and in 1893 it was finally abandoned, though its buildings survived and were used to house a government Indian school for the nearby reservation. The barracks were torn down in 1930 but the school farm, 200 acres of fine bottomland, is still worked by members of the tribe (Abeloe, 1966). Indian colonies are maintained here and at Eagleville.

Between Upper Lake and Goose Lake a back road leads over the mountains through Fandango Pass. That name is rooted in legend, which tells of an emigrant party composed of Mexicans who chose the place to make camp and celebrate with dancing their safe passage across the desert. Supposedly, in the midst of the "fandango" hostile Indians appeared and killed them all, after which word of the "massacre" spread. But historians have been unable to substantiate any of this and give the more plausible explanation that California-bound goldseekers, possibly the Wolverine Rangers, had camped there overnight and set fire to some abandoned wagons. A later party, seeing the partly burned remains, jumped to conclusions and started the rumor.

In 1846 Jesse and Lindsay Applegate came through Fandango Pass with a 15-man group looking for a shorter route to the east than the old Oregon Trail. They established the Applegate Cutoff, heavily used in 1849 but very dry and rough, and it otherwise never became popular. The Humboldt River-Forty-mile Desert approach to California was much more widely used.[1] By 1852 the emigrant trains to southern Oregon were traveling over the Noble Emigrant Trail, avoiding the hardships of the Applegate and the Lassen; this

[1] The California-bound emigration of 1849 numbered about 21,000 people, mostly men. Three trails then existed: the Carson, the Truckee and the Applegate-Lassen. An estimated 7,000 to 9,000 traveled the latter, and 2,000 wagons turned into it, but relatively few ever made it through (Helfrich, 1971).

crossed from the Humboldt to the vicinity of Honey Lake, thence north of Mt. Lassen to Shasta (now a State Park). In 1859–61 this came to be known as the Fort Kearney-South Pass-and Honey Lake Wagon Road.

The southeast quarter of Oregon was not well known until Israel Cook Russell surveyed and described it a century ago. A professional geologist employed by the u.s.g.s., he understood the Ice Age and correctly interpreted much of its vestigial evidence. He roamed a wide area, identified the Oregon lakes, the Lahontan profile and the Mono Lake relict, and published definitive works on them all. He also studied the Sierra Nevada and its glaciers. Mt. Russell (14,190) and Pluvial Lake Russell (Mono) were named after him. His Oregon survey is still the most accurate and useful work in its field.

East of Surprise Valley and wholly within Nevada, Lake Meinzer filled a depression now called Long Valley—one of three or more so named in the Great Basin.[2] A series of playas remaining from its eastern arm shows on the map as the Massacre Lakes, and to the north lies the Sheldon Antelope Refuge. The Pluvial lake, 355 square miles at maximum, was designated for O. E. Meinzer, another geologist of note and an authority on the Pleistocene hydrology. Beach terraces are very evident here along the bare hillsides, and there are hot springs in the vicinity. At Massacre Lake Cave elements of the Lovelock culture have been found. The name Massacre Lake (and Spring, Cave, etc.) comes from an unverified story like the one involving Fandango Pass; a mass grave is mentioned in guidebooks but no really authentic record of any massacre seems to exist.

The Applegate Cutoff passed through the Meinzer lakebed and on down through High Rock canyon to the lake of that name on its way to the Humboldt River. I. C. Russell observed that High Rock Lake forms seasonally in the stream channel obviously once occupied by a Pleistocene tributary of Lake Lahontan's Soldier Creek arm, and that damming of this stream by a landslide produced

---

[2] The name Long Valley was given three important basins that carried Pluvial lakes: one in White Pine County, Nevada; one in Mono County, California; and the one mentioned here, in the northwest corner of Nevada. Many other valley names are repeated: Grass, Clover, Pine, Paradise, for example, and creek names such as Cottonwood, Willow, Hot, Deep, Dry keep recurring. There are many lakes named Blue, Clear, Twin, Summit, Bear, etc. Indian and Warm Springs flow in many places. Pine Mountain, White Mountain, Old Baldy, Sawtooth Ridge and Red Rock are common and one might think the pioneers lacked imagination. Mineral associations are everywhere, with Gold (Acres, Creek, Hill, Point) and Silver (Lake, Peak, Creek) widely scattered. Iron, Lead, Copper and Salt dot the map—even Diamond. Eureka denotes many areas of discovery. (See George R. Stewart, 1945).

a considerably larger lake than the present one. Its size can be estimated from the height of the visible slide; Hardman thinks it covered about 11 square miles. In the course of time this Pluvial lake overflowed to the northeast and in draining created Fly Creek Canyon.

Within this dry and almost treeless region the remains of many extinct mammals have been discovered. These include two types of horse, cameloids, a mastodon and a large cat. Petrified wood lies exposed in many places, has been widely vandalized, but is now protected by law. Southwest of High Rock Lake about 15 miles, gold was discovered in the Granite Range in 1910, and Leadville, now a ghost town, flourished temporarily. No railroad or highway of consequence has ever penetrated this remote corner of Nevada but 30 miles south of Leadville sits the community of Gerlach, reached by the Western Pacific as it crosses Smoke Creek Desert to the west and Black Rock Desert to the east; both are portions of Lake Lahontan's dry bed.

Summit Lake, 20 miles northeast of High Rock, had a Pluvial ancestor no more than four square miles in area. It is permanent and contains Lahontan cutthroat trout. How they got there remains a mystery, for the waters are isolated and have never to our knowledge enjoyed any outside connection. Ichthyologists speculate that these fish may not be indigenous but were introduced in some unrecorded manner. In any case, this is the last reservoir of the subspecies in Nevada (La Rivers, 1962). These fish seek the waters of the only tributary, Mahogany Creek, to spawn and the area is protected in order to insure a favorable habitat.[3]

Hot springs are active in Soldier Meadow, far below, and may receive a flow from Summit Lake seepage (Hubbs and Miller). A "geyser" (actually a drilled well) on the Fly Ranch about 15 miles north of Gerlach in Hualpai Valley attracts visitors who come to see its lofty tufa accretion and periodic spouting. An army camp, Fort McGarry, was established at Summit Lake in 1877 to keep order, and an Indian reserve has surrounded it ever since.

At this point we might mention some of the Indian Reservation history in the northwestern Great Basin. No areas were set aside prior to 1860–61 when the Pyramid Lake and Walker River Reservations were given informal status. Their development, like that

[3] Gianella (correspondence) suggests that the trout in Summit Lake, which was once connected to Lake Lahontan, were trapped there by a landslide. He observes that Mahogany Creek was once a tributary of Soldier Creek (which fed Lahontan) but was dammed long ago by this slide, the scar of which is still quite conspicuous.

of the others, was a very slow process. In 1875 the Malheur was created in eastern Oregon for the benefit of the Northern Paiutes; some Bannocks also gathered there. But after the Nez Percé took the warpath under Chief Joseph in 1877, Bannock hostilities smoldered for two years and enthusiasm for the reservation concept cooled. Ranchers envious of the Malheur reserve obtained its abandonment by 1882; meanwhile many Indians settled around military posts such as Camp McDermit and Fort Bidwell for protection and employment (Forbes, 1967). But the Paiute reservation at McDermitt, Nevada, has been in formal existence only since 1936.[4]

Just north of Susanville, California, three Pluvial lakes made their appearance and their traces may still be seen. The long flat stretch from Ravendale through Termo to Madeline, crossed by the Southern Pacific Railroad and U.S. Highway 395, is known as Madeline Plains and here Lake Madeline's arid playa remains. At its peak it was 125 feet deep and contributed to Lake Lahontan, as did Lake Eagle and Lake Horse, small neighbors to the southwest. In this immediate vicinity, on the western border of the Great Basin, the forests and crags of Lassen Volcanic National Park provide a notable and dominating background to the desert condition. They indicate the southern limit of the Cascade Ranges. There are snow streaks even in late summer on Mt. Lassen, the last volcano to be active in the conterminous United States. In May 1915, its crater erupted with rumblings that did not subside altogether until 1921, but the effluent consisted mainly of large and destructive mud slides rather than hot lava. However, a small lava flow did materialize on the west slope just below the peak. Experimental drilling for geothermal energy has been conducted from time to time nearby. Over the plateau areas of the northwest most of the thick underlying lava beds were laid down in the Pliocene epoch more than a million years ago.

Susanville marks the western end of Lake Lahontan, to be treated in later chapters, and a modest stream passes through this town—the Susan River, which feeds Honey Lake residually. This is a playa body that fluctuates with good and bad water years but seldom goes dry. Long Creek comes into it from the south and there is

---

[4] Fort McDermit, on the Oregon-Nevada state line, was named for Colonel Charles McDermit, killed by Indians in 1865. However, the people of the settlement established there have, over the years, spelled it with two T's and loudly protested a recent move by the U.S. Board on Geographic Names to restore the original spelling. In January, 1972, the Board reversed itself, bowing to popular desire, and McDermitt became official (*Wall Street Journal*, 4-3-72).

good surrounding forage for a thriving livestock industry. East of
the lake at Herlong, the Sierra Army Depot, established in 1942,
stores military ammunition and employs many civilians as well as
Army personnel.

Pluvial Lake Truckee and the ancestor of Lake Tahoe both
belonged to the Lahontan system, which will be covered in subsequent chapters, so our attention now passes to the little basins
around Reno that once supported lakes but are now almost waterless. The winters of 1952 and 1969, however, were exceptionally
wet, brought unusual inflow, and resulted in a number of temporary
fillings. Four Pluvial developments occurred north of the city: Lake
Laughton in Cold Spring Valley, Lakes Fred and Lemmon in valleys
with the same names, and an unnamed lake in Spanish Springs
Valley. Lemmon, the largest of these, was the site of a wartime
air base and its flight strip occupied a part of the wide lakebed
(the actual sump lies a few miles south). Dry Lake, remaining from
Laughton, smooth and hard in most years, has been used for auto
racing and flying model airplanes.

In Washoe Valley half way between Reno and Carson City year-
round Washoe Lake is fed by spring freshets and returned irrigation
water. During Pleistocene times the surface extended over 25 square
miles but much of it even then was very shallow (today the lake
has a maximum depth of only 13 feet). Catfish and geese are still
plentiful, attracting sportsmen in spite of the rather considerable
settlement of the valley. Through it the Virginia & Truckee Railroad
built its main line in 1872, and for 75 years the mournful whistle
of steam locomotives echoed across the flat. They were years of
varying prosperity. In the end the highways and automobiles came,
rail traffic dwindled, and attrition set in. V & T dividends ceased
in 1924, yet miraculously the road survived World War II, only
to be abandoned in 1950.

Of lesser fame is the Nevada-California-Oregon Railway, built
by fits and starts from Reno to Lakeview and known at various
times by other labels. Inevitably it was nicknamed the "Narrow,
Crooked and Ornery." Ground was broken in 1880 with the announced intention of reaching the Columbia River! Two years later
it had come only 30 miles to the foot of Beckwourth Pass. By 1890
the terminus was at Amedee north of Honey Lake, 80 miles from
Reno; and Susanville was very bitter about having been bypassed.
Financial panics interrupted the growth of the NCO, yet by 1899
the tracks had been laid through Madeline Plains to Termo. Regular
service to Alturas began in December 1908, and finally the rails

arrived at Lakeview 238 miles from Reno on January 10th, 1912. Some of this line is still in operation with standard equipment, having been converted by the Southern Pacific, which purchased the road in 1927. The Western Pacific had taken over the portion from Reno to Herlong ten years earlier.

This concludes the account of the Pluvial lakes that appeared west and north of the Lahontan system. The mountain structures adjacent to their sites remain favorable catchments for snow, serving to fill the streams seasonally, as before. Thus a number of basins still collect water, and but for the diversions to benefit agriculture these remnants might be much more substantial and lasting today.

DESERT WATERS REMAINING FROM LAKE LAHONTAN

A   Lake Lahontan System
B   Dixie Basin

CHAPTER III

The Lahontan System
Lake Tahoe

The Great Basin lies like a wedge between Utah's Wasatch Mountains and the Sierra Nevada, attaining its broadest width in the northern flare, and here in the Pleistocene epoch the two largest lake developments received waters perennially draining from those ranges. To the east there was Bonneville, which will concern us later; to the west Lahontan filled a chain of valleys rather like a necklace in form, supplied by numerous rivers and creeks. Though less than half as big as Bonneville at its maximum, its watershed was comparable in size for it received not only the snow melt of the northern Sierra but also that of various ranges across the state of Nevada.

The rivers remaining from the Lahontan system that now descend the eastern slopes of the Sierra in California consist of the Truckee, the Carson and the Walker. The Susan River, already mentioned, enters from Mt. Lassen, and along the border of the Lahontan basin below Oregon the Quinn River and its several tributaries flow south to the site of the ancient lake. These are much longer today because Lahontan had occupied a very considerable portion of their streambeds. By far the longest and most involved basin segment is the Humboldt, bringing down water produced in the East Humboldt, Ruby, Independence, Toiyabe, Shoshone and Santa Rosa mountains with a concentration naturally emptying into the Humboldt Sink—a system today impaired and altered by artificial diversions. Little of this water is wasted, thus the terminal sinks of all these rivers, other than Pyramid and Walker Lakes, no longer contain substantial fluctuating waters.

Some of the river channels, however, were occasionally blocked, though in general the intermediate lakes that evolved in this manner were short-lived. We shall concern ourselves especially with two that were not. Both formed along the course of the Truckee River and one, Lake Tahoe, remains to us in much the same shape and size that it has had for many thousand years. The other, Lake

Truckee, will be the subject of our next chapter. Few people think of Lake Tahoe as a remnant, yet there are ample surviving indications to confirm a Pluvial history and place it among the relics of the Lahontan system.

Although much evidence that Tahoe attained greater size has been erased, what remains has stimulated the minds of many observers. I. C. Russell asserted it was once surrounded by glaciers. Joseph LeConte thought it might have been entirely filled with glacial ice. Hubbs and Miller (1948) point out that the fish fauna, *Salmo regalis* (a relative of the Pyramid Lake trout) and Lahontan chub, are typical of the whole Lahontan system and feel that Tahoe could have been raised to its present level subsequent to the origin of these species. This would have been caused by tectonic displacement though most of the major faulting that created the basin took place much earlier than the Pleistocene.

The definitive water parting between the Pacific and the Great Basin follows the summit of the main range, on both sides of which extensive snow fields built up. The huge Rubicon glacier overflowed toward the lake through Rubicon Pass, a thousand feet higher than today's lake surface; at that time its waters likewise stood much higher. Lindgren (1898) writes that lavas dammed the main basin to a level that had to be 700 to 1000 feet above the present stage, but no beaches remain because glaciers wiped out the shore records. Distinct beaches, not easy to find, occur only up to 100 feet above the lake.

Tahoe was created in the first instance by a heavy andesite flow that blocked the basin's opening during a late Tertiary period of volcanic activity. Hardman puts its greatest area at 211 square miles, not much in excess of the present 193; he gives no depth figure, but the one long accepted for the modern lake and verified by the National Ocean Survey (formerly the U.S. Coast & Geodetic Survey), is 1,645 feet, based on a "normal" level of 6,228 at the surface. Recently scientists from the University of Southern California measured the bottom sediments and found them extending at least 2,600 feet below the lake floor. This sublacustrine fill was created by glacial scouring and deposited by entering streams; it indicates a profound chasm between the main range and the eastern ridge, known as the Carson Range, crowned by Freel Peak (10,881), Mount Rose (10,778) and lesser summits. Thus the bottom of this cleft lies far below the elevations of Reno and Carson City.

Tahoe has a single outlet—the Truckee River, at Tahoe City.[1]

Supplying the lake around a mountainous margin are 63 separate creeks and minor drainage basins. The chief tributary among these is the Upper Truckee, which rises in Round Lake at an altitude of 8,000 feet and runs some 15 miles northward to debouch near Al Tahoe in marshy ground. Trout Creek and Taylor Creek, also at the south end, contribute appreciably; together with Ward and Blackwood Creeks these five streams carry more than half the basin's water production.

The rim at the northwest outlet formed by the andesite flow is now somewhat worn down but still determines the point below which no natural outflow can occur (6,223). Thus Tahoe is one of the highest water bodies of any great size in the world. A dam was built here in 1870 by Col. A. W. von Schmidt,[2] raising the level six feet. Its purpose was to float logs and regulate the river current, accommodating irrigation ditches and power development. Since that time the dam has been rebuilt and the top six feet of lake water pre-empted by the U.S. Government for downstream use. Regulation is under a 1915 court decree, administered by a Federal watermaster who has jurisdiction over releases at the dam. The level of Lake Tahoe has been maintained within the six-foot limitation save for a few dry years when it dropped below the natural rim and pumping was instituted to sustain a minimal river flow.[3]

The beauty of Lake Tahoe lay concealed from all but Indian eyes until very recent times. It was not until 1844 that John C. Frémont, first white man to behold the scene, came struggling up the wintry slopes north of Elephant Back on St. Valentine's Day (Gianella, 1959). With his cartographer Charles Preuss he climbed a nearby summit—probably Red Lake Peak (10,061)—and looked across its broad and sparkling expanse, recorded the sight in his diary, and called the water Lake Bonpland after the French botanist

[1] Lake Tahoe once had a different outlet, west of the present andesite lip, where the dam and gates are located. Gianella (correspondence) maintains it overflowed about where Tahoe Tavern stood. Beyond this point extends a marsh which is lower than the andesite rim. Long ago the lake was much higher than now and formed a bar which blocked that outlet, forcing the lake to discharge thereafter as it does now.

[2] Colonel Alexander von Schmidt, who built the original dam at Lake Tahoe, had an illustrious engineering career. He ran the 1863 boundary survey between California and Nevada, among other accomplishments, and also blasted a rocky obstruction in San Francisco Bay.

[3] The first recorded instance of the lake's dropping below its natural rim occurred in 1889 following a number of dry years. The year 1924 was the first in which pumping over the rim was instituted. This happened again in 1929, 1930 and 1934.

who accompanied Baron Alexander von Humboldt on his western hemisphere explorations.[4] But Preuss labeled it "Mountain Lake" on his narrative maps and it was generally known by that name for a number of years (Scott, 1964). A week later the Frémont party viewed the lake again, en route to Sutter's Fort.

Nine months after this discovery six young men and women detached themselves from the Stevens-Townsend-Murphy emigrant group, rode up the Truckee River from Donner Creek, and were the first of their race to set foot on the lakeshore. Among them was Daniel Murphy. It is thought that they passed on down the west side, headed for Sacramento Valley, but they left no descriptive account.

Others of importance have not been so perfunctory. Mark Twain and Dan DeQuille, in and apart from the columns of the *Territorial Enterprise,* gave Lake Tahoe extravagant praise. Joseph LeConte, the geologist, in his *Journal of Ramblings* under the date of August 22, 1870, penned the following: "This lovely lake! I could dream my life away here . . . Of all the places I have yet seen, this is the one which I could longest enjoy and love the most." He described its phenomenal clarity and mentioned that he had observed a white dinner plate resting more than 100 feet below its surface.

Long before Frémont came to this relatively secluded basin a small tribe of Indians adopted it for their home. These were the Washo, less aggressive than the Northern Paiutes and relatively exiguous, inhabiting this high harsh forested country and valleys adjacent thereto. Peripheral lands of the Washo extended from the headwaters of the Carson River north to Honey Lake and east beyond the Pinenut Range (Hickson, 1967). They were a gentle people with a way of life quite like the Paiutes' and excelled individually in the making of baskets; these were used to transport pine cones, acorns and seeds, or when pitch-lined, water. Babies were carried in basket-cradles. Cooking baskets, their contents heated by rocks from the fire, winnowing trays and storage baskets, receptacles for offerings to the spirits used by the shamans (medicine men) in the course of treating the sick—these were among the types created and utilized regularly. Their most famous craftsman was

[4] Brevet Captain Frémont was a well-read man. In naming the Humboldt River and suggesting Lake Bonpland as a name for Lake Tahoe, he doubtless had in mind the lengthy work entitled *Voyages aux régions equinoxiales du Nouveau Continent fait en 1799–1804, par A. de Humboldt et Aimé Bonpland* (12 volumes, Paris: la Librairie Grecque-Latine-Allemande, 1805–26). Neither the author, von Humboldt, nor his botanist, Bonpland, ever explored in the western u.s.

Louisa Keyser, known also as Dot So La Lee, and her *degikup* masterpieces (spherical, small-mouthed) were so fine, uniform and beautiful that they have become collector's pieces and immensely valuable. Most of the authentic examples of her skill are now owned by museums.

One very interesting distinction of the Washo is their linguistic association, inasmuch as they speak a form of Hokan language. Most of the Great Basin is inhabited by Numic Indians, speakers of Uto-Aztecan dialects: that is, the Northern and Southern Paiutes, and the Shoshones. However, Jacobsen (1966) observes that "the only non-Uto-Aztecan (except a few Yuman dialects) is Washo. They are on the wrong side of the Sierra." This linguistic anomaly remains enigmatic.

The years since 1844 have brought substantial change to Lake Tahoe and its environs, for the wilderness that Frémont first penetrated soon became widely known and open to exploitation. Its forest resources attracted lumbermen, whose markets included the voracious mines of the Comstock and the fast-growing cities of the West Coast. Resorts sprang up at Tahoe City, Glenbrook and elsewhere. Homes, hotels and stores were built, roads extended, steamboat lines instituted and narrow gauge railroads graded.

During the first half-century of occupation mountainsides were logged off and all but the most remote stands of virgin fir and pine fell to the axe. A tramway 4,000 feet long was built up a very steep grade near Incline in 1880 to carry timbers which, at the summit, were dumped into a flume: this sluiced the wood to a destination in Washoe Valley where there were mills. By 1896, having run out of suitable trees, the operations were shut down. But since forests are renewable, continually replenishing themselves where permitted to do so, this most obvious impact was only temporary, and a heavy growth has since developed. The sawmills and small logging railroads meanwhile disappeared. Even the branch line of the Southern Pacific which had been servicing the lake for more than 40 years was abandoned by 1942. The growth of a summer resort economy then dampened by wartime restrictions tapered off and population became relatively stabilized.

Throughout the nineteenth century the name of the lake was in dispute, since no one had accepted the original and capricious choice of its discoverer. Aimé Jacques Alexandre Bonpland was almost unknown in America. Frémont himself used Preuss's "Mountain Lake" in further references. Dissatisfied with so vague a label, a local group decided in 1852 it should be called Lake Bigler, in honor of California's third governor, and the state's Surveyor-General gave his approval the following year. But John Bigler was sympathetic to the Confederacy and the name of an avowed Secessionist did not sit well with many; thus other names were suggested, some of which actually appeared on maps of limited circulation. Gradually "Tahoe" took over, yet it was not until 1945 that the California Legislature cleared things up by rescinding the act of 1870, which had made "Bigler" official, and legally proclaiming the present designation. Its origin is shrouded in legend and doubt. Possibly it derived from the Spanish *tajo*, meaning a cut or cleft. Mark Twain, in deep dislike of it, insisted tongue-in-cheek that "Tahoe" meant "grasshopper soup" in Digger dialect. No one knows for certain where it came from.

Dispute was not limited to nomenclature, for the lake has been a center of wrangling almost since it was first settled. Radical proposals have been made, quarreled over and discarded, including schemes to tunnel from either Washoe Valley or the American River and tap the stored water. Though reasonably constant it has undergone considerable variation in level, not just seasonally but between wet and dry years too, and this has caused lakeshore and downstream flooding, dislocation of wharves and marinas, and an assortment of riparian troubles. The interests of lakeside property owners and proprietors of camps along the Truckee below the dam were often ignored or considered subordinate to those of others with earlier rights. But new reservoirs have been constructed in this mid-century that facilitate exchanges of stored water, relieving some of the dependency on Tahoe, and though there are still problems today, they do not seem quite so acute.

The principal area of existing controversy is relatively new and revolves around the problem of maintaining environmental quality. Soon after the close of World War ii, with the settlement of Lake Tahoe entering its second century, the basin became a cynosure for heavy resort development. Highways were modernized, California's population shot up, and widespread increases of affluence and leisure time stimulated the recreational proclivities of society. The influx began in earnest. Outside corporations, riding this trend, bought large tracts of land on which they developed high rise hotels, condominiums, residential clusters and retirement communities. Golf courses, ski slopes, lakeside facilities and shopping areas materialized as adjuncts of the housing splurge. Forested hillsides were slashed to engineer these "improvements" and the high speed highways they required; land was torn up and leveled to provide access and parking space. Very soon the seasonal life pattern changed to a year-round commercial metabolism, heralding an entirely new era of high human occupancy.

Conservationists became alarmed by increasing threats to the purity of the lake. Forming groups, they brought pressure upon legislators and county officials to set standards and limitations that would preserve its surroundings and water quality. At first the response was unenthusiastic. Meanwhile a movement was started to withdraw for park purposes a considerable portion of the Nevada shore and the land behind it; of the 71-mile total lakeshore a third lies in Nevada and half of this belonged to a single owner, who had kept it intact for many years. Small park areas had been dedicated elsewhere, mostly in California, but the recreational needs of the expanding population could hardly be satisfied by these. So after lengthy proceedings, purchase of a portion of this land was funded, the state acquired it by condemnation, and long-range planning for its development began. Initially, at the end of 1967, title to 5,300 acres along the eastern shore was passed; other parcels were subsequently obtained, and the total park acreage came to 13,461. The facility was dedicated in October 1971, in ceremonies at Sand Harbor.

Most of the riparian ownership other than parkland is in private hands, whereas the higher portions of the basin belong mainly to the Federal government. Holdings of the U.S. Forest Service alone account for almost half the entire basin's area. Four state parks in California total 3,500 acres and some additional land has been set aside by various county or municipal divisions for public recreation; these consist of campgrounds, picnic sites, boat ramps and similar dedications.

Astride the main ridge southwest of the lake lies the Desolation Valley Primitive Area, a high rocky wilderness reserved for limited use, barred to motor vehicles and power boats and reached only by trails. This glaciated and relatively barren expanse, once remote from the mark of any human presence, might have provided the setting for Wotan's farewell to Brunnhilde in the Wagner opera, *Die Walküre*. At its center Lake Aloha rests between Jack's Peak, Mt. Price and Pyramid Peak, each about 10,000 feet a.s.l., one of countless glacier-scoured lakes scattered along the Sierra crest—which is here somewhat ill-defined; part of the wild area belongs to the American River system and lies outside the Great Basin. This landscape was formed in Pluvial times and earlier by lava flows and grinding ice, with moraines or fans that blocked the existing drainage. Accessible only to strong hikers and horsemen, Desolation Valley nevertheless now receives heavy summer impact from campers, rock climbers, fishermen and scouting groups.

It was in and around the Lake Tahoe basin that Dr. James E. Church, professor of classics at the University of Nevada and enthusiastic outdoorsman, pioneered the science of snow surveying during the first decade of this century. In 1901 he began studies and measurements on Mt. Rose's summit and discovered that figures showing the water content of snow over a wide melting area could be used to forecast with great accuracy the likelihood and degree of flood or drought below during the following season. Dr. Church formulated a simple equation, the nucleus of what he called the Percentage Method. This involved water content measurements taken over a snow course annually on April 1st and weighted for both soil moisture on that date and precipitation on the snowfield during the melting (J. E. Church, Jr., 1960). New techniques and equipment have since been developed but the essential relationships determined by this imaginative scientist remain fundamental and accepted. Often associated with him and long in charge of the Nevada Cooperative Snow Surveys was his University colleague, Dr. H. P. Boardman. Both retired in 1939 but continued to study and publish for almost 20 years.

As the 1960s progressed the sharp increase in population and the alteration of physical surroundings intensified the concern for Lake Tahoe's future. Dumping of raw sewage and erosion products into its waters were bringing about noticeable degeneration that more and more people recognized. Two processes were at work: eutrophication, which implies an increase of nutrients in the water and results in a lack of dissolved oxygen; and siltation, caused by abnormal erosion. The first produces great blooms of algae,[5] with growths covering the rocky surfaces of lake shore and bottom; the other carries in sediments that foul the margins and have unpleasant effects on beaches. If unchecked, such deterioration can lead to a soupy lake, opaque, discolored and malodorous.

[5] Dissolved oxygen content varies greatly with the algal cycle, being excessive during the period of bloom; but when the algae die off in late summer a decrease in oxygen takes place (C. T. Snyder, correspondence). Pollution control studies have been undertaken by the Nevada Bureau of Environmental Health to determine such factors as algal growth potential, temperature, conductivity, and content of nitrogen and phosphorus. It was found, for instance, that seeding control samples with iron doubled the algal growth. AGP bioassays were conducted with calculated addition of nutrients; inorganic nitrogen did not create a different growth response but phosphorus did. It is one of the primary stimuli in the growth of algae (E. Gregory, 1970).

In 1962 a test was conducted similar in principle to the informal observation of LeConte, but with precise controls: scientists used an 8-inch disc and a hydrophotometer; they found the disc was discernible at 136 feet and light was detected at 500 feet (*Report of the Lake Tahoe Joint Study Committee,* March 1967). But Dr. R. C. Goldman, limnologist at the University of California, Davis, who has been studying the lake for more than a decade, predicts a slow death for Tahoe unless efforts to stem the inflow of nutrients and silt succeed; otherwise he believes it will only be a question of time before it turns totally green in warmer months. In 1969 the secchi disc was lowered again but found visible only down to about 100 feet; this would indicate an annual 4 per cent reduction and, at that rate, complete opacity in 25 years. While an increase in nutrients might benefit the fish life—a mackinaw trout weighing over 35 pounds was taken in 1970—siltation has an adverse effect, smothering food organisms and ruining spawning beds. The Tahoe basin is uniquely fragile; its ecology could easily be upset. One remedy would be the complete elimination of septic tank-cesspool systems, together with total export of sewage. Considerable progress here has been achieved.

As rapid, intensive development spread through the basin the need for a single controlling authority grew more and more apparent.[6] The political structure had been chaotic, with two states and five counties having jurisdiction, besides which 61 overlapping governments administered a variety of interests. A Joint Study Committee was created in 1965 by the two State Legislatures and in due course this body issued a scientific and convincing report detailing the dangers to the environment, the balance of nature, and the quality of the lake. Then in 1968, after great argument and foot-dragging, a bi-state agreement was finally reached and passed by both sessions. The following year came Federal approval and in March of 1970 the initial meeting of the Lake Tahoe Regional Planning Agency took place. This body began auspiciously with assigned duties and powers but has since become hamstrung through lack of funds and legal entanglements. The high hopes that were held for it in the beginning have been seriously dimmed, and it remains to be seen if the ideals of orderly development of the bi-state area and preservation of the lake itself can be achieved.

[6] Great impetus was given the basin's growth in 1960 by the selection of Squaw Valley as the site of the VIII Winter Olympic Games. Nordic events were held at McKinney Creek, a west-shore tributary of the lake; Alpine and jumping took place at Squaw Valley. Tahoe facilities were taxed to the utmost in handling the huge crowds of spectators and staff concentrated only seven miles by road from Tahoe City.

The fate of all alpine lakes where populations have multiplied, Switzerland displaying prime examples, is maximum biological fertilization. Whether or not Lake Tahoe can be saved from that dismal prospect, only the future can tell. A fate like that of Lake Erie is not wholly improbable, but if immediate and rigid measures could be taken the loss might be postponed. Otherwise our progeny will be denied the spectacle and the delight of sharing what Mark Twain once called "the fairest picture the whole Earth affords."

CHAPTER IV

The Lahontan System
Lake Truckee and the River

From the gates at Lake Tahoe where it starts, the Truckee River pushes northward for a dozen miles before swinging east and into its upper canyon. Many small streams enter: Bear, Squaw, Deer, Silver, Pole, Deep and Cold Creeks are among those with names. All along this stretch there are ancient stream terraces 20 or 30 feet above the river, from drainage associable with the Pleistocene glaciers. Thereafter the influx is greater from Donner, Martis and Prosser Creeks and at Boca the largest of the feeders, the Little Truckee, adds its flow. This in turn is formed by seven branching rivulets, with Webber and Independence Lakes the more notable sources.

The upper portion of the Truckee River basin resembles a funnel with a remarkably broad flare, 50 miles north-south from Henness Pass to the vicinity of Carson Pass, and all draining eastward into Nevada. The 790 square miles lying in California gather most of the water in the system from melting snow and rainfall on the surrounding slopes and ridges, and the 1340 square miles lying in Nevada—including Pyramid Lake—use most of it up. This unbalanced condition has been the basis of sporadic dispute ever since the political boundaries were determined; we shall examine this situation in due course.

The river is as short in recorded history, a century and a quarter, as it is in length, 105 miles. At the state line it has traversed only 40 miles but has descended 1,700 feet, which is about two-thirds of its total fall to the Pyramid Lake terminus. The aspect of this upper segment is that of a mountain torrent lined with alders, rushing through canyons in a succession of pools and rapids, delightful to fishermen and picnickers. Summer cabins have risen along its course and houses cluster at Boca, Hirshdale, and Floriston, but the only town of consequence in California is Truckee, where the river turns abruptly eastward.

This was the site in Pluvial times of a temporary glacial lake. "West of Lake Tahoe and the Truckee River the mountains were covered by vast névé fields above which only the highest volcanic peaks protruded, and beyond which glacier tongues projected in every valley," Lindgren (1898) writes, in his description of the quadrangle. "Today over 1,000 lakes, large and small, dot the summit region of the main range, nearly all of them of glacial origin (moraine or lava blockage)." There had been an earlier lake in Neocene times when sand and clay from the adjacent hills were washed in, and these deposits in the vicinity of Truckee were thereafter covered by lava flows. Lindgren's data substantiate a Pleistocene body of water 73 square miles in area, and one may infer a depth of 465 feet at Boca though this is not stated. It extended upstream from a basalt flow that dammed the canyon below Hirshdale and reached an elevation of at least 6,000 feet, remaining during part of the glacial period until the river wore down the outlet and the lake disappeared.

Beach gravels of Lake Truckee are found all around the basin, generally at a constant maximum altitude. On its western shore the wash gravels begin a little above 5,900 feet; these can be seen near the town of Truckee and at Sage Hen Creek. In Stampede Valley the shore materials run a little higher, up to 6,000 feet, in river terraces where tributaries entered the lake along the Little Truckee River; and east of Boca there is a beach at 6,200 feet that indicates a small uplift. Coarse gravels in Martis Valley show where the shoreline reached and finer sediments occur on the valley floor. All these features point to the existence, late in the Ice Age, of this vanished body of water.

Apart from the forming and draining of Lake Truckee, the river has remained in place and relatively stable since pre-Pleistocene times. The snouts of the glaciers never quite reached down to it, Lindgren asserts, and little else could have disturbed its relatively steep descent between closely restricted limits. There is no evidence that any Pluvial lake persisted in the Truckee Meadows, now the site of Reno and Sparks. Here moderate runoff from the eastern slopes of the Carson Range enters by way of Steamboat, Thomas, White's, Dry and Evans Creeks; Hunter and Alum Creeks also provide a continuing trickle.

Below Truckee Meadows, at Vista, the augmented river again becomes canyon-bound and continues another 30 miles to and beyond Wadsworth where it resumes a northward course approaching its destination in Pyramid Lake. This lower section lies in very

arid country with an average annual rainfall of only about six inches
and the small side canyons, gulches and washes rarely contribute
any input. Prolonged totally dry spells of up to ten weeks are
common in summer months. At Lagomarsino Canyon a monument
might be erected to the hydrological climax attained with Lake
Lahontan's farthest reach up the Truckee; here its highest level
intersected the riverbed at 4,380 feet a.s.l. about 65,000 years ago
(Morrison, 1964).

The river was discovered by John C. Frémont on January 15,
1844. Five days earlier he and his party had come upon Pyramid
Lake, first of the white race known to have seen it, and had journeyed down the east shore to the Indian village located near the
river's mouth. Impressed by the huge and very numerous fish teem-
ing in the stream he named it after them—the Salmon Trout River.
He followed it no further than the big bend at Wadsworth, for
he was hoping to locate the mythical Buenaventura River that should
have been flowing in the opposite direction—westward to the Pacific
Ocean. Thence he bore south to the Carson and Walker River basins.
Quite possibly trappers had preceded him, working the watersheds
as early as 1832, but they left no record. Frémont's account in his
published diaries is detailed and accurate, and it was he who opened
up this area.

The section from Truckee to Wadsworth is important historically
because it served as part of the transcontinental route most often
chosen by the emigrants from 1844 on. That was also the year
Caleb Greenwood conducted the Stevens-Townsend-Murphy group
upstream, blazing the trail to California. Elisha Stevens and Greenwood were the first to cross Donner Pass. One of their members
was Matthew Harbin, who had been acquainted with a French
Canadian trapper known as "Truckee" when they were both with
the Bonneville-Walker expedition in the 1830s. Harbin called their
Paiute Indian guide after this trapper and the party, presumably
regarding the stream as this Indian's home, named it after him.
Some confusion existed as to spelling: Trucky, Truckie and Truckey
were variously used; quite likely the trapper could not write it,
nor does it seem quite French, but other versions of the name's
origin seem less credible (Scott, 1964).

Other companies under Greenwood and Solomon Sublette took
this river approach to the Sierra and California beyond, the year
following. But the most dramatic passage, certainly, took place in

1846. In just two years the trail had become established and no more than moderate trouble had greeted previous travelers. But the people accompanying George and Jacob Donner came to the Sierra very late in the season, had lost much of their livestock, supplies and equipment along the way, and behaved as if unaware of the formidable hazards there awaiting them. Their story is well known; out of 87 who started from Fort Bridger only 47 survived to reach California (Stewart, 1960).

The first permanent settlement along the Truckee River took place in 1852 when a man named Jamison arrived and began supplying the emigrants passing through, about at the spot where Reno is centered. Seven years later C. W. Fuller built a small bridge and lived in a dugout home nearby, collecting tolls. He sold out in 1863 to Myron C. Lake, who then built an inn, and this accommodation was the real beginning of the city (Mack & Sawyer, 1965). Upstream that same year, Coburn's Station—precursor of the town of Truckee—was founded. Names changed again in 1869 when the Central Pacific Railroad pushed through and officials wanted short and simple ones for their maps and timetables. In the course of two decades the town named after General Jesse Reno, killed in the Civil War, had been successively Jamison's Station, Fuller's Ferry, Lake's Crossing, End of Track, Argenta and Reno (Myrick, 1962).

All sorts of changes were at hand. Nevada had achieved statehood in 1864. In the Carson River watershed the communities of Virginia City and Carson City were already active and growing, supported by the Comstock silver boom, and mining had become the main interest of the postwar era. Reno, enjoying other rail connections that included the Virginia & Truckee and the Nevada & Oregon, became something of a crossroads and expanded rapidly.

Yet the Truckee basin itself was never productive of minerals, unlike adjacent riverbeds and especially those west of the Sierra divide. Lindgren observes that mining was generally disappointing in the Truckee quadrangle; neither ore bodies nor placer were discovered, although deposits of coalshale with thin strata of lignite turned up in the Eocene beds of the Little Truckee and in the neighborhood of Verdi. Judge Frank Norcross of Reno owned patented claims to such but the deposits proved unworkable. If any auriferous gravels existed, they were very limited in exposure.

People should be thankful for the consequence of an unspoiled canyon. There are no rows of rockpiles left from vanished dredges, no landscapes torn and wasted by hydraulic mining. A few intruding enterprises came and went, like the river-polluting papermill at Floriston, the brewery at Boca, and all the ice houses that flourished along that part of the Truckee during the early days of railroading. They remain only in faded photographs and the memories of old-timers. Sooner or later the four small waterpower stations, now almost obsolete, will disappear along with their leaky wooden flumes, leaving the natural scene unsullied. It is one of the loveliest canyons in the West.

The section of the river east of Sparks has known mining activity from the time the Wilcox Mountains were initially examined by prospectors in 1860. Olinghouse, with hardrock showings and some placer gold, was the scene of a short-lived prosperity that revived again in the 1890s. A 10-mile rail connection with the main line at Wadsworth called the Nevada Railroad began operating to Olinghouse in 1906 but failed the next year. In non-metallics, extraction of diatomaceous earth near Clark Station and treatment in a mill at that location has been continuous since about 1940. Utilizing the river for condenser water, the power company has built a central station fueled by natural gas; but no industrial colonization of the lower canyon has otherwise been undertaken.

Beneath the Truckee Meadows along the foothills of the Carson Range lies a belt of hot water that issues to the surface in many places and has been tapped to heat some of the ranch houses there. A series of fumaroles at Steamboat vents columns of water vapor visible especially in winter, and beside the terrace that gives this area its picturesque name there is a spa where people have come for physical therapy presumably induced by its emanations. But thus far there has been no exploitation of the geothermal energy present.

Long after the rails were laid, the highways that share the Truckee River canyons began to take form, winding generally where the pioneers had brought their cattle and wagons through. But the automobile came late to Nevada, with its widely scattered population. Before the Great Basin was discovered a Frenchman named Nicholas Cugnot had, in 1769, developed the first mechanical "road wagon" (though that harbinger of modern transport could only go 2½ miles an hour and had to stop every 100 feet to get up steam). The first practical gasoline-fueled automobile is thought to have been the one that Krebs designed for Panhard in 1894, a year before the famous (u.s.) Selden patent was issued. In Nevada the first automobile appeared in 1903 but the state's earliest highway construction program dates from the close of World War I. A note-worthy transcontinental scheme of those times was the Lincoln Highway, never of uniform standard and soon completely outmoded; such as it was it bordered the Truckee for a considerable distance, close by from Wadsworth to Verdi but then veered off through Dog Valley at the state line. West of the town of Truckee, having returned to the river at Boca, it ascended to Donner Pass in what was considered in those days a triumph of highway engineering.

In arid country water has been coveted and fought over from immemorial time, and the Great Basin has a history of strong dispute where overlapping needs and claims have arisen. The exclusive right to use water is not only a valuable privilege; it is an essential element of worth in any inventory of land, and the oldest rights carry the highest priorities. Such rights are appurtenant to a given parcel; in Nevada they derive from putting a source to beneficial use.[1] The procedure is to develop the water and then make application to the State Engineer for a permit. He has records of all known waters, surface or underground, and can determine if any conflict exists. But as the mining of groundwater may impair another's supply, rights are often called into question, and some uses are not altogether settled. Arbitration may be required and often litigation in the courts may ensue.

Though it might be considered quite obvious, the user categories should be listed here in the light of contention for the Truckee's limited supply. Water being vital for human consumption, domestic use must come first; it is commonly linked with industrial use through systems sometimes referred to as "city water," otherwise municipal and industrial. Mining, which generally requires individual development, and agriculture, involving the preparation of special canals and structures, are other consumptive uses. Partial return is made from these but the waste water is usually polluted to some extent and downstream flow suffers loss of quality as well as diminution. Non-consumptive uses include hydroelectric power generation—where all the water is returned to the system and pollution is minimal—and public recreation in many forms: sports

[1] Under the traditional appropriations doctrine, recognized in Utah and Nevada, water may be used only for a present beneficial purpose, or at least must be put to beneficial use within a reasonable time, since the right is not perfected until the water is diverted and actually put to beneficial use. A reserved or future right to water may be applied for under some circumstances. Permits to appropriate water are issued by the State Engineer. Nevada water law policy has been to restrict groundwater withdrawals from a given basin to conform to the average annual replenishment. This views groundwater as a renewable resource, and minable (Ohrenschall, 1969).

fisheries, wildfowl hunting, boating, water skiing, skin diving, to name a few.

Flood control has in this century become a widely attempted objective. It might almost be called a non-use; yet in river management it gets much attention and has been generously funded at the Federal level. But channel modification is usually disturbing; structures and other provisions for upstream storage in emergencies require the relocation of existing facilities, and so proposals are likely to be very controversial. Furthermore, flood control works at cross-purposes with actual users since the ideal condition here is zero upstream storage, whereas maximum storage is what the irrigation, power development, recreation and municipal-industrial people want. Economic values have traditionally been controlling but today the esthetic ones are more and more being recognized as important. Potentially an asset, a river, when encroached upon or polluted, can just as vividly detract from its environment.

Throughout the Holocene epoch the Truckee River has been assuaging the thirsts of plant and animal life, including human, and furnishing a habitat for fish. Beyond this, it has replenished Pyramid Lake. Paiutes camped beside it for centuries before the first white contact, but they were non-agricultural; evapo-transpiration losses were caused by native species, not by crops. The planters and stockmen, with different needs and customs, changed all this and we find that as early as the 1850s they were diverting water and recording claims to it, even as the miners recorded and claimed their prospects. In 1861 the Cochrane and Pioneer ditches were completed, bringing irrigation to the Truckee Meadows ranchlands, and their pertaining rights are among the oldest in the Great Basin. Extensive diversion of the river followed. And although in recent years much land that was once served by the river has been transferred to other classifications, the ditch system still diverts a goodly portion of the river's flow during the six or seven months' irrigation season, to the raising of feed crops and potatoes—the staple products of the valley.

Domestic consumption has multiplied many times since World War II and the subsequent skyrocketing of population. The Reno-Sparks area has been unusual for conducting a non-metered distribution, required by a law that prohibited the use of any measuring device in charging for water. Whether or not this law will have to be changed remains to be seen but the philosophy behind it is that indiscriminate watering of gardens, trees and lawns will keep the city and its suburbs green. In any case the license encouraged by this method has resulted in a daily per capita use of 750 gallons or more during hot summer weather and such extravagance may not be tolerable indefinitely.

The present-day unit used to measure moving water at any particular point is one cubic foot per second (1 c.f.s.) and flow figures are stated thus in "second feet." Prior to this mid-century the Western unit of measurement was the miner's inch, which is the quantity of water flowing in a certain time through an orifice one inch square under a specified head. It varied from state to state, but in Nevada the miner's inch amounted to .025 c.f.s., or 11.22 gallons per minute; and by statute 40 miner's inches equaled one second foot (A. M. Smith, 1940). To give these figures practical application it may be observed that the minimum flow that some Fish and Game people consider necessary to support fish life such as trout in a river year-round is 20 c.f.s., with 35 c.f.s. needed during the spawning season. As a matter of fact, the Truckee River between the gates at Lake Tahoe and the town of Truckee, being a stretch with many gravel beds where trout like to spawn, is normally kept at a minimal 50 c.f.s. When those gates are fully opened the flow may increase to 1,800 c.f.s. but trout will tolerate this. An extreme flow figure, one that was reached at flood peak, provides interesting contrast: in December 1955, the river was gauged at over 20,000 c.f.s. as it passed through Reno, causing great damage. Many trout were then flushed all the way down to Pyramid Lake.

Measurements of this sort have their uses but in apportioning rights to water on a seasonal basis a larger unit is essential and the one most commonly applied in the West is the acre foot, the amount required to cover one acre one foot deep—equivalent to 43,560 cubic feet. Expressed in gallons, this comes to 325,850. When one considers the annual input of a lake or the water content of a snow pack, the acre foot provides a most practical unit; for large as it may seem, the quantities expressed in such terms often run to hundreds of thousands. So it is the one most often encountered in court decrees and similar allocations, in water storage figures, and in annual flow data.

The official who sees that court decrees covering water allotments are carried out is the Federal Watermaster. His duties include measurement and regulation of streams and adjudication of disputes that may arise between contending parties, subject of course to further court action on appeal. He presides in a chamber resembling a courtroom, where formal hearings are held, but more often is out along the river attending to the details required of his office.

Among decisions he must make are when and to what extent available controls should be applied, decisions that can be critical in time of drought or flood threat, which he must anticipate. In addition to the Tahoe outlet, Prosser, Martis, Boca and Stampede dams have associated gates, and at Webber, Independence and Donner Lakes the electric utility operates regulatory devices since it owns primary rights to their storage. All these controls must be balanced and coordinated to maintain proper volume throughout the system.

The condition most likely to trigger a flood prevails when the ground has been frozen hard prior to the accumulation of a snow pack; then when prolonged rainfall comes, lasting for as much as several days, none of it is absorbed, melting snow adds to the runoff, and the streams are loaded beyond their capacities. Floods here are mostly produced by rainfall, seldom by melting snow alone.

If in his judgment conditions require it, the Watermaster provides upstream cushion to reduce a flood potential. He does this by releasing a portion of the stored water behind dams, but he does so in a manner that prevents or at least minimizes downstream damage. Conversely, when precipitation has been scanty he holds back flow and hoards as much as he can against summer needs. So he must frequently act as a weather prophet, quite literally a man for all seasons.

The employment of a computer might seem to be indicated in order to achieve these functions, what with all the variable and interacting unknowns in the hydrographic profile.[2] But computer time is expensive and the results never transcend the quality of programming, so that here the human mind fortified by intuition and years of experience may perform the necessary calculations faster and better, as well as at lower cost. Moreover, they can be worked out on the job; thus the process is flexible and simple.

Mankind is often at the mercy of some whim of nature. When disasters like a flood or prolonged drought impend, people are filled with dismay and high resolves. But these conditions pass, and recede from memory. Regardless of how much damage there may have

[2] The Desert Research Institute of the University of Nevada, under the leadership of Dr. George B. Maxey, has prepared two "models" (computer programs) for the Truckee River. One deals with volume and flow, the other with water quality. The first one utilizes over 45 years of data and has been extended to cover the Carson River system; its capabilities include providing instantaneous answers to the many problems capable of mathematical analysis. The water quality model, it is hoped, will lead to improved methods of safeguarding public health and a better environment. Thus far these aids have not been incorporated into the actual river management, but as they are built up from year to year with continual additions of information, their potential usefulness increases. They could become instrumental in determining control procedures.

been, the public's concern dies away—the tendency is to forget. These events being relatively uncommon, reluctance to spend money resumes. Yet after the severe flooding of 1950 and 1955 considerable progress was made toward controlling the Truckee's excesses.

A comprehensive plan called the Washoe Project had been advocated in the hope that it would provide better management of both the Truckee and the Carson watersheds. Many of its key features have been adopted. The weir at Lake Tahoe was rebuilt, new dams have been constructed on the Little Truckee, Prosser Creek and Martis Creek,[3] and the clearing of channel obstructions including removal of "reefs" at Vista (transverse ledges) was accomplished. These rock sills at the valley's single outlet tended to maintain an unduly high water table in the lower meadows and this aggravated conditions whenever minor flooding took place. The Corps of Engineers and the U.S. Bureau of Reclamation were instrumental in effecting these improvements.

Some provisions of the Washoe Project were dropped, others were postponed. Meanwhile the Army Engineers advanced some highly controversial proposals for flood controls upstream from the Reno-Sparks metropolitan area. Four alternative sites where very massive structures might be built, with large storage basins designated behind them, were recommended in February 1969. There had been major inundations at intervals: 1907, 1928, 1937, 1950, 1955, and 1963, with minor flooding in years between and since; the Engineers insisted that provisions of this sort must be undertaken to avoid such catastrophes as the "once in a hundred years" engulfment they confidently predicted. Any of these alternatives would be enormously expensive, as well as disruptive to the properties involved. Federal appropriation would be inadequate, structures would disfigure the landscape, and facilities such as the railroad, highways, ranch establishments and some businesses would have to be moved, though if left unprotected their existing sites might not be endangered in a single lifetime—if ever. All proposals were summarily rejected, since most of the responsible citizenry took the position that presently adopted measures should suffice to ward off predictable emergencies and beyond that the calculated risk must be accepted.

At the start of this chapter we noted that the portion of the

---

[3] Martis Creek contributes about one-ninth of the Truckee River volume, compared to one-sixth for Prosser Creek and one-third for the Little Truckee.

basin lying in California gathers most of the system's water, whereas it is largely consumed or dispersed in Nevada. Due to this situation many quarrels have arisen over the years, and gradually through Federal intervention or otherwise the flow has been assigned to specific purposes. But water cannot be doled out unless it is in being. It must first descend in the form of rain or snow and then drain into the normal channels. In order to reach an equitable division of available supplies, negotiators from both states began meeting in 1956 to promulgate an agreement that would be acceptable all around. Thirteen years later, after prolonged political maneuvering and compromise, an interstate compact dividing the water between the states finally was agreed on and legislation ratifying it introduced in both the state legislatures. Eventually the bills were passed and signed into law, but not without much public clamor; and the Pyramid Indians brought suit, insisting the compact would deprive them of their lake by causing it to dry up. Just how the compact could do this was not explained, nor how it might be amended to satisfy the tribe. The agreement simply recognized legally established priorities and allocations, most of which were already binding. But this dispute served to focus attention on the problem of the lake's recession and the Indian interest in maintaining it. And underlying the dissension, all the old rivalries for Truckee River water simmered, intensified by the annual extra-basin transfer required to supply the Newlands Project. We will look into this matter in subsequent chapters.

Wave-cut Terraces Remaining from Pleistocene Lake Lahontan
Spectacularly in evidence at the north end of Pyramid Lake, Nevada.

Tufa Construction at Pyramid Lake
These rocks were formed under water during Lake Lahontan's floruit.

CHAPTER V

The Lahontan System
Pyramid Lake

The aqueous chain that linked the valleys of northwestern Nevada during Wisconsin time reached its climax development early in the period. Lake Lahontan's surface then covered 8,665 square miles (somewhat more than does Lake Ontario) and stood at least 886 feet deep where Pyramid Lake, the lowest point in the system, now remains. The area draining into it was five times as large, but the fact that it did not overflow this basin is evidence that the climate 65,000 years ago was only moderately humid (Russell, 1885). Long arms and bays extended into California beyond Susanville and almost up to Oregon, near McDermitt. Hawthorne marks about the southern limit and the Stillwater Mountains in general the eastern, beyond which an inlet went up the Humboldt River past Golconda and an embayment occupied Eightmile Flat beyond Fallon.

Though Lahontan consisted mainly of filled and connected valleys rather than a uniform body, it attained great extent in the Carson Desert area where about one third of the total surface was concentrated. One should not think of its decline as having been a steady diminution following the early Wisconsin peak, for the lake rose and fell with swings of climate; volume, area and shores changed likewise. As the lake aged it built up bottom sediments, in some places hundreds of feet thick (Morrison, 1964), and at times it nearly dried up. Two prolonged stillstands took place at the 3873 and 3855 levels. Pluvial oscillations included at least three peaking enlargements: about 65,000, 45,000 and 30,000 years ago *(ibid.)*. Generally, precipitation was high when low temperatures prevailed—even as today, when most of it derives from cyclonic storms passing through between October and June, with a winter maximum. Inflow came mostly from normal runoff inside the drainage basin, with only negligible amounts due to melting ice. Fluctuations paralleled those of the Sierra Nevada glaciers. Morrison concludes that Lake Lahontan (and probably Lake Bonneville too) dried up entirely between the two greatest deep-lake intervals, and that the Sierra Nevada was then probably completely deglaciated for long periods.

The Great Basin has been peppered with irrelevant names, and we have Clarence King to thank for the one applied here. Baron La Hontan never made camp within 1,000 miles of the lake site, as I. C. Russell points out, and made no contribution to the world's knowledge of this region. But King's exploration along the 40th Parallel did add much to that knowledge and established him as a geologist of importance. As for Russell, who came on the scene somewhat later than King, his well-written observations were penetrating and have largely withstood subsequent professional scrutiny.[1]

This complicated inland sea has left us two substantial remnants and a number of lesser vestiges. Pyramid and Walker Lakes are the living waters of Lake Lahontan, whereas Carson and Honey Lakes persist well-filled during wet cycles only; also there are several playa-lakes that are just seasonally wet. A large enduring lake that dried up quite recently was Winnemucca, companion to Pyramid and dependent upon the same Truckee River supply. It is still remembered for a perennial surface that finally disappeared about 1938. A considerable land area west of Humboldt Sink, completely surrounded by Lahontan, carried two small internal lakes during the Wisconsin: Granite Springs and Kumiva Valleys, lying between the Sahwave, Seven Troughs and Trinity Ranges. These have playas remaining where they existed.

Among the mud-flat termini that usually carry some expanse of water in the springtime, the most noteworthy are Humboldt Sink, where what is left of its river comes to a destination, and the final run of the Quinn River to its ending in the Black Rock Desert. These are alkali flats devoid of any vegetation at the foci and fringed about with salt-tolerant shrubs. They exhibit all the phenomena of an extreme desert condition—the mirages, dust devils, dune patterns, etc., which presented such a forbidding aspect to the pioneers.

[1] Baron Louis Armand de Lom d'Arce de la Hontan, born in 1666, explored French Canada from 1683 to 1693 and claimed to have discovered the "River Long," describing Indians he said he found at its headwaters. Given command of a fort near the present city of Detroit, he abandoned it out of sheer boredom and in 1693 deserted the French army altogether. His very popular memoirs, New Voyages to America (1703) were often republished, but authenticity of portions of it is suspect. His admiration for Indian life influenced European thought. Actually, it was Arnold Hague who in all probability first coupled his name with the Pluvial lake, in 1877, in an article called "Truckee River Region" which appeared in volume 2, "Descriptive Geology," of King's Report, 1877. King treated the lake in greater detail the following year and received credit for applying the name. A classical monograph on Lake Lahontan was published by Russell in 1885.

Hot springs were observed by Frémont near Black Rock,[2] a dark, non-volcanic outcrop 400 feet high used as an aiming point on the Applegate Trail. A number of thermal outlets in the vicinity produce small ponds of crystal-clear water bubbling just below boiling temperature. Double Hot Springs consists of two pools five feet apart, one clear and the other almost black, surrounded by grass and rushes which attract animals and birds. In the 1840s and 1850s these places served as oases for weary travelers. Some of the pools contain brilliant travertine, in delightful contrast to their settings. Russell (1885) wrote: "The absolutely desert mountains stretching north from Black Rock . . . are so gorgeous and varied in color that they merit the name of Chameleon Hills." The first articulate pioneer to cross the length of this vast alkali plain—80 miles of naked level hardpan—was J. Goldsborough Bruff. His voluminous account replete with accurate sketches includes a good description of the playa. During the wet season this expanse may carry a lake up to 60 miles long and 20 miles wide, greenish-yellow in hue with silt in suspension, very shallow, stirred by the slightest wind. In one portion of the sump a polygonal suncrack system, called "giant desiccation fissures" by geologists who have studied this particular spot, develops following complete evaporation. Russell is worth quoting further:

> When the heat of summer drives every drop of moisture from these deserts a white saline efflorescence appears, which is formed by the crystallization of various salts brought to the surface in solution by . . . capillary attraction and left as the water that disssolved them is evaporated. Incrustations of this nature sometimes cover many miles in extent, especially along the borders of the playas, and render the surface as dazzling as if covered by snow.

Pyramid Lake itself, a body over 30 miles long and from 4 to 11 miles wide, is situated between the Lake Range on the east and the Virginia Mountains to the west, with Pah Rah Peak lying south. A low ridge forms the division between its northern end and the Smoke Creek Desert, an adjacent part of the Lahontan

---

[2] There has been confusion about the name "Black Rock Point," Gianella (correspondence) insists. Historians, he says, have used it quite incorrectly for the tall, dark eminence that gave travelers a landmark across the empty sands, rising next to the pool called Boiling Spring. The proper name is "Black Rock" and the pool is not actually boiling but probably registers no more than 180 F. Various writers including Frémont have referred to the crag as a "volcano," in error, but Gianella—who made several visits there—identifies it as "sediments standing almost vertical . . . of andesite tuff on the north and south sides, with light-colored calcareous rock between." In 1959 he collected fossils from this rock, including "brachiopods, clams and corals, of Permian age."

lakebed that is in reality an extension of the Black Rock Desert. The normal runoff in the immediate basin is almost non-existent, so that from a practical standpoint the Truckee River can be considered the only source of input other than direct precipitation on the lake. It enters near the Indian settlement of Nixon from the southeast. There is now only one island, Anaho, of about 750 acres, and it lies seven miles north of the rivermouth, just off the eastern shore.

The lake varies considerably in both size and elevation due to wide fluctuations in the annual input. The trend has been generally a shrinking and lowering of the waters, though in years of heavy runoff this tendency has been reversed, as in 1952 and 1969. During the latter season over half a million acre feet spilled in from the Truckee River and brought the level up five feet. The annual evaporation rate is assumed to be about 48 inches and this is almost the only escape of water since there is no outlet whatever and very little transpiration via the sparse and scattered lakeside vegetation. Modern maps usually put the lake area at 108,000 acres, rounded off, the the elevation similarly 3,800 feet.[3] Public outcry over the prolonged recession has been vehement, motivated by recreational and esthetic interest in the resource, as well as sympathy for the rights of the Indians whose home it is and whose livelihood depends on its continued existence.

The attraction of Pyramid Lake issues from its spectacular beauty and accessibility, offering to visitors the rare and unlikely sight of extensive water in a very arid setting, all within 30 miles or so of Reno. The usual approach by way of State Highway 33 through the Virginia Mountains brings a sudden impact as the lake comes into view when the sun rides high in cloudless weather, for its indigo spread makes a startling contrast to the bony cinnamon hills

---

[3] The first actual measurement of Pyramid Lake appears to have been made in 1867 by the 40th Parallel Survey under Clarence King. It showed a surface elevation of 3,876 but the method employed—interpolation based on barometer readings at Reno and the lake—was faulty. Gianella writes that it involved "untold errors and also the elevation at Reno was incorrectly noted at the time." In 1941 Hardman and Venstrom, using accurate methods, found the 1867 level to have been 3,867. Based on the revised figure the drop amounted to 78 feet in 100 years. The final report of the Pyramid Lake Task Force (1971) sheds light on the causes and gives these 40-year figures:

1929–69 average annual Truckee River inflow,	+ 250,000 a.f.
Average annual precipitation on the lake,	+ 55,000 a.f.
Total annual input,	+ 305,000 a.f.
Average annual loss due to evaporation,	− 440,000 a.f.
Annual water deficit,	− 135,000 a.f.

beyond. The treeless shores, the totally uninhabited prospect, excite responses not soon forgotten.

These colors maintain no constancy accorded the hour or the season, and the face of the lake may be quickly transformed by changing winds and altered daylight. A dazzling blue becomes a slate gray, or a green expanse grows flushed with the brilliance of the sunset. Algae blooms often give it this greenish hue, and the vertical movement of water in one place or another may produce adjoining patches of surprising dissimilarity. At the end of the day there sometimes comes a series of bewildering transformations when the peaks redden with the departing sun and their slopes pass through the lower prismatic range—pomegranate deepening to egg-plant, reflected across the intervening mirror.

All around the basin there are marks of the ancient presence. Highest terraces made early in the Pluvial period lie some 550 feet above the waves now lapping the shore. Pyramid was then no more than a wide link in the Lahontan chain and lacked individuality. The physical features of today's shoreline were beginning to take shape and among them the most visible and specialized forms are the tufa constructions of calcium carbonate ($CaCO_3$) that have withstood natural forces through the intervening millennia. Of these, the Pyramid itself together with the Needle Rocks seen at the northwest end are the most striking examples. These were created by precipitation from supersaturated waters entering the cold lake from thermal springs.

Some of the shoreline tufa was created by an algal process in which carbon dioxide was extracted by the algae to produce insoluble calcium carbonate; this was then precipitated as aragonite (not calcite). Russell described three main kinds of tufa: 1) Lithoid, deposited in superimposed layers, compact and stony; 2) Thinolite, made up of elongated skeletal crystals; and 3) Dendritic, the most abundant variety, of branching structure. Thinolite is unique to the Lahontan and Mono lake basins and is conspicuously absent in the Bonneville region. It is non-algal, created in offshore waters probably 10 to over 100 feet deep, and is composed of orthorhombic crystals of aragonite.

Other ways in which tufa came into being were by mechanical deposit through wave action against existing rocks, sticks, bones, etc.; concretion in bottom muds from rising supersaturated solutions; and general precipitation as the waters receded in arid phases of the lake cycles. Morrison adds two kinds to Russell's three: cellular tufa, found as coatings, and a coralline type occurring in heads and also as coatings. Antevs (1948) describes two stages of Lake Lahontan in tufa terminologies, calling the first interstadial the Thinolite Lake, and the second peaking the Dendritic Lake.

As geomorphology goes, these constructional forms are relatively small and uncommon, but here along the lake front they loom conspicuously. Frémont observed the triangular erection (then) offshore, midway along his passage, and likened it to the Great Pyramid of Cheops, which structure dates from about 5,000 years ago and is 481 feet high, comparable in size if not precisely in shape. The natural one is of course many times the age of the Egyptians'. The Needle Rocks, a cluster of more than a dozen miniature mountains, share the dramatic aspect though they are not as high or as compact. A striking feature of the littoral is the white band of tufa coating referred to in Chapter I. It is 10 or 12 feet high (at 3,855) and is prominent all around the eastern extent and the base of the Pyramid. At widely spaced intervals rise domed and crenellated jumbles of spheroidal tufa containing shafts and caverns alluring to children; today these are picnic spots and targets of photographic interest. A number of caves have been washed out along the high and long-abandoned beachlines, each inviting exploration.

Winnemucca Lake occupied the valley immediately east of the Lake Range and was ephemeral. When quite full it was still considerably smaller than Pyramid Lake, for although almost as long it was very much narrower. Russell recorded that during the summer of 1876 all the water of the Truckee River emptied into it, the outlet to Pyramid having been closed by a gravel bar; but the following spring the annual rise of the stream removed this obstruction and the normal flow to Pyramid resumed. These transfers seem to have been periodic as accumulated trash or alluvium caused the channel to wander. The Winnemucca lakebed now receives only modest runoff from its own limited basin; wet places form each spring but many people recall when there was water enough to support pleasure boating and a fish life. Today a highway permanently blocks its inlet. The lake will not form again.

There are a number of important archeological sites associated with the Desert culture in the Lahontan basin, most of them located distantly east of here. But two quite important discoveries were made near Winnemucca Lake. Fishbone Cave on its eastern shore, with four levels of different material, is representative. In the lowest level horse, camel and marmot bones were found as well as evidence of a fire (ash); but most importantly, two choppers resting on vegetable fibre that yielded a C-14 date of 11,200 B.P. The cave also contained human bones, partly burned (Orr, 1956). Falcon Hill Cave northwest of the lake and above its highest terrace yielded signs of an occupation almost as old (Tuohy, 1965) plus bones of a prehistoric shrubox *(Euceratherium collinum)*. Both caves shed light on a much earlier lifeway than the better known Lovelock culture, but we still know little about the Paleo-Indians who lived beside this part of Lake Lahontan at the end of the Wisconsin period. Hunting points, animal bones and examples of rock art abound but other indicators are conspicuously lacking. Later oc-cupants were basketmakers and it seems probable that their lives were lake-oriented much like those of the subcultural groups who inhabited the Lovelock area. We will examine this horizon in a forthcoming chapter.

On January 10, 1844, John C. Frémont and his party of 25 (includ-ing Thomas Fitzpatrick[4] and Kit Carson, mountain men acting as guides) "discovered" Pyramid Lake. They had left Fort Vancouver on the Columbia River early in November, passed down through Oregon as we have mentioned and crossed the Black Rock Desert near Boiling Springs, not far from the present town of Gerlach. The pages of his diary are colorful and explicit as he describes the countryside, problems and events at this stage of his journey. His astonishment and pleasure at coming upon the unexpected lake were profound: "It broke upon our eyes like an ocean " he wrote, and observed that this body clearly possessed no outlet. He recorded a great many Indians skulking about, flocks of bighorn sheep, quan-tities of ducks and many very large fish. His party descended to the shore from the head of Sweetwater Canyon, north of Tohakum Peak (8,174), and continued along the east side to the Indian village where, on the 15th, they were cordially received, and dined upon cutthroat trout, which delighted them. All this time they were hauling and considerably encumbered by a mountain howitzer which never was of much use to them and eventually had to be abandoned.

[4] Thomas Fitzpatrick, known as Broken Hand, was a trapper and very capable guide who served many parties moving in the West. Bernard DeVoto (1952) linked him with Kit Carson and Jim Bridger, calling them "the supreme triumvirate of Mountain Men," and observed that the success of the Frémont expeditions to which he was attached stands in marked contrast to the failure of those from which he was absent.

The expedition proceeded. Frémont complained in his diary that he received little information about the country but described a map that the Indians drew on the ground which seems to have been quite accurate; had they followed the Truckee River as drawn they would have saved much time and effort. But instead of reaching Lake Tahoe in three days, as the Indians had promised, they went south beyond the riverbend at Wadsworth, continued across the Carson watershed to the Walker River, and floundered around rather aimlessly for almost a month before they actually saw that lake.

After Frémont's visit the village and the lake remained relatively undisturbed for the next decade. The tide of emigrants passed by, out of sight and reach, for Pyramid lay well off the beaten track. Forty-niners and Mormons hurried on. Then came the Comstock silver strike at Virginia City 40 miles to the southwest, and a horde of adventurers who knew no restraint moved in. Clashes with the Indians became inevitable and these culminated in the "Battle of Pyramid Lake." Major William Ormsby with a force of 105 men undertook a punitive expedition against the Paiutes in May 1860, following the massacre of four men and burning of Williams' Station on the Carson River. For this there seems to have been some provocation, but the white men were determined upon revenge. On the 11th they camped at Wadsworth and next day, a few miles south of the lake, were ambushed and routed by a large force of Paiutes. Major Ormsby was killed and only 29 of his men survived. Army troops and volunteers undertook to retaliate two weeks later; a second battle was fought on June 2nd, the Indians then retreated northward, and on June 4th the white army reached the Indian village only to find it abandoned (S. S. Wheeler, 1967). Later in 1860 Fort Churchill was built on the Carson River and Col. F. W. Lander negotiated a peace treaty with Chief Numaga.[5]

The lands surrounding the lake had been given an informal reservation status after 1859 when the Indian Affairs agent, Frederick Dodge, requested they be set aside for such purpose. But it was not until March 23, 1874, that a presidential order signed by Ulysses S. Grant made the designation official. This reserve, property of

---

[5] Colonel (later General) Frederick W. Lander came west to explore for a railroad route in Oregon, was then assigned to survey and build a wagon road across the Great Basin and the Sierra Nevada. In 1860 he worked the region between Willow Springs and Rabbit Hole with a large crew, improving the roadway and watering places along the Fort Kearney, South Pass and Honey Lake Wagon Road (Helfrich, 1971). Like Gen. Jesse Reno, he died in the Civil War, of wounds received in Virginia in 1862.

the tribe, amounts to almost half a million acres and except for a few inholdings has been continuously owned and occupied by them ever since. Their livelihood is precarious, for they are non-agricultural and no longer are able to conduct a commercial fishing industry: the construction of Derby Dam across the Truckee River and the dewatering below it deprived the trout of their essential spawning grounds, after which the once huge and prolific population died out. Some Indians now run livestock, others find work in neighboring towns. The lake has been restocked with hatchery fish which grow to considerable size but do not breed, so that a fishery of sorts has been reconstituted. It supports the tribe only to the extent that sportsmen who come must buy permits to fish. A 180-acre park at Warrior Point was dedicated in 1971 but there have been no resort developments or leased enterprises that might bring income to the Paiutes, though many possibilities have been explored and proposals offered.

At this point we may concern ourselves with the lake's biotic assemblage. The fish fauna it supported was unique for the quantity, quality and size of its trout and also for the cui-ui, a peculiar kind of sucker, which survives. The Lahontan cutthroat (*Salmo clarkii henshawi*) developed to a maximum length of four feet and over 40 pounds. The largest recorded fish, caught in 1925, weighed 41½ pounds but it is thought much larger ones were taken in preceding years before anyone made note of such matters. Some figures indicating the quantities this fishery yielded may be appropriate. A *Nevada State Journal* article dated November 26, 1889, stated that one W. D. C. Gibson bought and shipped 23,000 pounds of trout from Pyramid and Mud (Winnemucca) Lakes during the preceding 8 weeks. In 1888–9 during the 6-months winter-spring period 100 tons of trout caught by commercial fishermen were shipped via Wells, Fargo Express. The supply of fish was considered to be inexhaustible. As late as 1912 Fred Crosby was shipping 10 to 15 tons a week (S. S. Wheeler, 1967). What wrecked this resource, however, was not so much the overkill as interference with the reproductive cycle. When habitual spawning areas became denied, the species was bound to disappear from Pyramid.

Several other species inhabit the lake. The surviving cui-ui (*Chasmistes cuius*) is a second important food fish which the Indians have caught for centuries by snagging or spearing at such times as they entered the river to spawn—which they still are able to do. They do not respond to ordinary lures, weigh up to 9 pounds, and none less than 12 inches long have ever been seen; where they go between spawning seasons is not known. The species is unique to Pyramid Lake though relatives are found in Klamath and Utah Lakes.[6]

A sporting variety in addition to reintroduced trout is the Sacramento perch *(Archoplites interruptus)* which was brought in about 80 years ago. Also there is a minnow, classified as a lake-type chub *(Siphateles bicolor obesus)* of ancient origin. Plankton and small crustaceans are plentiful in the lake and figure importantly in the food chain, supporting a highly favorable habitat for the larger forms. The lake water is somewhat brackish—not really potable—with 5,000 p.p.m. of dissolved solids, three-fourths being sodium chloride. A pH of 9.15 (strongly alkaline) was measured in 1961 and this remains fairly constant; cutthroat trout have a tolerance considerably in excess of this figure (S. S. Wheeler, 1967).

The sports fishery of Pyramid Lake was revived by artificial means in recent years with stock bred in Nevada state fish hatcheries. The Lahontan cutthroat had been considered extinct but then specimens were unexpectedly obtained from Walker Lake, the other associated remnant, and these provided the eggs needed to revive the species. But in view of their continuing inability to reproduce naturally, they must be replaced from hatchery stock as they become depleted through harvest. Individuals now being taken approach in size and weight, though not in quantity, those originally present. In 1971 many trophy fish were measured in excess of 30 inches long and up to 18 inches girth, and in 1973 a specimen of 19 pounds, 8 ounces broke the modern weight record.

Many fish of riverine habitat were swept down by flood waters in 1950 and 1955 and thrived in the lake. These, mostly rainbow, gave an early stimulus to fishing, having grown to good size in the less confining and nutrient-laden Pyramid. Experiments in cross-breeding at hatcheries have produced good types for stocking: the cutbow and bowcut offer special qualities and excellent sport.

There is some hope that a natural fishway can eventually be reconstituted. Federal money has been appropriated to build a dam

---

[6] The cui-ui may be a clue to the continuing question: has Pyramid Lake ever dried up completely? Morrison contends that it did so and Russell thought that Pyramid owed its freshness to total post-Lahontan desiccation (when winds would have blown away the dried salt from its bed). But Hubbs and Miller contradict Russell and point to the cui-ui, maintaining that enough spring and creek water must have remained on the parched surface to support the fish fauna in this entirely closed basin. Some others take the view that the cui-ui could have persisted at the mouth of the Truckee after the lake became too mineralized for the fish to tolerate, but Hubbs and Miller do not agree.

at Marble Bluff, several miles above Nixon, and dig an adequate channel below it. Sufficient flow would be released during the spawning season from a reservoir above the dam to attract trout, it is hoped, and they would move to suitable beds. This work has gone forward but it remains to be seen if the scheme will succeed in restoring a natural breeding cycle.

A varied birdlife comes and goes here. The largest known nesting colony of white pelicans is situated on Anaho island, which has been designated a National Wildlife Refuge. But its isolated status is in jeopardy as the water level descends, and it may cease to be an island in the course of another decade or two unless some drastic precaution such as dredging a channel is instituted. Connection to the mainland would provide access for predators and probably end its usefulness to the pelicans. A 1965 government inventory listed 7,500 pelicans, 1,500 double-breasted cormorants, 4,500 California gulls, 150 Caspian terns and 200 great blue herons living on Anaho (Woodbury, 1966). The pelicans commonly arrive in June and nest throughout the summer. Migratory waterfowl stop over seasonally and mud hens are perennial.

Coyotes, jackrabbits, cottontails, mule deer and bobcats are indigenous to the shores and adjacent slopes but the bighorn sheep have long since disappeared. The kangaroo rat runs abroad at night. Horned toads (properly horned lizards of the genus *Phrynosoma*) and several other kinds of lizard, as well as the Great Basin rattlesnake, live among the rocks and sagebrush; and there is a species of tarantula—also nocturnal, rather shy and inoffensive—that can be observed. Another arachnid, rarely encountered, is the scorpion.

Besides the everpresent artemisia, rabbit brush and shadscale occur all through the basin, with cottonwood and willow *(Salix)* where moisture is sufficient. There is a dark planting of salt cedar *(Tamarix gallica,* not native locally) where U.S. Navy personnel, hoping to camouflage a World War II installation, succeeded in establishing the most conspicuous living landmark in the countryside. It is the only remaining evidence of this intrusion.

In 1912 the Southern Pacific Railroad began building a branch line from Fernley to Westwood and its tracks passed along the west side of the lake. Completed in 1914, its main purpose was to carry lumber, but passenger trains were also operated for some years. Connections with private lumbering roads served the Westwood region (Myrick, 1962) but as the mills ran out of timber in the late 1960s and shut down, revenues shrank; so in 1970 the Fernley and Lassen Railway, as this branch line was called, ceased operations. When the railroad came to salvage their rails the Indians laid claim to them as fixtures of the tribal property, and for a time prevented their removal. The matter has since been re-solved—rails and ties have disappeared.

Although the Indian lands were doubtless thoroughly prospected in the early days, no workable mine was ever found. However, just outside the reservation boundary southwest of the lake, deposits were located at least a century ago in what became known as the Pyramid Mining District. There a stamp mill was built in 1876 and the Monarch mine enjoyed a degree of activity. The ore con-tained mainly copper and silver, with some gold.

During the years when the reservation existed informally, that is to say between 1859 and 1874, a number of white families settled within it and began ranching. Though told to leave they failed to do so, and finally in 1924 legislation at the Federal level was passed which permitted them to obtain legal title in return for certain payments. Some of them did make payment and stayed on; others did not and were eventually dispossessed.

The tribe has a legal right to a specified amount of water from the Truckee, provided it is used for agricultural purposes. But these people are not farmers and have failed to use this allocation. Some ditching was once undertaken but no sustained agricultural effort has been conducted and the present Indian demand is for enough water to keep their lake from diminishing. Such an amount has been estimated at 385,000 acre feet, at a minimum, but nothing like that is normally available after the legal upstream demands have been satisfied. These demands have been called into question, and the entire matter is in the hands of the courts. In most years there is insufficient water in the Truckee to meet the needs of all the users and to keep the level of Pyramid Lake from dropping.

CHAPTER VI

The Lahontan System
Carson River and the Sink

The Carson River, like the Truckee and the Walker, receives snow melt from a portion of the eastern Sierra slope and flows down into a desert sump. Nowhere along its descent is there convincing evidence that any Pluvial lake persisted, such as the two that formed in the channel of the Truckee; any damming would have been very brief. We have no reason to think that in their adjoining basins these modern streams are much different, other than in length, from those that were in place there 65,000 years ago. Lahontan then being very broad and full, the entering rivers were naturally much shorter.

Tributaries of the Carson River system rise along 50 miles of the main Sierra crest and the southern end of the Carson Range, beyond the Tahoe basin in California's Alpine County, and joining, flow down across the state line into Nevada where most of the beneficial use of their waters is made. The east and principal fork begins right under Sonora Peak (11,462); its descending course trends north and east, with a volume much augmented by Silver King, Wolf, Silver and Markleeville Creeks. The west fork rises in Lost Lake south of Kit Carson Pass and also probing north and east past Woodfords enters Douglas County short of Minden and Gardnerville. The two branches meet near Genoa, the oldest town in the state.

This source area of the two forks is very high and handsome country, forested and relatively uninhabited, but sought out in summertime by campers and fishermen spending their vacations along the trout streams. The lofty form of Highland Peak (10,955) stands vis-a-vis Ebbetts Pass at the head of Wobe Canyon. Heavy winter snows usually close this pass for as long as six months but in recent years Kit Carson Pass has been kept open the year around and traffic crossing the Sierra can use this adjacent route to Stockton and the San Joaquin Valley. Both passes are over 8,500 feet above sea level.

Beyond Genoa the river skirts Carson City, the state capital, swings eastward through Brunswick Canyon and almost to Fallon, then turns north into Carson Sink, where it ends. This segment is about 100 miles long, without allowance for meandering. At a point some 15 miles past the capital near Dayton, Lake Lahontan's Carson arm made its farthest upstream advance at the height of the Pluvial influence, but no signs of that presence remain there now. Downstream some distance lie the remnants of Fort Churchill. These crumbling adobe structures are protected in a state park, and near this site the narrow Walker arm of the old lake joined its main body. Artificial Lahontan reservoir next breaks the river's march and thereafter under control it passes to the ranchlands of Lahontan Valley. The waste water supplies Carson Lake, Stillwater Marsh, and a National Wildlife Refuge in the Carson Desert and Sink. Here are located the Fallon Indian Reservation and a U.S. Naval Air Station.

During early Wisconsin time the Humboldt, Truckee, Carson and Walker Rivers, together with shorter and less important streams, all led to the one extended and integral body of Lake Lahontan, which then filled a score of connected valleys in northern Nevada. As its volume dwindled and its area shrank, the principal basins were detached and one after another dried up until only Pyramid and Walker Lakes maintained perennial existence. These ancestral waters attained their widest dimension where the Carson Desert now spreads out and over 30 per cent of its surface developed in this locale. Around and about the southern half of this broad plain are mountain clusters called the Cocoon, Blowsand, White Throne, Dead Camel and Desert Ranges; on them the marks of the ancient water levels are very plain. Terraces can be seen in many different parts of the valley and they often occur one above another up to 515 feet higher than its present floor. With bottom sediments as much as 200 feet thick deposited in some places, water depths in the earliest Lahontan times must have exceeded 700 feet. Sorted gravels lie along the beaches, and other lacustrine evidence includes alluvial cones, dry deltas and shelving at hard horizontal strata.

I. C. Russell noted that in 1882 water had accumulated in Carson Sink covering 40 square miles but only four feet deep in the middle. At the same time Humboldt Sink, a few miles to the north and not then connected—nor is it normally—carried a 20-square mile spread that was 12 feet deep. Today these bodies come and go, rarely drying altogether, yet seldom as extensive as the ones Russell (1885) wrote about.

Much information can be deduced from studying the sediments built up in a lake or sink such as this one. Rivers swollen by melting ice, coming into existence at the snouts of glaciers that are scouring troughs in the rock, are commonly burdened with pebbles, sand, clays and rockflour and so are of a milky hue. These may be seen worldwide in high regions still favored with permanent ice: the Rhone, the Athabaska, the Dudh Kosi, and hundreds of others. In situations where the melt water enters a lake, momentum is lost and some of the suspended material is dropped, so that the bottom tends to build up in annual layers called varves. By counting and measuring these, much information can be gained as to preceding river life, climatic conditions, and glacial activity. But over the longer divisions of geological time more practical methods of analysis are desirable.

The nature and source of material, with implications of ancient climatic conditions, can be studied in detail thanks to a whole new science called soil stratigraphy. Its very sophisticated techniques have become standardized in quite recent years, and it is particularly valuable here because the highest lake stages tend to obscure or wipe out earlier evidence, occurring at lower elevations. New ways of determining geological history were long needed. Roger B. Morrison, a pioneer in soil stratigraphy, developed a series of weathering profiles for the entire Lahontan existence (1963 et seq.) and he conducted his basic studies in the southern Carson Desert. Briefly, the method is as follows:

The soil-stratigraphic unit is the geosol. This is a laterally traceable and mappable layer of weathered mineral material maintaining a constant age relationship with associated deposits (older below, younger above). Geosols are nearly time-parallel, valid markers for long-distance correlation as well as for defining time-stratigraphic units within the Quaternary. Each soil horizon has chemical and physical characteristics that distinguish it. A most important chemical property is the acidity or alkalinity of the material, the degree of which is indicated by its pH value. Among the physical characteristics are feel, cohesiveness and tactility; these determine the textural class in which the sample fits. Primary soil particles are known as peds, and soil without structure is described as apedal. Organic soils are amenable to carbon dating. Fossil soils are those without organic content and the study of them is called paleopedology. Analysis and comparison of geosols usually result in quite accurate knowledge of the conditions under which they were deposited and as to when, relatively, they were laid down.

In the valley south of Fallon, Morrison found evidence of many lake cycles and prolonged intervals between them, and he interpreted the sequences in detail. He identified the various layers of soil and named them after local geophysical features. For instance, there is the Eetza formation, 100 feet thick, deposited during the highest lake cycle when the 4380-foot maximum was attained, 65,000 years ago. Another soil, of even earlier origin, called Cocoon after the range of mountains south of Eightmile Flat, has been correlated with Dimple Dell soil in the Bonneville basin and Sangamon soil in Illinois, all of a similar nature and timing. Toyeh soil, parallel with Utah's Midvale soil, has been proposed as a logical marker between the Pleistocene and the Holocene epochs in the Great Basin. A soil named after Sehoo Mountain is widespread, and there are many more layers, all being specialized and recognizable wherever they may occur (Morrison, 1964).

Conditions in the Carson Desert are typically arid and only the unnatural introduction of a substantial irrigation source has altered them appreciably. At Fallon Agricultural Station the mean annual rainfall has been measured at just over five inches, and a maximum evaporation rate of 64 inches a year has been recorded. Carbonates, sulfates and chlorides left after the lake waters evaporated have put the ground in poor condition for agriculture and limited the natural flora to salt-tolerant desert types. The prevailing cover consists of shadscale, little greasewood and bud sagebrush, with scattered hopsage, white sage and *Ephedra*. The latter is also known as Mormon tea or joint fir, and is a relic unchanged from the Mesozoic era. The plants that adapt themselves to this sort of environment fall into one of two categories usually: either they are xerophytes, shallow-rooted species like some cacti that spread their underground elements widely and close to the surface to catch precipitation before it sinks, or phreatophytes (well-plants) which send roots down to the water table, anywhere from 8 to 50 feet below the surface (Jackson, 1928). O. E. Meinzer established this latter term, and the commoner species include big greasewood, big rabbitbrush and saltgrass *(Distichlis stricta)*.

Perennial herbs and annuals are generally sparse or absent in such an area, where precipitation in a year's time can run as low as one inch, never more than nine inches. Summer temperatures in excess of 100° F. are not unusual, and the diurnal temperature range is phenomenally large: a 65° rise from pre-dawn hours to mid-afternoon is occasionally recorded in summer. For Great Basin communities east of the Sierra Nevada within 50 miles of Reno the annual precipitation averages 5 to 7 inches, except for Carson City, which receives 11 inches (Thomas, 1964), Minden with 9, and Doyle with 12.

A fossil is defined as any evidence of former life. The Great Basin has revealed a diffuse and varied fossil incidence derived from all epochs when life of one kind or another existed here—from the earliest Precambrian invertebrates and simple plants down to man himself. We shall be concerned in this work with only the late Pleistocene animal forms, many of which are now extinct but whose fragments (bones or the mineral replacements of them) remain as proof they once inhabited the region.

When the climate was much cooler and wetter, a different kind of vegetation thrived in the Basin. It supported species that disappeared when conditions changed. A number of bison species (*B. antiquus, B. taylori*), a mammoth (*Elephas* species), a camel (*Camelops hesternus*) and a horse (*Equus occidentalis*) were fairly widespread. Fossil remains in Gypsum Cave near Las Vegas, Nevada, included the ground sloth (*Nothrotherium shastense*), dire wolf (*Canis dirus*) and long-legged llama (*Tanupolama stevensi*). Also, the largest flying bird[1] known to have lived, a long-extinct vulture with a wingspread of 16 to 17 feet called *Teratornis incredibilis*, was a Nevada native (Fisher, 1970). During the last 32,000 years at least 60 species of mammals and 33 of birds have become extinct in North America, most of them in the last 15,000 years (*ibid.*) but the presence of only a few has been established for the intermontane West and much work remains to be done in this field.

One of the richer fossil finds in Nevada was the mud flat pattern exposed in the yard of the state prison at Carson City. Here a stone terrace carries the imprints of many long-extinct varieties; horse, elephant, ground sloth and camel walked the soft terrain that eventually became petrified, and we have rather surprisingly clear and uncluttered tracks that serve as a map of these species' wanderings. Footprints of different birds also crisscross the yard floor. The tracks must have been made at almost a single moment

---

[1] In 1975 the fossil remains of a pterosaur with a "wingspread" of 51 feet were discovered in the Big Bend area of West Texas. This extinct animal, like the previously-known pterodactyls, was not a bird but a reptile. Moreover, it is thought that such forms did not actually fly, but glided with set wings toward their objectives. Several true bird forms larger than *Teratornis incredibilis* existed but were incapable of flight. Among these the extinct *Aepyornis maximus* of Madagascar was probably the most imposing. He weighed half a ton and stood 9 feet high. Another huge species, this one from New Zealand, was the Moa, who stood 10 feet high, but was not as heavy. Both had only vestigial wings.

in time, after which the mud soon hardened, or was covered and then much later exposed, so the record remains to us. Fortunately someone recognized and valued the traces sufficiently to make an accurate diagram of them and we have a surviving identification even though new building has covered or defaced some portions of this very special register.

The presence of man in the Carson drainage area, though not evident in the State Prison fossil tracks, is amply attested otherwise. Projectile points and rock drawings have been found in many localities at open sites, but most importantly a number of caves have been excavated that show early and very interesting occupancy. In the adjacent Humboldt and Carson Sinks three different horizons of the Desert culture are clearly distinguished by artifacts found in these repositories: Lovelock Cave, dating from ca. 4,500 B.P.; Leonard Rockshelter, 4,000 to 6,000 B.P.; and Humboldt Cave, somewhat later, perhaps 2,000 B.P. (Heizer and Krieger, 1956). All three horizons were established in the Leonard Rockshelter 11 miles south of Lovelock, in Pershing County. Each was distributed in strata at appropriate levels and yielded rich material. Obsidian flake scrapers, atlatl darts and shell beads belonging to the Humboldt culture turned up in the lowest provenience. More recent indicators of the Lovelock culture, included many textile items such as nets, duck decoys, fishhooks and baskets; there were hammers, scrapers, tubes and grass-cutters, awls and similar tools, made from a variety of materials (Tuohy, 1965).

The Leonard Rockshelter's older levels, together with contents of most of the Oregon caves and those of southern Nevada (Gypsum and Etna) are classed as Protoarchaic, whereas the earlier Great Basin sites at Fort Rock, Danger Cave, the Death Valley complex and Lake Mojave complex are called Paleo-Indian (Krieger, 1964).

In this Carson Sink-Humboldt Lake vicinity the more recent occupations left proof at Lovelock, Ocala and Humboldt Caves of a lake-oriented lifeway; each contained duck decoys and fishing indicators. The first of these three, 22 miles southeast of the town of Lovelock, for which it was named, was discovered in 1887 but not scientifically investigated until 1924. Meanwhile it had been dynamited, mined for guano and otherwise vandalized so that the upper layers were thoroughly destroyed, yet much below remained intact. A considerable number of specimens, perhaps 2,000 were removed in 1912 by L. L. Loud on behalf of the University of

California and the Nevada Historical Society and were preserved
by these institutions (Mack and Sawyer, 1965). Then in 1924 Loud
and M. R. Harrington completed the excavations professionally
and established the inventory on which our knowledge is based.

Lovelock Cave itself is 150 deep and up to 35 feet wide. Until
Danger Cave (Jennings, 1957) was published, Lovelock was the best
known and most prolific site in the Great Basin. Its use seems to
have been primarily as a cache site from 2,500 B.P. on (Heizer,
1964), though 60 or more burials were also found.[2] Cressman (1956)
collected a series that subsequently yielded a date of 3,400 B.P.
(± 260). Inasmuch as its position was well above any Holocene
lake level it was a dry cave with well-preserved contents. Individual
cache pits were generally lined and covered with basketwork held
in place by stones. Mammals found within, all of them modern
species, included deer, antelope and mountain sheep, wolf, bobcat,
beaver, skunk, mink, weasel, marmot and badger, jackrabbit and
cottontail. Scores of plants such as hemp *(Apocynum)*, rush, cane,
grasses, willow, cottonwood and greasewood, provided raw material
for various purposes (Jennings, 1968).

Humboldt Cave—not to be confused with the much earlier Humboldt cultural horizon—dates from about 2,000 years ago. It contained 31 cache pits and yielded a rich assemblage of specialized
artifacts. Among them were sickles made of mountain sheep horn,
bone awls, drills, fishhooks strung on lines, bundles of feathers,
olivella shell beads, bone whistles, stone pipes, dart and arrow shafts,
obsidian points, cottonwood bowls, string aprons and many other
items. A shaman's kit consisting of articles for making magic[3] and
766 pieces of coiled basketry were unearthed. Food bones from
eight bird species as well as many of the mammals found in Lovelock
Cave were identified (Heizer and Krieger, 1956). But at neither
of these two places were any manos or flat milling stones reported
although they were plentiful nearby in the open. This fact and

---

[2] Heizer made further studies at Lovelock Cave on coprolites (fecal material) and found
a diet consisting of baked cattail pollen, parched bulrush seed, whole baby birds, raw and
cooked ducks and geese, beetles, antelope, bighorn sheep, squirrel and chub. One coprolite
contained the bones of 51 chub, presumably eaten in a single meal, and these would have
weighed at least 3½ pounds. (*Britannica Book of the Year*, 1970).

[3] The shaman, or medicine man, was a functionary of many if not most tribal groups in
North America. His magic-making sometimes employed quite elaborate forms, using such
aids as the Tsimshian soul-catcher (made of bone and abalone shell), the spirit whistle,
the charm necklace, and other figures whose purposes have not in all cases been deciphered.
Intricate designs were often incised upon these objects.

the absence of midden discards at Humboldt Cave suggest that it was seldom used as living quarters but rather almost entirely for storage.

Ocala Cave, four miles away, was another source of Lovelock cultural material, as were Hidden Cave and Hanging Rock Cave. The latter, quite recently discovered, yielded a very interesting painted wooden owl effigy plus other perishable artifacts found by two collectors in 1966 and turned over to the Nevada State Museum. A single C-14 date of 1,700 B.P. (±100) was obtained (Tuohy, 1969). This rockshelter is located at Grimes Point, in the Carson Sink at the southern end of the Stillwater Range. Hundreds of petroglyphs and at least 26 caves or shelters, mostly containing some trace of prehistoric use, have been located and studied in the general vicinity of these caves.

Many open sites have been identified along what was once the Lahontan shoreline. These were campsites used seasonally or perhaps as substitute camp locations when traditional ones were flooded. Near the old railroad siding at Toulon west of Humboldt Lake an arch of 16 house pits of late origin—dated perhaps about 600 A.D.—was uncovered in the late 1960s and given archeological study. It was probably a fishing village at lakeside. Hunting points indicated the use of bows and arrows here, and spears, knives, tools, hammer and grinding stones, basketry and ornaments turned up. Among such was an effigy with the features of a resting frog.

Gathering centers, chipping grounds and quarries, hearths, waterholes and hunting lairs lie scattered throughout the well-watered Carson Basin. The commonest indicator of human occupancy is probably the projectile point; these have been found in many forms, distributed in every part of the region.

The Indian population diminished considerably during the first decades of the historical period, probably reaching its minimum in the 1860s. Undermined by starvation resulting from depletion of the always-marginal biota and disruption of the ecosystem by the white intruders, and lacking any built-up immunities, the Northern Paiute and Shoshonean bands were unable to resist disease. Cholera decimated them. Ailments like measles, justifiably regarded by those of European stock as mild, were serious and often fatal for the Indian. In order to survive he tried to adapt to changing situations but seldom succeeded. With the old customs and dependencies shattered his predicament became grave, and the Federal authorities who might have assisted him, had they been enlightened and philanthropic, instead often perpetuated or intensified his problems.

Today the Indian people are more numerous and in a somewhat better situation. They tend to congregate in this basin at colonies in Dresslerville, Carson City and Fallon. Like those on the Pyramid Lake Reservation, a few run cattle or do some gardening but the men are more likely to find work in the towns. Some have become excellent craftsmen and substantial citizens, but clannishness and the pull of tradition are barriers to their becoming completely assimilated.

At Stewart, south of the state capital, the Carson Indian Agency maintains a school, established in 1890, where young people come from neighboring states as well as from around Nevada to learn various crafts and trades. Two dozen or more stone buildings house the facility, which is located about where Clear Creek joins the Carson River. Some of the craft work has been sold at a trading store connected with the school.

The first white man to enter this watershed was probably Jedediah Smith, along with his two companions Silas Gobel and Robert Evans, late in May 1827. We cannot be certain because the record is incomplete, but it seems likely that he entered at the head of the East Carson and crossed over to the Walker basin. Peter Skene Ogden stopped short of Carson Sink two years later, reluctant to encroach on the territory of Alexander McLeod and lacking proper maps of the area. He returned to Oregon without investigating either the Carson or the Truckee although his interpreter had learned about both from the Humboldt Lake people. Late the same year Ogden came this way again, but his route is known only through a surviving letter indicating that he came down from Humboldt Sink and on to the Walker River.

In 1833 Joseph R. Walker's party of explorers, numbering 30 or 40, came to the region of the sinks in early autumn, rested a day or two, and regrouped. Here "eight or nine hundred Piutes" confronted them, Zenas Leonard wrote in his journal. A parley followed but when the Indians continued to threaten, insisting on coming into the camp, a decisive blow seemed necessary. The whites opened fire and the Indians dispersed, leaving at least 25 dead, with many more wounded. The next year in about the same vicinity Walker and his men camped on their return journey to the Bear River rendezvous in Utah. Again the Paiutes gathered, twice as many as before. A second "Battle of the Lakes" then took place, actuated by the same dire encroachment, and 14 were killed, many others wounded. After this the explorers encountered no further trouble.

The Bartleson-Bidwell party, first emigrant train to the West, paused in passing beside Carson Lake in 1841. Two years and some months later John C. Frémont, Kit Carson and Thomas Fitzpatrick, en route from Pyramid Lake, examined the lower Carson River and camped there on January 18th. The waters were very high at that time, the sinks were flooded and joined, and so it was not possible to tell in what direction the rivers were flowing since motion depended on which one was then in spate. Frémont, bemused by the notion of the Buenaventura, was further perplexed. The triumvirate shortly went on to the Walker without tarrying longer.

Next came the main company of Frémont's Third Expedition under Theodore Talbot, in 1845, with Joe Walker as their guide. The route being known, they did not linger. By 1846 more emigrant groups were coming west along the Humboldt River and down through Carson Sink; during the next decade this route became heavily traveled. The section from Ragtown on the Carson River northward to the Humboldt, known as the Fortymile Desert, turned into a disaster area for hordes of people. Scattered along its dry and dreary waste were the bones of oxen and cattle, the broken and abandoned wagons, and a sad miscellany of equipment discarded by the pioneers. "Let your horse or oxen rest on Sunday," wrote one pious migrant in 1850, "for they will make up in six days more than you can travel in seven." To go from Indiana to the Mother Lode country took four months or more.

In 1847 Brigham Young brought his followers into Utah and founded the Mormon capital at Salt Lake City. Three years later California was admitted to the Union and H. S. Beatie set up a trading post for immigrants near the confluence of the Carson Forks. This was the beginning of Genoa, first permanent settlement in Nevada. John Reese and 20 men from Salt Lake built a fort thereabouts the following year. Utah Territory extended all the way to the Sierra, and Brigham sent his deputy Orson Hyde to the newly created Carson County in 1855. Hyde set up his court and administered territorial law throughout the valley, but not for long, as these were troubled times for the Latter-day Saints and Brigham feared intervention by the Federal government. Judge Hyde was recalled in 1856 and a year later the whole Mormon colony was ordered home (Hulse, 1965).

Capt. James H. Simpson left Camp Floyd, west of Utah Lake, on May 2nd, 1859, with a company of 44 officers and men to set up a new route to California. Guided by John Reese, they went by way of Skull Valley to Ruby Valley and thence across Nevada to Carson City, using the Churchill-Carson River approach. Genoa, end of the line for the main group, then boasted a population of 150 to 200 people. Simpson's return trip began late in June, passed 40 miles south of his earlier operation, and ended August 1st back at Camp Floyd. Relay stations of the Pony Express (1860) were set up along his northern route whereas the Chorpenning Mail, the Overland Telegraph, and the Majors & Waddell transport utilized the southern, which was 260 miles shorter than the Humboldt trail and 390 miles shorter to Sacramento than the Los Angeles roundabout. It was employed daily by emigrant trains and stock movements, and the Overland Stage & Mail line used it, beginning July 1st, 1861. Today, U. S. Highway 50 runs approximately where Simpson made his southern survey.

The discovery of the Comstock Lode in 1859 changed the pattern of living in the Carson Valley. Previously there had been sporadic placer mining in the vicinity but only a few ranchers had settled along the river to raise wheat and potatoes. Then with the sudden mining boom came population growth and a great activity. Virginia City, Silver City, Gold Hill and Dayton sprang up. All are in this drainage basin, and it was natural that mills treating ore from the mines would be built along the Carson River, quantities of water being required in the separation process. Many of these mills, a dozen in number and eventually dismantled, have left substantial rock foundations visible along the banks today.

Statehood came to Nevada in 1864, largely as a result of the Civil War and Abraham Lincoln's desire to add two more free state senators in support of the Union. More mining centers materialized across the land with new discoveries, trade boomed and towns expanded. When the war was over, Congress decided to finance a transcontinental railroad. Surveys for it had been conducted during the preceding decade and even before then much discussion of competing routes had taken place. When the Central Pacific construction finally reached across the Sierra Nevada to the Truckee basin it was rapidly pushed eastward and at Wadsworth the roadbed left the river and started out across the desert. Thousands of Chinese were used in grading it, many of whom later turned to mining. They ran the CP by way of Hot Springs over White Plains Hill to Brown's Station (Toy) that hot summer of 1868, approaching the Humboldt River, which would provide a favorable right-of-way as it had for travelers since the coming of man. It was necessary at one point to haul water 84 miles to the railhead (Myrick, 1962). The branch lines via Hazen to Fallon and to the connection at Churchill with the Carson & Colorado would come much later.

Two other railroads are important in the history of this river basin. Oldest in the state apart from the CP and much the most successful of all the small regional roads was the Virginia & Truckee, for which ground was broken at American Flat on February 18th, 1869. It ran from Virginia City to Carson City at first and in 1872 was extended to Reno. Considerably later the line was given a branch to Minden and thus until May 30th, 1950, it served the half dozen communities in its territory. For most of its 81 years it showed a handsome profit. A typical early day cargo consisted of 35 carloads of lumber, and in addition, upwards of 20 cars filled with merchandise, hay, machinery and ice destined for the mines. The 80 to 100 outgoing carloads a day would be almost entirely ore from the mills *(ibid.)*.

The tracks of the V & T dropped from the elevation of Virginia City 1,575 feet to the Carson River by way of a maximum 2.2 per cent grade and they contoured the steep slopes of Sun Mountain and its shoulders through a series of tortuously winding curves. Myrick asserts that these were equivalent to 17 complete circles in the course of traveling 13½ miles to the Carson. Seven tunnels and a 500-foot trestle across Crown Point ravine were features of this civil engineering masterpiece.

The other railroad to festoon this countryside was the Carson & Colorado. It was projected to operate between the rivers of its name, but while it did run along the Carson from Mound House, ten miles east of the capital, it failed to come close to the other. Instead, it veered off at Tonopah Junction to cross Montgomery Pass and go down the Owens River to Hawley (Keeler). Its narrow gauge construction was started in 1880 and its destination 293 miles away was reached three years later. Purchased by the SP in 1900, the C & C was in due course converted to standard gauge and a link was built to the main line at Hazen. The stretch from Mound House to Churchill along the river survived, nevertheless, until 1934 in intermittent operation.

A small (8-mile) connecting railroad called the Dayton, Sutro & Carson Valley lasted 15 years from 1881, hauling ore and tailings to the Lyon Mill. A railroad into the Como Mountains and one up Gold Canyon were proposed but never built. In Chapter IX we shall have more to say about the C & C and its Owens Valley extension. As for the Comstock, before the lode pinched out it produced more than half a billion dollars worth of gold and silver, as well as prolonged prosperity and lasting settlement of an otherwise unpromising mountainous hinterland.

The rivalry for water in the contiguous Carson and Truckee basins has been keen and often bitter since the mid-19th century. In its normal course each river was integral and carried meltwater from its own portion of the Sierra crest to separate destinations in the desert. Then in 1903 an act of Congress established the Newlands Project, named after its author, Senator Francis G. Newlands of Nevada. This was the first of many reclamation schemes to be instituted by the Federal government throughout the West.

The Newlands Project consisted mainly of the following features: a new weir at Lake Tahoe, the Derby dam 25 miles east of Reno on the Truckee, a dam on the Carson River creating Lahontan reservoir, a canal 31 miles long connecting the impoundment behind Derby dam with the Lahontan reservoir, and a system of irrigation canals and laterals in Lyon and Churchill counties some 550 miles in length. The act creating this project guaranteed to the ranch areas it served a minimum 406,000 acre feet of water annually, and inasmuch as the Carson River could not be expected to provide this amount even in the most favorable years, the remainder had to come from the Truckee. Thus the Truckee-Carson Irrigation District (TCID) came into being, with full authority to operate the project's various controls to the end that the ranchers received their legal quotas. The Truckee Canal and irrigation network were completed in 1906 and have been serving the district ever since.

Over the years the supplemental basin transfer has amounted to an average 235,000 acre feet. This is the amount of water leaving the basin annually, water which otherwise would have passed downstream and into Pyramid Lake. Ranches in Lyon County along the Truckee canal receive some of this water but most of it reaches Lahontan reservoir where a dam 121 feet high, completed in 1915, holds back 293,600 acre feet when this reservoir is full. A small hydroelectric plant below the dam has been in intermittent service, and in recent years the artificial lake with 10,000 acres of surface above it has become a recreational resource with very heavy use.

It was thought that the various rivalries for water had been settled when, in 1944, a series of court actions culminated in the so-called Orr Ditch Decree that affirmed existing rights including the 406,000 acre feet allotted the TCID. However, in the late 1960s the Indian protest grew stronger, based on the shrinking size of Pyramid Lake, and pressures were brought against the Interior Department to cut back TCID water transfers; a lawsuit in the Indians' behalf was filed. In 1973 the Department announced it would take over management of the project and reduce the water it received to 350,000 acre feet, whereupon the ranchers became very aroused and with them the sportsmen who had been using both the Lahontan reservoir for boating and fishing and the Stillwater-Carson Lake areas for wildfowl hunting. Without the 90,000 acre feet of water wasting from the canals and irrigated lands to the National Wildlife Refuge and Game Management marshlands it was felt this resource would vanish, also that the usefulness of Lahontan reservoir would be greatly impaired without the full flow from both the Carson River and Truckee Canal. There were accusations of extravagance and waste leveled against TCID[4]—and the ranchers retorted that saving Pyramid Lake was a lost cause in any case. The matter seems likely to drag on in the courts for many years, probably to be settled by compromises that please no one.

Many ideas have been advanced toward limiting water losses caused by evaporation, leakage along canals and ditches, ordinary seepage to groundwater, and extraction by trees and other vegetation; not all are practical. The transparent fact is that existing sources are inadequate to supply the needs which are increasing with each passing year. A recent inter-agency study estimated the annual increase in the Great Basin water needs of society at 2.6 million acre feet over the next 50 years and submitted that withdrawals to meet this increase will necessarily come from the existing stream flow to Pyramid, Walker and Great Salt Lakes. This study found the greatest use will continue to be for irrigation but the greatest increase will occur in the area of municipal and industrial use.

So unless new sources can be developed some uses will have to be curtailed or abandoned. These new sources might conceivably lie outside the basin. A continental transfer redistributing water

---

[4] The Newlands Project withdrew 391,700 of its allotted 406,000 acre feet from the rivers in 1971, a fairly typical year. Of this amount, 56% came from the Carson and 44% (or 172,348 a.f.) from the Truckee. The net supply available to ranchers was 362,612 a.f. but of this only 213,705 actually reached their lands; the rest was lost to seepage or spilled to the wildlife areas. This represents a water efficiency of only 59%. These figures were given in the Annual Report for 1971 of the TCID to the Bureau of Reclamation, which went on to say that Newlands water traveled an average 100 miles from source to point of use.

now being wasted to the ocean by northern rivers, such as the $100 billion North American Water and Power Alliance scheme, could solve the problem, but in view of the expense and political difficulty it may be considered at best very remote, at worst wholly fanciful. Mining the groundwater other than in emergencies is no answer since this would deplete river flow and soon exhaust the supply, recharge rates being very slow. About all that can be said for groundwater is that it is not subject to evaporation.

The stakes are high in this battle for water. On the one hand the ranches of Churchill and Lyon Counties constitute the most productive agricultural area in Nevada and their water metabolism supports the recreational facilities at Stillwater, Carson Lake and Lahontan reservoir. On the other hand, Pyramid Lake is unique and beautiful. It is the ancestral home of the Indians and lies wholly within their reservation. Their priority of use may be at least 10,000 years. One may reason that it has been dwindling during all that time, that even if the white man had not interfered with the lake it would inevitably diminish, for it shows little evidence of stability throughout the march of geological time. But keeping it "full" may be considered an extravagance in the light of today's total population need, and who can say at what level it is "full" or at what point it might be called unacceptably depleted? Some geologists think it may stabilize at about two-thirds its present size, in 150 to 200 years' time, but they also believe that in 100 years it will have grown too saline for the cutthroat and cui-ui to survive (Dept. of Interior: "Pyramid Lake Recreation Study," 1969).

Multiple use of our natural resources was an objective given much lip service during the 1960s. Something of a political slogan, its concept has been replaced to an extent by the idea of dominant use, since not all uses are compatible. Normally there is an optimum purpose well recognized for any particular resource, to which it should be put were the public interest to be well served. A water supply is an excellent example of a resource put to multiple use, and the rivers here illustrate a sharing of this sort. But gradually a single need tends to grow and dominate, and it seems likely that in the Carson and Truckee basins the thirst of the cities will eventually dominate, as populations and their thirsts expand. Certainly in dry years the residual uses will be the ones to suffer.

Conceivably, more economical use of available supplies can be achieved and wasteful practices eliminated. Stream management can be improved. Stampede reservoir on the Little Truckee was designed to assure a municipal supply for the Reno-Sparks community and a similar facility, the Watasheamu, on the East Carson has been planned (though not yet funded) to satisfy Carson City's future needs. Yet the ultimate solution may lie in massive regional water importation. The wealthy megalopolis of southern California could afford it and western Nevada might exact a small transit fee in acre feet.

CHAPTER VII

The Lahontan System
Walker Lake and the River

There are two main forks of the Walker River, just as there are of the Carson, and the systems are alike in other respects: both rise in lakes and springs along the Sierra Nevada crest and flow about the same distance northeast to destinations once widely covered by Lake Lahontan. Indeed the Truckee, Carson and Walker Rivers are remarkably similar. The peaks along the crest here have elevations of 10,000 to 12,000 feet generally, and this indented barrier along 25 miles of its southern extent separates Yosemite National Park from the Walker River drainage.

The headwaters of both the Carson and Walker Rivers lie wholly within the Toiyabe National Forest and the latter, particularly, is in almost roadless country. South of the Sonora Pass route across the Sierra Nevada only short dead-end roads give access to the lower reaches of the Little Walker, Buckeye Creek, Robinson Creek at Twin Lakes, and the Green Lake and Virginia Lake clusters. Pack stations are located at some of these road ends. In summer and late autumn, fishing and hunting groups go deep into the mountains to camp, for this is a very high quality recreation area. In the Robinson Creek-Green Lake surroundings the Hoover Wilderness Area has been designated to protect a fragile biota. Here on the edge of Yosemite Park the bighorn sheep had long been considered extinct, but in 1969 a ram and at least two ewes were observed, with a good chance that others might be around.

The uppermost branches of the West Walker rise in Kirkwood and Tower Lakes just under the divide, below Hawksbeak, Ehrnbeck and Tower Peaks. The flow is due north to Leavitt and Pickel Meadows, and three miles north of Sonora Junction it is joined by the Little Walker. The more important feeders are Molybdenite and Hot Creeks of the Little Walker, Leavitt and Silver Creeks of the West fork. (Note that this is the third Silver Creek we have thus far recorded.) The river now continues to Little Antelope Valley where it picks up Lost Cannon and Mill Creeks, then Slinkard Creek just before it crosses the Nevada line. Passing close to Topaz

Lake, an artificial reservoir, the West Walker next drops into Smith Valley where in the neighborhood of Wellington it supplies a number of irrigation canals; these are also served by Desert Creek, which drains the west slopes of the Sweetwater Mountains.

Here in Smith Valley the only Pluvial lake known to have formed in the Walker drainage was created by stream blockage five miles east of the town of Smith; it covered 90 square miles to a maximum depth of 300 feet. Lake Wellington lasted long enough to leave unmistakable traces, and its overflow continued to Lake Lahontan which lay just beyond in Mason Valley.

The East Walker River is somewhat longer and less abrupt in its descent from many small lakes of indescribable beauty nestled in rocky niches high above the lush meadows of Bridgeport Valley. Snow, Crown and Peeler Lakes at the head of Robinson Creek feed down into Barney and Twin Lakes above the Hunewill Hills. California's Matterhorn Peak (12,264) and the Sawtooth Ridge rise above Yosemite Park's Burro Pass, Avalanche Lake to the east, and four small glaciers; two more rest in cirques beneath Twin Peaks (12,314) to the south. All along this magnificent crest these sparkling waters recur in galactic profusion: the Green Lakes with Bergona, Par Value, West and East Lakes hanging above Green Creek, and the Virginia Lakes—about a dozen of them—reposing high in the vicinity of Dunderberg Peak (12,374).

Buckeye and Swauger Creeks meet Robinson in the Bridgeport Meadows; Green and Virginia Creeks converge and all come together at Bridgeport reservoir, which regulates the downstream supply. Among the several high domes of the Sweetwater Mountains a creek of the same name flows down to the East Walker; across and some distance below that influx, Rough and Bodie Creeks add a final infusion.

In the higher valleys such as Antelope and Bridgeport, forage is the chief crop and land is widely used for pasture. In Smith and Mason Valleys, at lower altitudes, the milder climate favors the growth of hay, grains and the hardier fruits; there is also some truck-farming. But Nevada, of all the contiguous states, has the lowest proportion of its land area under cultivation. Even in the comparatively well-watered Walker basin the crops must be irrigated and the growing season is remarkably short. Light frost can occur in any month, and killing frosts come late in the spring and early in the fall.

The two main forks of the Walker system merge six miles south of Yerington, and from that point the river describes a hairpin loop

50-plus airline miles to its mouth at the north end of Walker Lake. The lower portion passes through the Walker River Indian Reservation. At a point above Schurz the flow is collected in Weber reservoir, which has a 13,000-acre foot capacity for the needs of that Indian settlement. This reservation is the oldest one in the state and celebrated its centennial in 1969.

From the mouth of the river, Walker Lake's only significant supply, it is 18 miles to the south end. Width varies from 5 to 6 miles at its middle, and the area is about half that of Pyramid Lake. Depth being relatively shallow, it seems likely that Walker will dry completely within the next century or two. Here the black-spotted (Lahontan) cutthroat trout somehow managed to survive, being able to spawn presumably in the rivermouth. Less than 150 years ago this species occupied the entire Lahontan system including Tahoe, Pyramid, Winnemucca and Walker Lakes and the Humboldt, Truckee, Carson and Walker network of rivers. It was certainly the most common and widely distributed game fish in the state (LaRivers, 1962). As mentioned in Chapter v, after these trout had disappeared entirely from Pyramid in the 1930s a number of specimens were unexpectedly taken in a net at Walker and then placed in a hatchery where they were used to revive the strain. Other fish have thrived in this lake habitat, especially a local variety of crappie, and fishing today is very popular. There are boat landings at the Sportsman's Beach Recreation Site and at Tamarack Point Campground, both adjacent to the west shore highway.

The effect of river diversion for agriculture over the past 100 years is evident at many points on this western shore, where successive beach contours of very recent origin mark resting levels sharply. The higher strandlines of Lake Lahontan's Pluvial history are less readily discerned, but at the north end they can be seen along foothills of the Wassuk Range. This high barrier culminates to the south in Mt. Grant (11,239)—very abrupt and massive, and decked with snow for much of the year. Precipitation increased by the altitude of this mountain wall has resulted in a heavy erosion which wiped out most lacustrine features. Across Walker Lake the Gillis Range, much less impressive, lies back beyond the gentle shore declivity.

Walker Lake has much in common with its fellow Lahontan survivor, Pyramid: the high evaporation rate, meager rainfall regime, the somewhat saline waters, tufa formations and similar vestiges of Pluvial existence. Mankind has inhabited both vicinities for at least several millennia. A rich petroglyph site is located in the northern Wassuk Range at 7,000 feet. Though we have as yet found no cave record here like that of the basins further north, mentioned in the last chapter, some distribution of artifacts in open sites has come to notice and I. C. Russell found mastodon bones along the river in 1882 with a hunting point in association, which would indicate very early occupancy. Since men converged wherever the waters gathered we may assume further archeological search will be rewarded.

Three men in particular are associated with the earliest history of the Walker basin. Unfortunately none of them has left a definitive account, and we must establish their pathways mainly by conjecture. Jedediah Smith's astonishing thrust across the Great Basin in 1827 with two companions probably constituted the first deep penetration by any white man. Francis Farquhar (1966) concludes that Smith crossed the mountains "not far from the present Ebbetts Pass" and most historians now believe he continued south of Walker Lake without seeing it. This would have taken him across the headwaters of both the Carson and Walker Rivers to a desert passage 30 miles north of Tonopah and around the southern extremities of the Shoshone and Toiyabe ranges. The section of Smith's journal describing this part of his journey is missing; only letters and fragmentary references survive. In any case we know he crossed the Great Basin at its widest extent, being the first to do so, in 44 days and without any maps, guides or previous information about this incredibly difficult and almost waterless terrain.

The second entrant, generally credited with the discovery of Walker Lake, was Peter Skene Ogden, who in a letter mentioned passing a large body of water. It could hardly have been any other, for he had come down the Humboldt trapping beaver and crossed the sinks. The year was 1829. But the caprice of history has slighted Ogden and none of the lakes or streams he found now carries his name.

Joseph R. Walker, who opened a new route to California and made the first east-west Sierra crossing, received the honors here. Despatched with a large, armed company by Captain Bonneville in 1833, he like Ogden came down the Humboldt but as an explorer rather than a trapper. It is not known if in aiming for the Sierra Nevada he ever saw the lake, inasmuch as the lively account set down by his clerk Zenas Leonard is imprecise regarding routes. No desert lake is mentioned after the party left Humboldt Sink.

Rather, they seem to have gone rapidly up river to pasturage and mountain water, crossing the cordillera above Yosemite Valley. Here in its lower reaches Leonard recorded and described the Sierra big trees *(Sequoiadendron giganteum)*. His published journal is the earliest account of them.

In 1841 the Bartleson-Bidwell emigrant train came down the Humboldt River and reached the base of the Sierra Nevada on the West Walker in October. They continued up the river and cleared the crest at about Sonora Pass. Two years later Walker led the Chiles party through, and then came Frémont. Throughout January 1844, the snow lay very deep beneath the peaks and in the forests, and Frémont and Carson wandered about the lower valleys looking for a practical way to cross over into California. From the sinks they rode south to the East Walker, ascended it as far as the site of Bridgeport reservoir, turned northwest up Swauger Creek, and passed through what is now called Devil's Gate. They then veered north to stay high above the West Walker's rugged canyon and for a time followed Deep Creek where, it is believed, they abandoned the mountain howitzer brought all the way from Missouri. This field piece was recovered some 18 years later and taken to Virginia City where it remained for many years (Gianella, personal contact). During World War I it disappeared, no doubt sold for scrap. By the third week in February, having discovered Lake Tahoe and finally managed to negotiate the crest, the Frémont party descended the western slope and proceeded to Sutter's Fort.

The following year a rendezvous was made at Walker Lake. The Third Frémont Expedition had divided at Whitton Spring,[1] east of the Ruby Mountains, and the main section under Theodore Talbot, guided by Joseph Walker, had journeyed down the Humboldt River while the smaller one with Frémont in command went off exploring to the south. It took them only 19 days to reach the lake and the Talbot-Walker group caught up three days later. At this point the impetuous leader once again abandoned his main force, sending it south via the Owens River valley, while he headed west up the Truckee River canyon and over Donner Pass.

For 15 years only transients came to the lush meadows of the

---

[1] Whitton Spring, now known as Chase Spring, lies in Independence Valley 10 miles north of Spruce Mountain. It was already December when the Walker Lake rendezvous was made but no great amount of snow had fallen—in contrast to the following year when by mid-October the Donner party had already become immobilized by deadly winter conditions. Frémont was very fortunate, as indeed he had been the previous year when he crossed in February.

Walker River basin. Then in 1859 a stockman named N. H. A. Mason who had noted the favorable conditions when driving cattle through some years earlier returned to settle in the valley now bearing his name. Smith Valley was occupied later the same year by four herdsmen, two of whom were named Smith. Then in August 1860, gold was discovered at Aurora and about the same time a camp sprang up at Bodie, 12 miles away. No one was sure where the state line ran and for a time Aurora was claimed both by California and the Territory of Nevada. In 1863 people voted in both state elections amid great hilarity, but three weeks later the boundary was set half way between the towns by an official survey party, and the California records were taken to Bridgeport.

Mining booms have played a quite considerable part in the region's development, with the Rawhide and Leonard districts northeast of the lake and the Lucky Boy, Pamlico and Garfield districts south of it. Most of these enterprises flourished during the first decade of this century with major production in gold and silver, but Leonard (Sunnyside) was important chiefly for its tungsten. Mining here and elsewhere was undoubtedly the principal stimulus to railroad-building. In 1880 the Carson & Colorado's three-foot wide track was spiked along the eastern lakeshore, and in October that year the town of Hawthorne was laid out by its superintendent, H. M. Yerington. The following April train service to that budding community was inaugurated. However, in 1905 when the main line was converted to standard (four-foot, eight and one-half inches) width, the spur into town was abandoned. Citizens expressed outrage, but to no avail.

At the north end of Smith Valley there is now a marshland filled in wet years where waterfowl are lured by growing tules and nut grass. Nearby ranches carry pheasant and quail, so hunters are attracted to the area. On the east the Singaste Range extends northerly from the river and here in the 1860s deposits of copper ore were discovered. A German immigrant named John Ludwig worked the first important mine, and in 1881 he erected a smelter, but soon afterward he went bankrupt. After the turn of the century the copper mining revived and in 1909 the Nevada Copper Belt Railroad was built here. For years it maintained freight and passenger service but the vicissitudes common to small feeder lines eventually caught up with it and by 1947 it went out of business.

The U.S. Navy selected the Hawthorne-Whiskey Flat portion of the Walker Valley as the site for its ammunition depot in 1930 and since then has greatly expanded it. This storage ground for explosives is the Navy's largest such facility. A 200-mile network of railroad tracks connects the various bunkers, warehouses and handling installations. The town of Babbitt was built adjacent to the north to house required personnel, and this installation has contributed heavily to the growth of Hawthorne.

Included among the lands withdrawn for the Naval Ammunition Depot is the section of the Wassuk Range that includes Mt. Grant. A placer claim staked on its very summit tested high in values and in spite of formidable problems involving access and water supply was considered very promising, but Naval security requirements precluded such use and claims were never developed.

Nevada's Fish and Game Department chose Cottonwood Canyon in the same locality for experimental planting of the Himalayan snow partridge, in March 1970. Forty-six birds were released. To aid in following up their movements, five carried radio transmitters, secured by rubber bands and weighing only three ounces each including diminutive transistor batteries. They purportedly do not handicap the bird in any respect. Released at 8,500 feet, the partridges headed straight up Mt. Grant, right into the snow. There they remained at home and were easily traced through emitted signals. Other plantings of this species followed in the Toquima Range and elsewhere.

The bi-state water compact adjudicating interstate waters between California and Nevada specifically covers the flow of the Walker River and its tributaries.[2] Management is provided by the Walker River Irrigation District, which operates like the TCID mentioned previously, and it has its own special watermaster and set of regulations. A court decree of 1936 governs water storage at Topaz (85,000 a.f. maximum), Bridgeport (57,000) and Weber (13,000) reservoirs, and diversions for this and other purposes within the river system; the compact recognizes and confirms the court decree. There had been a long record of controversy over the years as to how the water should be allocated, and the compact represents a big step toward permanent settlement of these differences.

Proposals to dam the tributaries for one or another purpose have been put forward from time to time. A new major storage project on the West Walker River upstream from Antelope Valley is one

---

[2] The annual inflow to Walker Lake from Walker River is about 85,000 a.f. on the average, but simultaneously some 140,000 a.f. is being lost through evaporation. Solids and dissolved salts are increasing steadily. Water available to the lake is very limited due to upstream priorities and no prospective remedies are in sight. A special Task Force formation has been urged upon the Nevada Legislature, similar to that provided for Pyramid Lake.

of them and receives consideration in the compact. New dams to make lakes for recreation use have been promoted but not yet authorized. Any of these might increase the evaporation loss and hasten the eventual desiccation of Walker Lake. This residual depository has survived, though not without considerable loss, the arid swings of the rainfall cycle during a dozen decades of human interference with its supply. We know the wet years tend to come in sequence—and so do the dry ones. The next generation or two will be measuring the lake's decline, better able to foretell its end or, one hopes, to forestall that calamity by means not now available.

CHAPTER VIII

The Lahontan System
Humboldt River and the Sink

Sixty thousand years ago, when ice lay heavy and lasting in the snow bowls of the Ruby Mountains, the Humboldt River flowed much as it does today in a westward wandering passage toward its sump. But in those late Pleistocene times a narrow arm of Lake Lahontan extended up river beyond Golconda almost to Red House, shortening today's course by over 100 miles. As the lake receded the riverbed lengthened until finally it ended in the playa lying south of Lovelock; this is shown on many maps as Humboldt Lake. Water stands here in some depth and extent during most of the wet years. A low divide projects southwest from the West Humboldt Range and separates it from the broad alkali flats that mark Carson Sink. On several occasions in modern times when very heavy flooding occurred the river has overflowed this divide and mingled with the waters of the Carson; this happened in 1971.

The Humboldt cut its channel at least a million years ago across many intervening ranges and it may have formed temporary lakes in the process,[1] but we find no evidence of sustained lake existence during the Pluvial episodes anywhere along its principal course. A number of adjacent basins, however, contained bodies of water that spilled into the system at peaking development during prolonged lives. Two were quite substantial.

In Diamond Valley directly north of Eureka a lake of 294 square miles supported by a drainage basin more than ten times as large stood at 130-foot maximum depth; the overflow descended by way of Huntington Creek, a tributary of the Humboldt. Lake Gilbert, forming in Grass Valley northeast of Austin between the Toiyabe Range and the Simpson Park Mountains, was almost as big (209 square miles) and achieved a depth of 250 feet. Together with a

---

[1] Long before the Pleistocene epoch began, the Humboldt may have flowed to the Pacific by way of the Pit or Feather River. Gianella has noted east-west channel gravels in ancient riverbeds on top of the mountains south of Gerlach and thinks they would be worth a study. "Certainly the Humboldt has a very unusual course crossing numerous north-south ranges while it is flowing westerly," he writes. Could it not have once continued across the Sierra?

tiny lake in Carico Valley it spilled into Lake Crescent and thence at Beowawe into the main system.

Crescent at maximum measured 77 square miles. Another about half that size filled in Buffalo Valley 20 or 30 miles southwest of Battle Mountain and overflowed for a time into the Reese River. Other north central Nevada lakes were not connected to the Lahontan pattern but occupied isolated basins of their own. The largest, named Lake Dixie, extended over 420 square miles and was some 235 feet deep about where the settlement of Dixie Valley and the nearby Humboldt Salt Marsh are situated. Just to the south the flat in Fairview Valley surrounding Frenchman Station was the site of diminutive Lake Labou. Big Smoky, Edwards Creek and Smith Creek Valleys held other sizable lakes.

The Humboldt rises in low hills northeast of Wells, Nevada, and flows about 280 airline miles west and then south. For every airline mile it meanders about three and so is almost 1000 meander miles long (Hardman, 1960). Historically and economically it is without doubt the most important river—as well as the longest—in the Great Basin. The main tributaries, beginning with Bishop and Tabor Creeks, number at least 30 and spring from various canyons and couloirs where snow collects along a score or more of lofty ranges. Some are brief and modest but a few, such as the Reese River, come great distances. The beautiful Jarbidge Wild Area near the Idaho border contains a divide that delimits the Great Basin, and the south slopes of these peaks and ridges drain to the Humboldt by way of Mary's River, which joins it at the town of Deeth.

At the upper end of the Humboldt basin along its southeastern flank are the Ruby Mountains, a very noble and impressive range from which numerous torrents descend that supply the hay meadows where Elko County's grazing industry is centered. A spur extending northward beyond Secret Pass is known as the East Humboldt Range, and Hole-in-the-Mountain Peak (11,276) is its loftiest summit, with Clover Valley flanking its eastern footings. The major streams originating in the Ruby Mountain snowfields run northwesterly and not all of them actually reach the Humboldt River; but rising in a chain of glacial lakes just east of the main crest, Lamoille Creek describes a sweeping curve before dropping into the valley where, near the town of Halleck, it adds its small share. This tributary supports a modest hydroelectric station and is regularly stocked with trout by the state. So too is the South Fork of the Humboldt, which rises near Wines Peak, and here many alpine lakes are clustered amid spectacular pinnacles. Just to the north the highest of all, Ruby Dome, attains 11,387 feet. Another is Pearl Peak, where a stand of bristlecone pine many thousand years old has persisted throughout much of the Neothermal ages. This region has been proposed for inclusion in the National Park system by reason of its high scenic and environmental quality.

North of Elko the Independence Mountains provide the source of the Humboldt River's North Fork, which enters below Halleck, and also flowing down from that quarter are Susie, Maggie, Boulder and Rock Creeks. At Battle Mountain the Reese River is joined, and this by a wide margin is the longest subsidiary of them all, for it rises at the base of Toiyabe Dome (11,788) far south in Nye County and struggles through a desert valley for about 150 miles. Its life is strictly seasonal and much of its bed is perennially dry. Ordinarily it adds no surface flow at all to the Humboldt's volume.

Evans Creek comes in from Midas and at Winnemucca the Little Humboldt, with a network of rills draining the Santa Rosa Range easterly, makes its approach. It may be observed, though, that this feeder has actually brought water into the main Humboldt only three times during the past half century (1953, 1958 and 1969— Nevada Division of Water Resources report). Sand dunes choke it off a few miles north of the city. In 1969 it was necessary to cut through these dunes to allow 20,000 acre feet from this source, in that very abundant water year, to pass down. Humboldt waters are impounded in Rye Patch and Pitt-Taylor reservoirs, constructed just below Imlay, and designed to conserve a total of 240,000 acre feet (but limited in practice to 210,000).

The problems of water storage are again brought into focus at this point and it may be noted here that the Humboldt has been studied, analysed and managed about as thoroughly as any stream in the United States. All its water has been appropriated by users for many years. The dam at Rye Patch, completed and dedicated in 1936, stores water for ranching in the lower Lovelock Valley but this storage takes place where conditions are least favorable for conserving the supply: the evaporation rate is maximal. Heavy losses are also due to leakage to the groundwater storage and transpiration via parasitic vegetation along the channels. A representative example of these losses may be found in the 1969 figures of 154,540 acre feet released at Rye Patch, of which only 95,000 acre feet reached the headgates on individual farms and ranches—a loss of almost 40 per cent (Goldsworthy, 1969).

There are two small holding ponds upstream where lower temperatures and greater cloud cover are likely to occur, namely, on Bishop and Willow Creeks (others have been proposed) but these two are relatively small—30,000 and 18,000 acre feet capacities, respectively—and primarily of local value. A Desert Research Institute study has shown that two underground basins, in Winnemucca and Boulder Valleys, would be ideal for holding water without appreciable loss but, because the Humboldt is under court decree, established water rights preclude their development for such purpose and furthermore the economics of the region are too low-grade to support the necessary expenditures.

Since the principal water-producing area of the Humboldt is the mountainous upper third of its drainage basin, the river commonly attains its maximum volume in the vicinity of Palisade (Thomas, 1964). Because of diversions and natural evapotranspiration in the valley the flow has shrunk by almost a half at the point where it reaches Rye Patch reservoir, even though the drainage at that juncture is three times as large as the one contributing at Palisade. These figures are in graphic illustration: the measuring station there (100 miles from the source, 150 miles above Rye Patch) reported 2,300 cubic feet per second passing in mid-May 1969, while the inflow to the reservoir at the same time amounted to only 1,500 c.f.s. Admittedly, 1969 was an uncommonly bountiful year, but in less favored ones the figures would be considerably smaller and their disparity even greater.

By the time the waters reach Lovelock Valley they have been used and reused and have picked up enough alkali, dissolved or in suspension, to impair their value to agriculture. Canals and ditches are steeply graded on this account in order to maintain a rapid flow so this unwanted chemical material is not deposited. Here we have the phenomenon of "natural pollution" where the quality of the resource is degraded by substances not of human origin. The wasting remnant passed over the fields returns in part to its normal channel and continues on down, to disappear in the sink. It is, as Dale Morgan (1943) observes—disputing Swinburne—one very weary river that does not wind to sea.

The natural vegetation of the river basin is dominated by common sagebrush, *Artemisia tridentata* of the silver-gray leaves, an important forage plant. Giant wild rye grass once grew plentifully alongside the meadows and was of much benefit to the emigrant trains, but it has been largely replaced by greasewood *(Sarcobatus ver-miculatus)*. Both are phreatophytes. The spiny shrub does well in strongly alkaline soils and is also somewhat useful as feed.

There are four principal classes of vegetation throughout the Great Basin. In its higher reaches the pinyon-juniper community thrives, dominated in its virgin state by the singleleaf pinyon[2] and Utah juniper *(Juniperus osteosperma)* rather sparsely distributed in association with such forage plants as mountain mahogany, bitterbrush and cliffrose. Before the grazing era began, palatable grasses grew under and between these low-growing trees, which were not as thick or abundant as they are today. The proportion of browse was much higher in those times *(Nevada Wildlife, 1965)*.

The largest category, however, consists of the sagebrush-grass community covering vast areas of Nevada, Utah, Oregon and Idaho. The numerous grasses, all palatable, include wheat grass, Idaho fescue, needle grass, wild rye and Indian rice grass. Along with these, under and between the shrubs, grow a variety of forbs such as balsam root, phlox, hawksbeard and lupine. The major aspect, however, is common sagebrush, bud sagebrush and rabbitbrush *(Chrysothamnus nauseosus)*.

Second largest group in varieties is the salt desert shrub type and it covers large areas in the central and eastern Great Basin. The virgin growth at the time of the settlers consisted mostly of low shrubs like shadscale, bud sage, winterfat and rabbitbrush, among browse species. The grasses included wild rye and squirreltail, Indian rice and alkali sacaton; in the more alkaline areas the halophytes—salt-loving plants—such as greasewood, pickleweed and soapweed occurred. Intensive grazing has caused good basic grass cover in some of this type to disappear completely.

Finally, the southern desert shrub type is the least changed in the Basin because the region where it occurs—the southern counties of Nevada and Utah—is endowed with less water and this has inhibited usage either by livestock or by wildlife. The creosote bush is characteristic of this region, with its olive green hue and strong resinous scent, as are shadscale and mesquite. Yucca is found, and cacti of many kinds. The most dramatic form is the Joshua tree *(Y. brevifolia)* which grows up to 35 feet high, is very shaggy and angular with postured branches; south of Goldfield it is common.

[2] The *Pinus monophylla*, or singleleaf pinyon (also called nut pine, sometimes spelled pinion or pinon) gets its name from the Spanish *piña*, meaning "fircone." This tree was named and described by Dr. John Torrey from material collected by Frémont. It is the Nevada state tree, and its pine nuts constituted a staple Indian food.

The Paleo-Indian undoubtedly used the Humboldt River valley when traversing the Great Basin. We have little knowledge of these earliest people but some clues exist. An 8½-foot mammoth tusk was unearthed near Winnemucca in April 1971, which indicated a large-game hunting opportunity though its age (between 18,000 and 24,000 years) was much older than the known range of early man in the Desert West.[3] Of the Protoarchaic people in this valley more is understood, thanks to traits found at Leonard Rockshelter (Chapter VI) dating from 11,000 B.P. and other more recent inventories. An important site that revealed long cultural sequences relevant to environmental change and dependent lifeways is the South Fork Shelter near Elko. Occupation there began ca. 4,500 B.P., or about the end of the Altithermal age, and continued to recent times (Heizer, Baumhoff and Clewlow, 1968).

These primitive people used spears and, later, bows and arrows, were basketmakers but knew nothing of pottery. Like more modern tribes they developed no governmental organization and moved in small bands with the seasons, according to the availability of food. In summer the groups were small, amounting to perhaps no more than a single family, but in autumn and winter there were larger gatherings to share special activities.

When the white man arrived the Indian distribution along the Humboldt consisted of Shoshones moving in the headwaters and downstream as far as Golconda Summit; below that point the Northern Paiutes were dominant. But it should not be assumed that they observed any rigid territorial limits; these were roving bands rather sparsely scattered. The Bannocks were an offshoot of the Northern Paiutes, distinguished by their use of the horse and living with the equestrian Shoshones, from whom they were linguistically differentiated. They occupied the Snake River country and, except for occasional raids, came into the Great Basin rarely.

Game was scarce and elusive. The ground squirrel, rock chuck and jackrabbit were more commonly of their diet than antelope, bighorn sheep or deer. Today's herds of large game (other than elk and sheep) are much more extensive than those of a century ago and earlier, and this is undoubtedly due to the institution of scientific game management and the elimination of predators. Ducks were taken in the marshes, especially at such times as they

---

[3] The tusk, exposed by a bulldozer, remained in context until it could be examined and its association established: the Lower Member of the Sehoo Formation, composed of lacustrine deposits and older, late Pleistocene rocks. The tusk is of interest but not crucial. (Donald R. Tuohy in *Nevada Archeological Survey Reporter*, Vol. 5, no. 4, 1971.)

were moulting or when the ducklings were nearly grown but still could not fly. More often the prey would be coot, a slow and stupid bird that moves just off the water and can be captured in nets. The Indians also caught rabbits in nets, gathering in large numbers to conduct drives. Fish were eaten in the Pyramid and Walker Lake vicinities where trout or cui-ui had survived the Lahontan desiccation. Varieties of seeds, nuts and roots, especially cat-tail shoots dug in the springtime and pine nuts gathered in the fall, were esteemed and dependable sources of food. Buckberry and the small red fruit of the desert thorn *(Lycium pallidum)* were harvested in summer (Wheat, 1967).

Two reservations, the Te-Moak on the South Fork and the Yomba near the head of the Reese River in Nye County, continue as centers of the Shoshone People (although their principal concentration lies outside the Great Basin at Owyhee). Indian colonies have been established at Elko, Battle Mountain, Winnemucca and Lovelock, the larger towns along the Humboldt. There are today quite probably a good many more Indians in the river basin than there were in 1850 during the brunt of the white invasion. Disease and famine were the prime factors in tribal attrition, but today these destroyers are better controlled.

Had Jedediah Smith known about the Humboldt he might have saved himself and his companions much hardship and time. Passage across the Great Basin at its widest extent would have been far easier by way of the river's bottomlands and gentle canyons than threading the central ranges of Nevada. That he succeeded at all is affirmation of his stamina and resolve. Smith would have been a geographer, but he never quite made it; neither did Peter Skene Ogden, who followed. Smith having missed the Humboldt, it remained for Ogden to discover it while scouting down from Fort Nez Percés for beaver; this fort had been built by Donald McKenzie on the Columbia River at the mouth of the Walla Walla. Ogden's *Snake Country Journals* are reasonably clear, and we can trace his movements: seven weeks after leaving the fort he came to a region of sand dunes surrounding a marsh; here the Little Humboldt River vanished. Then Ogden rode over a low saddle and looked upon the main Humboldt's long willow-lined winding course through the broad flood plain beyond. The date was November 9, 1828. As far as we know he was the first white man to see it, and in all justice it should carry his name rather than a stranger's. Here he found the beaver he was seeking but the season was precariously late and conditions soon drove him east to winter quarters beyond Great Salt Lake where buffalo were available (Elliott, 1973).

Somewhere in the vicinity of Carlin there is an unmarked grave where Joseph Paul, the first white man known to have died in Nevada, lies buried beside the river. One of Ogden's trappers, desperately ill, he was brought into camp by an Indian. The entire party lingered in miserable weather for several days while their solicitous leader, recognizing the plight of the expedition—horses starving and provisions low—as well as that of Paul, grew increasingly restive. The man could not be moved so two were left to care for him while the remainder went on. As the year 1828 ran out, they reached the Malad River in southeastern Idaho and made camp. There the men who had been left behind caught up and related that Paul had died eight days after the main party left him.[4] Ogden returned along the Humboldt in March and followed it to the end. Trapping was productive and not until June did he turn northward, passing west of the Santa Rosa Mountains into Oregon, loaded with furs and headed for Fort Nez Percés (Cline, 1963).

John Work succeeded Ogden as brigade leader for the Hudson's Bay Company and came briefly to the Humboldt in the spring of 1831, but heavy floodwaters then made trapping impossible. Milton Sublette, accompanied by Nathaniel Wyeth and 45 men, worked his way into the Basin that year and came down river in 1832 while Wyeth wisely turned north and west into Oregon with a third of the party. Sublette and the remainder found no game and were forced to eat beaver meat. According to one story (Thompson & West, 1881) these animals had experienced a season of famine during which they had to consume wild parsnip which "poisoned their flesh," and the trappers who had partaken of it became violently ill. Sublette soon hurried north to the Snake River Country.

Captain Benjamin Louis Eulalie de Bonneville, on leave from the United States Army, camped at Bear Lake in the spring of 1833. From there he sent a group of about 40 men under Joseph R. Walker to explore westward as far as California. They made trail down the Humboldt, returning by the same route the following year after many adventures. Kit Carson, out of Fort Hall in 1838,

---

[4] Ogden referred to the Humboldt in his journal as "Paul's River," having previously called it "Unknown River" and "Swampy River," while others about that time used the name "Mary's River." Walker's men called it "Barren River" but Frémont's designation became final.

searched the Humboldt for beaver but found none left. Thus the explorers and mountain men utilized this ancient highroad even as the primitive people had for thousands of years before they came.

Captain J. C. Bartleson and John Bidwell led the first emigrant party west in 1841. Among the 32 people in this train were Mrs. Benjamin Kelsey and her small daughter America. Their route entered the Great Basin at the Bear River in Wyoming, skirted Great Salt Lake to Park Valley and Pilot Springs, crossed the Ruby Mountains through Secret Pass and reached the Humboldt River west of Elko. Having passed down this waterway to the sink, they proceeded to the Walker River basin and thence across the Sierra. They were extremely fortunate in avoiding trouble with the Indians and making the journey without loss of life.

In 1843 the emigrant group organized by Joseph B. Chiles, guided by J. R. Walker, arrived at the Humboldt by way of the Raft River-Goose Creek approach from Fort Hall; they also utilized its relatively easy grades and ample forage. Then the following year came Caleb Greenwood escorting the Stevens-Townsend-Murphy party, from Council Grove on the Missouri River to California. "Old Greenwood," he was called, and that year he reached the age of 81! From Fort Hall he had taken them by way of the Raft River and the City of Rocks to the head of Bishop Creek and on down all the way to the sink. Greenwood got them there by mid-September and they walked in to Sutter's Fort before winter shut down the trail.

John Charles Frémont avoided the Humboldt in 1845 but sent his main section under Talbot through Secret Pass with Walker guiding. He had left Washington in May with a very strong group, a potential armed force, and his true purpose was veiled. War with Mexico would begin the following year. President Polk had offered to purchase California from Mexico and many Americans hoped it would be annexed. Frémont was very ambitious and in great haste to reach the land of conquest. This time he was not accompanied by Charles Preuss, the expert cartographer who had served him professionally on his second expedition, but he did make sketches and kept a good record of his third one.

Bernard DeVoto, historian of the developing West, refers to it as "the plundered province" and his personal descriptions are equally pithy. He called Joseph R. Walker a "thirty-third degree mountain man," Captain Bonneville "an independent and interloper, trying to break into the mountain trade," and John C. Fré-

mont "Captain Jinks of the Horse Marines." Stegner (1969) refers
to the latter as "that large, empty figure." He was indeed inconsistent and controversial, Byronesque, a disappointment to his friends
on many occasions and an arrogant, capricious individual. Yet he
was first to organize an expedition strictly for the purpose of
exploring the Great Basin and though altogether outclassed by the
earlier exploits of Lewis and Clark in the Northwest, two of his
four exploratory trips opened up the last unknown region on the
continent to public knowledge. In these he displayed much determination and fortitude. Allan Nevins calls him a "pathmarker," rather
than a pathfinder.

After Frémont, came the deluge. Traffic thickened along this
"highroad of the West" (Dale Morgan's appositive). Most of it bent
westward to the Pacific, and there was every sort, from the fumbling
progress of the Donner Party of 1846 to the headlong rush of the
Forty-niners. The Mormons had founded Salt Lake City in 1847
and soon their colonists were fanning out, many to settle in other
watered valleys of the Great Basin and some to make California—admitted to the Union in 1850—their ultimate goal. John Reese
and 20 men from Salt Lake built the fort at Genoa in 1851; Utah
Territory then extended all the way to the Sierra Nevada. But many
of those who came west along the Humboldt in the early '50s
returned by the same route when Brigham Young recalled his
faithful to defend the homeland. In September of 1857 a string
of 130 wagons loaded with Latter-day Saints, their families and
belongings hurried back along the riverbanks toward Deseret (Hulse,
1965).

The 40th parallel of latitude passes 17 miles south of Provo, Utah,
and about 25 miles north of Nevada's Reno-Sparks community;
between them no other city of size lies along this dimension. It
crosses Utah just south of Utah Lake and Nevada below Ruby Lake,
then bisects Humboldt Sink and Pyramid Lake; this is the broadest
configuration of the Great Basin. By the end of the Civil War a
keen interest in this recently discovered province arose. Numerous
engineering surveys had been conducted to determine the best route
across it for a transcontinental railroad, but no one had attempted
any thorough geographic appraisal. Frémont's reconnaissance had
been spotty—much more was needed. So now came three giants
to write scientific history: Clarence King, Grove Karl Gilbert and
Israel Cook Russell.

After hostilities ceased in 1865 King, then only 25 years old,
obtained Congressional authority to undertake a definitive study

along the 40th parallel, and he accomplished that task during the years 1867–72. A brand new knowledge of the region and feeling for it, supplanting wild ideas and apocryphal legends, resulted from King's work. His report is a classic, and the very model of good scientific writing.

Grove K. Gilbert covered the Colorado River with John Wesley Powell in the mid-1870s and in our field of interest published two papers describing the Basin Range and Plateau provinces. He discovered the phenomenon of basin and range faulting, a new concept, and brought it to scientific attention. The Great Basin is the type locality for these structures which exist throughout the world. Gilbert named and defined Pluvial Lake Bonneville.

Russell, whom we mentioned in Chapter II, gave extensive scrutiny to many parts of the Great Basin and developed the kind of information for Pluvial Lake Lahontan that Gilbert did for Bonneville. In 1879 Congress created the U.S. Geological Survey and Clarence King was named its first Director; at the same time Gilbert was appointed senior geologist under him.

Ever since the drainage basin of the Humboldt was first settled the major interest and livelihood of its citizens has been stock raising and the related growing of feed crops. The focal point of this activity has always been water. Professor Walter Webb's view of the West in terms of an oasis civilization is nowhere more vividly reflected than along this river system. Here there are about 286,000 acres of irrigated crop and pasture lands with recognized water rights (Hardman, 1960) providing winter feed for most of northeastern Nevada's livestock production.

The first cattle to enter this region were herded through by Mormons in 1850, destined for Carson Valley. Then B. F. Huffaker of Kentucky introduced cattle (1856) in the Truckee Meadows. Perhaps the earliest stockman of fame in Elko County was John B. Sparks, later elected Governor of Nevada, who arrived in 1868. He, with various partners including L. R. Bradley, who also became governor of the state, ran very large herds that at maximum totaled over 70,000 head. Colonel E. P. Hardesty came with beef cows from Texas in 1869 and opened up the Bishop Creek area. Among the famous brands originating in those days were the Winecup, 25, YP, T Lazy S, and Shoesole. (Nevada Wildlife).

Sheepmen preceded the cattlemen on some of the ranges. Among the earliest was a Basque named Pedro Altube fresh from the Pyrenees who saw a welcome resemblance to his land of birth in the ranges at the head of the Humboldt. He established the Spanish Ranch in 1859, and in his lifetime he was responsible for many Basque herdsmen coming to the region to tend sheep (Hulse). John Garat was another pioneer in sheep from this ethnic group who had extensive holdings, and W. T. Jenkins who arrived in the 1800s prospered with substantial flocks. These operations involved many thousand head; at one time, 1907, the number of animals totaled well over a million (Hazeltine, Saulisberry & Taylor, 1960).

In those early days of grazing the cattle barons ruled the range, which was totally unfenced. There was no such thing as supplemental feeding. The native meadows along the Humboldt were irrigated by natural runoff, and although this wild flooding has been improved and the wet areas enlarged, the system remains basically the same. Precipitation averages nine inches a year along the river but in the mountains runs much higher, and sometimes violent storms disrupt the pattern. In August 1970, a single rainstorm deposited 4.13 inches at Elko in less than two hours—almost half a year's normal supply—and an official of the Weather Bureau said this amounted to 112,000 gallons per acre.

Small-scale farming has not been generally successful in most of the central Great Basin. For example, Nevada though the 7th largest state in area ranks 48th in total cash receipts from farm marketing (U.S.D.A., 1965). Only Alaska and Rhode Island derive less income from this source. Of the state's agricultural land, 90 per cent is in grain or hay and the minimal economic unit is likely to be a large and diversified operation.

Mining has figured importantly in the development of the basin. Mineral values occur in the two very different types of deposit—placer and hardrock. The first involves minute amounts of metal scattered in loose gravels and clays that must be washed out and concentrated. The process requires much water, is very inefficient in the use of it, and tends to disturb the countryside and to pollute streams. However, the ancient channels where these minerals were carried down long antedate the Pleistocene, their profiles having vanished or become buried through erosion, and their distribution is seldom directly related to existing watersheds. Thus much of the placer mining has been conducted at considerable distance from the main streambeds. Some placer has been reconcentrated in Humboldt tributaries such as Maggie Creek, at the head of which a little mining has been attempted from time to time but no large production was ever recorded. Most of the placer in Nevada has been found in the northern (Humboldt) and western regions. Two lucrative districts near the edge of the basin, Tuscarora (located in 1871) and Battle Mountain (1910), produced millions, and in Pershing county the Sawtooth and Spring Valley districts were very profitable.

Hardrock mining requires little or no water in the extraction of ores but involves sinking shafts and driving tunnels to reach veins or lodes where the metal is present. Once the direct-shipping high-grade has been removed, water is used in almost all methods of concentrating it. The earliest discoveries of ore in the Humboldt basin were at Mill City (1856) and Imlay (1860) where gold, silver and tungsten were found. Unionville, Austin and Cortez were silver bonanzas, with gold in association, developed during the next three years just as Nevada was about to be given statehood. The Potosi district (Getchell Mine—Kelly Creek) began in 1938 primarily as a gold prospect and produced about 17 million dollars worth, plus some 20 million in tungsten; the Nevada-Massachusetts mine near Mill City overlooking the lower Humboldt River likewise produced tungsten and at one time was the largest mine of its kind in the United States.

Many boom towns that flourished a century ago have disappeared entirely; some remain as ghost towns, but a few such as Austin continue quite lively though dependent on other affairs than mining. Tuscarora has mainly ranching families now. Mill City and Imlay, accessible from Interstate Highway 80, cater to the needs of the traveler. Tenabo, Rabbit Hole and Unionville are vestigial but Lynn (1907) and Cortez (1863) have been revived most successfully—the former on an open-pit basis. New mines in Copper Canyon and Copper Basin (Battle Mountain district) were opened in 1965.

In addition to the precious metals, copper and iron have figured heavily in recent operations along the Humboldt. Big Mike south of Winnemucca and Mineral Basin east of the sink have been profitable sources of these. Also, industrial minerals—non-metallics—are widely distributed: barite occurs extensively and diatomite, perlite and clays such as kaolinite in good commercial value are being mined. Pumice has been quarried at Palisade, gypsum and diatomite extracted near Lovelock.[5]

Coal occurs in Carlin Canyon but there has been no known

---

[5] Barite is an essential ingredient of the driller's mud used in sinking oil wells as is bentonite, a high swelling clay also used as a sealant for reservoirs and ditches. In oil drilling the mud mixture (sometimes containing as many as 74 different chemical constituents) is pumped into the well to lift cuttings from the hole and firm up the sidewalls prior to installing the casings.

production. Drilling for oil and natural gas has been tried all along the river but thus far the results have been uniformly disappointing. On the other hand the search for energy sources now appears ready to bear fruit with the development of geothermal steam at Geyser Basin in Whirlwind Valley, near Beowawe. Here a number of wells have been put down and capped, awaiting further study and exploitation.

Transport remained literally on a horse-and-wagon basis until the building of the Central Pacific Railroad. Legislation authorizing it was signed by President Lincoln on July 1, 1862. It was five years later, though, when the rails reached the Humboldt, displacing the stage lines and the teamsters who had been thriving on business from the mines but then found themselves unable to compete. The first train arrived at Elko on January 28, 1869.

Mining supported the new transcontinental route, and other lines were soon extended to connect it with the more promising centers of this industry. Two were of considerable importance and longevity, the Nevada Central and the Eureka & Palisade. Both were narrow gauge. The Austin boom started in 1862 and within ten years that town became Nevada's second largest. In keeping with such importance a railroad through the Reese River Valley was planned to connect with the CP at Battle Mountain; this line, 93 miles long, was finished in 1880. The Nevada Central served a number of mining communities besides Austin and also ranches along its right of way, served for 57 years and was abandoned in 1938.

The Eureka strike 65 miles east of Austin materialized in 1869 and very soon several smelters were functioning there, ore being hauled in from mines in the surrounding region. Tracks were laid northward in 1875 to Palisade where they met those of the CP and for 63 years this feeder existed usefully. The E & P ceased operations the same year as the Nevada Central, driven under similarly by improvements in cars, trucks and highways (Myrick, 1962).

Late in the game another transcontinental railroad, the Western Pacific, made its appearance. Sharing the valley of the Humboldt for 177 miles, it more or less parallels the Southern Pacific, successor to the CP, and serves the same communities of Wells, Elko, Carlin and Winnemucca. But the first WP train to reach Elko did so on Christmas Day 1908, almost 40 years after the CP event and long after most of the railroad history of the West had been written.

These two standard gauge systems, needless to say, still operate successfully across the Great Basin.

Many small railroads were projected and some actually built, such as the Golconda & Adelaide, vintage of 1898. It ran track three feet wide a dozen miles between copper mines and a smelter on the CP, but ores were difficult to reduce, production was spasmodic, and by 1914 it had expired. The Nevada Short Line operated from Oreana on the SP to Rochester for only 5 years, from 1913, negotiating a nearly impossible canyon grade with a switchback; a tramway that hauled the ore more cheaply dealt this road a fatal blow. The Battle Mountain & Lewis Railway ran from Galena on the Nevada Central 12 miles to mines in a canyon below Lewis Peak; there were three switchbacks here. It remained in operation for just four years from 1881 and carried passengers, silver ore and general freight.

The Mid-Pacific Railroad was a wild and woolly scheme envisaged by Andrew Stevenson as a merger or takeover of six existing roads and four new links to be built into a farflung system. Unhappily, the year was 1929. Stevenson enjoyed a substantial reputation in railroading and his plan was imaginative: a Y-shaped network with Barstow on the Santa Fe at the southern end, Reno and Battle Mountain the northern termini. He planned on spending ten million dollars and gained the attention and moral support of some very influential people, but financing proved impossible and it was quietly scuttled in 1934 (Myrick).

Lastly, two projects developed in late years at the head of the Humboldt, the first of them eminently successful. The Union Pacific created a subsidiary called the Oregon Short Line to build a link between Wells and Twin Falls, Idaho. I.C.C. authority was granted in 1923; the 124-mile road was completed and operating by February, 1926. As recently as 1962 it was still scheduling a "mixed train," the last such in the state in regular service, and it remains an important handler of freight.

The other project was unfortunate. In 1910 the Pacific Reclamation Company promoted a colonization on 25,000 acres at Metropolis, north of Wells, including a dam and irrigation development from three nearby creeks. The SP built a station and an 8-mile branch from Tulasco in 1911 at a cost of over $100,000 to serve the needs of the anticipated ranching community. But legal and other troubles, including serious droughts, beset the entire enterprise; only one creek could be dammed and but 4,000 acres brought

under irrigation. Most of the inhabitants, who at one time numbered
nearly 1,000, departed (Morgan, 1943). By 1916 the train schedule
was down to one a week, the line was abandoned in 1922, and
in 1925 the rails were removed and sold.

Metropolis was an example of misplaced confidence in the faulty
conservation techniques of those times and in people and government agencies. Under the Carey Act of 1894 this settlement was
created on land given the state by the Federal government for
such purpose. It turned out to be just another boom-and-bust land
promotion. Many substantial buildings and a big hotel had been
erected, sidewalks and parks laid out, Bishop Creek reservoir constructed, and crops planted widely. Then came the dry years of
1913–14 with the jackrabbits invading and eating. A few Mormon
families stayed on but most of the crops shriveled, the buildings
crumbled, and the trees died (Mack & Sawyer, 1965). Today there
is little to show for money spent and a dream forgotten.

Transportation was the social determinant of the Humboldt Valley. Coinciding with the waters, its routings positioned the habita-
tions and shaped the livelihoods of all who came, from the back-
packing Paleo-Indian to the airlines' personnel. The springs and
creeks sustained man and the wild game he depended on, alike;
their paths were worn along the riverbanks where habit took them,
and here the wagonroad went easily. What was good for wagons
was good for the Iron Horse. Towns were staked out at stagecoach
intervals, railroad shops and division points came into being more
widely spaced but where towns already flourished.

Change in the kinds of transportation marked the years: the
century of steam came to an end in the 1950s and much of the
grooming of engines was eliminated. Machine shops, round houses,
water tanks disappeared; car icing gave way to mechanical refrig-
eration and the ice houses went by the board. At the same time
the demand for passenger service dwindled steadily with the quick-
ening pace of civilization, and the desire for independent movement
put scheduled transportation at disadvantage. The family car, the
faster plane, the cheaper bus took over. The Pullman cars and the
glittering trains were retired and the rail industry thenceforth devoted itself to less complicated and more profitable cargoes.

Railroad housekeeping brought prosperity to Carlin, Elko, Wells
and Winnemucca. The shops and yards meant jobs, payrolls and
associated business. Now much of this is gone but other enterprise
has taken up the slack. Communications, as well as transportation,
have been revolutionized and towns are relatively much closer,

their restless populations are much increased, and dependence upon transient commerce has broadened. Now these towns enjoy a resort economy transcending the service function in a desert life zone. The oasis concept is realistic. Indoor and outdoor recreation draw new participants as an affluent society endowed with leisure time pumps the expanding flow of trade: wining and dining, show business, legalized gaming, hunting, fishing, skiing and snowmobile racing—these are some of the magnetic foci, and all depend upon the availability of water.

Along the Humboldt roadside rest areas appear. Geysers and ghost towns attract their visitors and the showy mountains draw scenery enthusiasts with cameras at the ready. Near the head of the Reese River, fossil beds containing the skeleton of an ichthyosaur, a marine reptile of Triassic age, are protected as a State Monument for those interested in paleontology. From the four corners of the earth people come to look, to pass through or linger, most of them giving no thought to the fact that their passage is one the river has traveled for at least a million years.

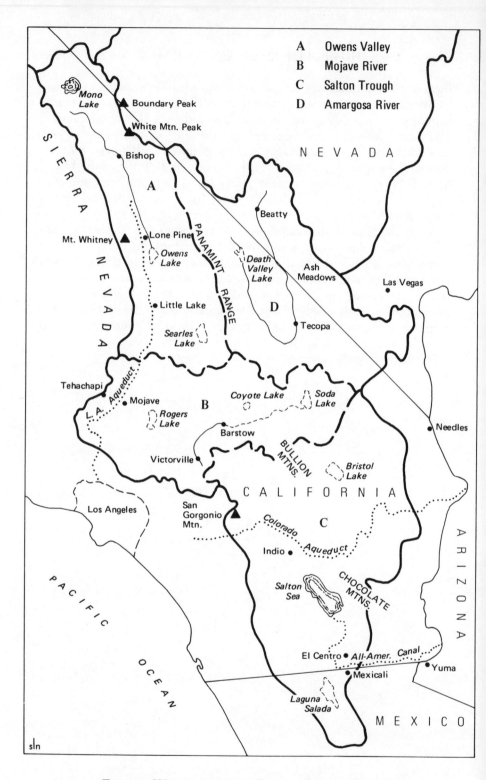

DESERT WATERS OF THE DEATH VALLEY SYSTEM

CHAPTER IX

The Death Valley System
Owens River and Lake Owens

South of the Lahontan site the Great Basin extends eastward from the Sierra Nevada, John Muir's "Range of Light." The crest of this massive barrier runs over 400 miles from a gap south of Lassen Peak to its designated southern end at Tehachapi Pass. It is comparable in size to the combined ranges of the Alps, rising higher above the surrounding country than even the Rockies: from sea level to over 14,000 feet on the west and from valleys on the eastern flank abruptly as much as 11,000. It consists essentially of a single huge block of the earth's crust, uptilted, with its broad surface slanted westward and its eastern scarp rising very steeply from a depressed trough. Most of the range bears evidence of the heavy and extensive glaciation that developed during the Pleistocene epoch, and the gorges of Yosemite and Hetch Hetchy are notable examples of this process.

Walker and Tioga Passes lie 177 airline miles apart and between them rises an impressive scenic barrier uncrossed by any river or highway. A dozen pinnacles over 14,000 feet high grace a 60-mile stretch from Mt. Langley to Thunderbolt Peak. Much the greater share of the runoff from this water parting drains to the central valleys of California and the glaciers that once adorned these heights bequeathed their principal sculptures to the western slopes. Yet along the eastern declivity they emerged into the open canyons, and the many rivulets and creeks descending into the Great Basin in Pluvial times supplied a group of lakes. The streams exist and still produce together a significant volume now mostly gathered to the Los Angeles aqueduct.

At the northernmost extremity of this drainage the largest of four lakes covered 267 square miles to a maximum depth of 750 feet. It lay immediately south of Conway Summit and has been named for the geologist I. C. Russell, who first mapped the surrounding region and authored extensive Pleistocene studies on various parts of the Great Basin.[1] Lake Russell at an early stage

---

[1] Russell described in his 1886–87 report the hot springs at Casa Diablo, near Mammoth Lakes, and the springs on the northeast shore of Mono Lake as well as those on Paoha

spilled briefly to the Owens River and is the only one of the four to have left any living reminder. It reached into Nevada at its peak through Mono and Aurora Valleys and came within 20 miles of Lake Lahontan.

The remnant is Mono Lake, as weird and fascinating a body of water as you will ever see, 10 to 14 miles in diameter and so full of salts (borax, sodium chloride and calcium carbonate) that no fish can live in it. But brine shrimp thrive here in countless numbers and water flies breed, attracting and supporting bird life. The shrimp are harvested to provide hatchery food and the flies form a diet for the tiny phalaropes that dart and pirouette about its surface. Mono has no organic shore growth of any kind but there are strange constructions of tufa, prolific and varied, rising where springs once furnished an environment suited to their formation. The columns, arches and battlements that ornament the shoreline like the ruins of an ancient Roman city were created by the action of algae congregating at underwater shelves and in locations where groundwater issued below a then much higher surface of Lake Russell.

Within the lake lie two volcanic islands. The smaller, darker one is called Negit, an Indian word meaning "blue-winged goose"; the larger, lighter colored one is Paoha, "hot springs" in Mono dialect. Both have craterlets and cinder cones, some containing water, and are areas of some geothermal activity. At the northern end of the lake short of the narrows rises a very steep and uniform bank of reddish black cinder material, an ominous countenance brooding over the landscape. The surrounding basin is littered with volcanic sand, pumice and obsidian. South of the lake and dominating the skyline, a series of igneous mounds called the Mono Craters line up beyond the highway and form an impressive panorama suggesting landforms of the moon. But in spite of being called craters they are actually domes that have few geologic associations with the crater phenomenon, whereas some miles south of them between Mammoth and Crestview there are two relatively minor vents called the Inyo Craters which are truly such and of very recent origin. Some scientists feel that this volcanic activity, which began somewhat less than four million years ago and built the imposing Mammoth Mountain as well as the Mono Craters, may not yet be ended (Rinehart and Huber, 1965).

Island in that lake. There has been some drilling here to determine the geothermal energy potential and a plant designed to generate 10,000 k.w. of electric power was scheduled for the Casa Diablo area, to cost $3.5 million. However, this has not yet materialized.

Looking out over the Mono basin from Conway Summit, one sees the magnificent peaks bordering Yosemite National Park on the east: Conness, Dana and Gibbs among them. Away to the south rises Mt. Lyell, like Dana exceeding 13,000 feet, and supporting on its slopes one of the largest and northernmost of the Sierra Nevada's three score surviving glaciers. Across Mono Lake the ancient terraces of Russell, not much in evidence elsewhere, are visible—picked out by lines of vegetation. A wooded ridge lies beyond and over it may be seen the distant mass of Boundary Peak (13,145), highest point in Nevada, and its companion summits—Mt. Montgomery, Mt. DuBois and White Mountain Peak—forming a long, dramatic phalanx.

Between Mono Lake and the White Mountains, Adobe Valley opens, with the Mono and Inyo National Forests surrounding it. Lower ranges, the Benton and Cowtrack Mountains among them, border this valley where a Pleistocene lake about 15 miles long and 75 feet deep at maximum gathered; at that stage it overflowed to the Owens River system through a very steep and impressive canyon. The Mt. Diablo Base Line, a prime surveyor's reference, cuts across its middle and small vestiges of the Pluvial development appear: Adobe Lake, Black Lake and a playa flat or two.

Southwest of Adobe Valley the drainage of the Owens River, largest of the three major permanent streams in the Death Valley system, begins. It rises in remote snowfed lakes along the Sierra escarpment and takes its name at the junction of Glass Creek and Deadman Creek, near Crestview. A copious source enhances the flow at Big Springs just below that point, and thereafter additions from Mammoth Lakes basin via Hot Creek, from Convict Lake, McGee Creek and other origins combine to supply the reservoir known as Crowley Lake. Here we have another of the several Long Valleys in the Great Basin; its vanished Pluvial lake has been given the valley's name (Mayo, 1934).

Lake Long Valley, more than four times the size of Lake Adobe but only a third as big as Lake Russell, occupied a comparatively narrow basin with a 90-square mile surface and a depth of 250 feet. Lacustrine deposits, wave-cut terraces and tufa remain. The modern Crowley reservoir (maximum capacity 183,465 acre feet) was created in 1941 and serves multiple uses: it acts as a regulator for hydroelectric facilities downstream, and provides recreation. The fishing, boating and swimming opportunities attract swarms of visitors and summer residents. It is one of the largest trout fisheries in California (Schumacher, 1959).

Below Crowley reservoir the river descends abruptly through a lava rim, dropping 2,400 feet in 20 miles; but most of its flow is diverted via penstocks to serve power stations in Owens Gorge. Rock Creek and Pine Creek enter at Birchim Canyon. Next come ponds in Fish Slough which drain southward 10 miles to where the river swings around the city of Bishop. Springs feeding these ponds were recently found to contain a specialized variety of pupfish *(Cyprinodon radiosus)* surviving from the Ice Age.[2] In 1969 when it became evident that the springs were beginning to dry up, probably because well-drilling in Chalfant Valley was lowering the water table, the California Department of Fish and Game transferred the population to an alternate site where they had built a permanent sanctuary. This move undoubtedly saved them from extinction.

Downstream from Bishop the Owens River flows between two very lofty and very different mountain developments and its valley narrows considerably. Vis-a-vis, the Inyos confront the Sierra Nevada, and the contrast is vivid. North and Middle Palisade, Thunderbolt, Sill and Split Mountains on the west, White Mountain Peak on the east, are all over 14,000 feet high. But whereas the Sierra enjoys a climate and expresses a quality appropriate to alpine regions, the Inyos are desert mountains and truly relate to the Great Basin. In spite of their comparable altitude they are very dry and are reached by only a very modest precipitation. No broad snowfields festoon their summit ridges, for the Sierra acts as a giant snow fence in the direction whence storms usually come, and the land east of the Inyos is all burnt out and relatively innocent of vegetation.

Westgard Pass crosses this range, separating the northern (White Mountains) and southern portions of the chain. Just to the east of this passage a steep-sided tight little depression known as Deep Springs Valley shows signs of having once held a lake about 17 square miles in area. The cognomen source lies north, and a playa occupies the southern end. The present arid condition undoubtedly maintained throughout most of the Holocene epoch and Lake Deep Springs was the single instance of a Pluvial accumulation between the Nevada boundary and the Sierra, south of Long Valley and short of Lake Owens. There are four desert basins to the east of

---

[2] Presence of the pupfish species, *C. radiosus,* in a number of Owens Valley springs is regarded as proof that a hydrological connection with Lake Manly once existed. This variety resembles other desert pupfish, but the male may be identified by its distinctive solid black ventral and anal fins. All male pupfish are bright blue; females are greenish, with black markings.

the Inyo crest, wholly enclosed and generally inaccessible, each with a large playa that fills up when the infrequent heavy rain materializes. These are called "lakes" on some maps; so besides Deep Springs Lake we have in today's cartographic inventory Eureka Lake, Saline Lake and Butte Lake (Hubbs and Miller, 1948). None of these last shows any evidence of Pluvial waters ever gathering though probably they had lakes that fluctuated without leaving identifiable shores.[3] Each is now fishless and apparently always has been.

From Bishop southward many clear creeks descend the western escarpment, pointing the high passes where only stock trails have access, some too steep and rough even for pack animals and frequented mostly by deer and the occasional backpacker. At sources under the high rock wall a long necklace of sparkling pools, partly or wholly iced during much of the year, lies below snowbanks and gives being to the streams. No Pluvial stands existed along these sharp declivities that underwent heavy erosion, and the year-round torrents swiftly cut through moraines and other barriers until only small ponds and tarns remained. But after coursing down its valley 100 miles or more the Owens, like all other Great Basin rivers, comes to a sandy destination.

Today nearly all the water of the basin has been pre-empted by the Los Angeles Department of Water and Power; this is a situation we shall examine later on in the chapter. At Aberdeen the Tinemaha reservoir and intake now collect to an aqueduct almost the entire flow of the river at that point. And so Owens Lake is bone dry and barren, the totally desiccated bottom of what was once an elongated sea 33 miles by 12. It once covered ground where Olancha now stands and ran northward well beyond the city of Lone Pine. These modern settlements lie well below the higher strandlines of the Owens predecessor (Gale, 1915). Olancha Peak (12,123) and Mt. Langley (14,042) are among the bastions beyond which a setting sun shone down upon that once extensive water.

At its highest level this sea spread over 205 square miles and sounded 220 feet. For our purposes the Owens River may be considered separately, even though at this development it was connected all the way to Death Valley by a continuous waterway: across a saddle next to the Coso Range to lakes in Indian Wells, Salt Wells,

---

[3] C.T. Snyder writes: "There has been a large amount of debris washed into Saline Valley by torrential storms. This would have destroyed any lake relics. Lake features on the eastern side are not readily evident." (Personal correspondence.)

Searles and Panamint Valleys, from which the discharge proceeded to Lake Manly.[4] None of it ever reached the ocean. The Lake Searles and Lake Panamint were substantial and Death Valley's Lake Manly, the subject of our next chapter, was the fourth largest and one of the deepest of all the Great Basin's Pleistocene lakes.

The Mono-Owens region, lying as it does along an extensive boundary of a specialized province, offers a wide variety of habitats for all sorts of living things. Three major animal and plant communities impinge: mountain, steppe and desert. Among birds and mammals, perhaps a hundred species of each can be identified, including migrants. The region's unique mammal is the Tule elk (Cervus nannodes), a dwarf variant native to the Central Valley of California but hunted very nearly out of existence there (Hock, 1962). In 1933 they were introduced in the Owens in order to save the species and they range from Lone Pine to Bishop on both sides of the river up to 8,000 feet. Controlled hunting has been permitted so that the number may be kept within limits inasmuch as the elk compete with domestic cattle for available forage and tend to encroach upon ranching property and gardens. A group of conservationists has been formed to study and protect the Tule elk and to work for the establishment of refuges here and elsewhere in the state. An interesting feature of this study has been the use of radio transmitters similar to those attached to the Himalayan partridges mentioned in Chapter VII, in order to chart elk movements and determine range use. At least two animals in each of the valley's five subherds were so equipped. A 1971 count put the number of elk at about 300 here, but two smaller herds additionally may be found in California's Kern and Colusa Counties.

Other mammals, indigenous types, are widely distributed and include such familiar species as mountain lion, bobcat, bighorn sheep (quite scarce), mule deer, porcupine, coyote, kit fox, beaver, marten, marmot, striped skunk and a number of small prowlers such as ground squirrels, rats and mice. Of particular interest is the kangaroo rat, completely adapted to the desert and never drinking any water; moreover, it eats only dry seeds and therefore must produce internally what little water its system requires, by a function of its metabolism. Three kinds of hare or rabbit in addition to the ubiquitous black-tailed jackrabbit (actually a hare) are worth

[4] Some miles northeast of Little Lake en route to Coso Hot Springs, a "fossil" waterfall may be seen, with potholes formed thousands of years ago when the Owens River ran through there via Indian Wells Valley to Lake Manly.

noting: the Sierra hare *(Lepus townsendii)*, often mistakenly called a snowshoe rabbit since it turns white in winter, occurring normally above 9,000 feet; the cottontail, genus *Sylvilagus*, with its mountain (darker) and desert (paler) forms; and the little pika, or cony *(Ochotoma princeps)*, that newcomers to the high country often regard as some kind of squirrel.

Birdlife varies with altitude—as indeed the mammals do. In the valleys the most spectacular fellow is the widely distributed magpie, in black and white dress with long tail; he is a social bird and valuable as a scavenger but also destructive, stealing eggs and eating the young of other species. Raven, nighthawk, sparrow hawk, meadowlark, horned lark and roadrunner are native and common. The chukar partridge has been introduced and, well-adapted, provides good hunting along with the mountain quail. Clark's nutcracker and Steller's jay are flashy, noisy and bold around campsites, alpine in habit. Mountain bluebird, western tanager, purple finch, white-crowned sparrow, Oregon junco, chickadee, hermit thrush and water ouzel are among the commoner varieties, and indeed there is material for ornithologists and birdwatchers everywhere, from hummingbirds to eagles.

Of the plant communities the creosote bush scrub is found below 3,500 feet, indicated by thornbush, beavertail cactus, ephedra, apricot mallow, brittlebush and the creosote bush *(Larrea divaricata)* from which it is named. These endure the frost and dryness but cannot stand salt conditions. Those which enjoy the salt, the halophytes, include saltbush, saltgrass, glasswort *(Salicornia rubra)* and a variety of dodder *(Cuscuta salina)* which is parasitic on the glasswort.[5]

The intermediate community, growing up to 6,000 or 7,000 feet, includes sagebrush, bitterbrush *(Purshia tridentata)* and rabbitbrush, shadscale, hopsage, lupine, desert peach and a variety of ceanothus. At higher altitudes the differences between the Sierra and the Inyo-White Mountain species of vegetation become more evident; the mixed coniferous families of the former are much more varied than the pinyon-juniper growth of the drier eastern slopes.

Above 7,500 feet one finds the Jeffrey and lodgepole pines, with

---

[5] Dodder also infects clover and alfalfa and is something of a pest in growing sugar beets, onions and flax. Though it feeds on crops it is non-poisonous and does not attack cereals. Sheep are useful in grazing dodder, and crop rotation has been found effective in controlling it. Other names for this plant include love-vine (used widely), strangleweed, devil's guts, pull-down, hellbind and hairweed. Of 54 different species of *Cuscuta*, 49 are native to North America (Hansen, 1923).

white and red fir, abundant up to the subalpine forests along the Sierra. Timberline may occur above 11,000 feet anywhere along the crest; at levels just below this we encounter whitebark pine (*Pinus albicaulis*) and may also find specimens of lodgepole, western white pine, foxtail pine and mountain hemlock. Especially does the *albicaulis* typify the sylva of the high Sierra, shaping itself to the exposed situations where it flourishes. The form may be prostrate or up to 45 feet tall; it may hug the slope in knee-high mats (called elfinwood) or send up multiple trunks to top out like a broom. This is *the* timberline tree of the Sierra Nevada.

The quaking aspen is the most widespread tree on this continent (D.C. Peattie, 1955). In the Great Basin it may be found at most altitudes, from sagebrush country up to the red fir-lodgepole community of the Sierra; but most often it occurs in high, cool, dry places, forming in open sunlit groves. It may reach a height of 90 feet but has little value as timber. It trembles (says Peattie) because the leaf is hinged upon a leafstalk longer than the blade, flattened contrary to the plane of the blade. Thus the stalk acts as a pivot and the leaf is agitated by the slightest breeze. Early in autumn, touched by the frosty nights, the aspen foliage turns from light green to shining gold, and the glittering groves become visible from great distances upon the shimmering heights of land.

The pinyon-juniper woodland of the Inyos is rather sparse and leads above 8,500 feet to the bristlecone pine forest, which is characterized by mountain mahogany, low sagebrush, limber pine (*Pinus flexilis*) and the bristlecone (*Pinus longaeva*). Of all the specialized forms in the Great Basin this last is particularly intriguing, for it has longer life than any other known species of tree (with the possible exception of the Formosan sun tree) including the sequoias.[6] Thriving under the most severe conditions of drought and exposure, this gnarled and battered hulk of a pine looks half dead when healthy and remains in place often for centuries after its total demise.

There are two varieties of bristlecone pine: the Great Basin kind, *longaeva*, quite recently differentiated; and *aristata*, found in the high country of Utah, Colorado, Northern New Mexico and the San Francisco Mountains of Arizona. The bristlecone was first collected by F. Creutzfeldt, in the course of a railroad survey in 1853 near Cochetopa Pass, Colorado, on the Continental Divide

[6] In November 1973, Prof. Chow Hui-yen of the College of Chinese Culture on Taiwan reported finding a Formosan sun tree growing 30 miles southwest of Taipei which he believes is more than 6,000 years old. It measured 88.4 feet in circumference.

CHANNEL OF THE PLEISTOCENE STREAM FROM LAKE OWENS
SOUTH TO INDIAN WELLS VALLEY, LOOKING NORTH (see page 131)
U. S. Geological Survey, 1920 photo: D. G. Thompson, no. 566.

SPECIMEN TREE OF THE BRISTLECONE PINE
U. S. Geological Survey photo: V. C. La Marche, no. 39.

250 miles east of the Great Basin (D. C. Peattie, 1953). The species lives in scattered stands on the highest windswept slopes, growing in limestone soils under dry conditions; its beaten, often crippled-looking appearance results from climatic severity. Trees such as this are known as "wind timber" and in Switzerland are called *krummholz*. They persist around the world. Here on the rooftops of the Basin they must bear the sandblast of tearing winds and blizzard-born ice crystals, the desperate cold and the prolonged aridity. If a drought continues for several years they die back to conserve moisture, with channels of bark maintaining the circulation necessary to support surviving foliage. The growing season for this species is no more than three months of the year and the mean annual temperatures of its habitats exceed freezing by hardly more than a degree or two.

Here the bristlecone lives from 8,500 to 11,000 feet a.s.l. along the White Mountain crest north of Westgard Pass, mostly in association with dolomitic rock. One specimen has been dated at 4,600 B.P. and a score or more have been found with an age in excess of 4,000 years. Determining the age of a tree involves a reasonably simple technique of measuring and correlating tree-rings, called dendrochronology.[7] A long slim cylinder is driven to the heart of the wood and then withdrawn to extract a core, which is then glued along a trough-like matrix, sliced in half, and stained for easier reading. The succession of bands of different widths revealed by this process represents the tree-rings, and examination is made with a microscope since these lines are often too fine to be seen by the naked eye. The pattern of bands is compared with previously identified configurations and in this way cross-dating may be accomplished. Band widths are indicators of growth and therefore to some extent of precipitation, annually over the centuries.

The crossdating is reliable though the weather record may not be, inasmuch as the rings only show available moisture during the growing season. Antevs (1948) observes: "The rate of tree growth is a disputed indicator of rainfall and moisture—radial growth of trees is determined by winter and spring precipitation, little if at all by summer rainfall." Holdover snowmelt and soil moisture after a wet winter could produce good rings in a dry summer.

Ten miles north of Cedar Flat on the back road to White Moun-

---

[7] The father of dendrochronology was Dr. A. E. Douglass of the University of Arizona. From 1910 on, he worked out the basic method of applying tree-ring data to chronological problems of archeology. He was not only a dedicated scientist but an inspiring teacher as well (Gianella, correspondence).

tain Peak the U.S. Forest Service has designated the Schulman Grove and picnic area, honoring the late Dr. Edmund Schulman of the University of Arizona, a dendroclimatologist who conducted early tree-ring research. Recently Dr. C. W. Ferguson, dendrochronologist of the same institution, has been engaged in studies that involve bristlecone pines of this area and of the Pearl Peak stand in the Ruby Mountains (Chapter VIII). He has also worked with specimens growing in the Wheeler Peak environment, Snake Range, and determined the ages of some very old trees there. The White Mountain Research Station, operated by the University of California in conjunction with the Office of Naval Research and the National Science Foundation, conducts high altitude studies at three sites on or near the summit of White Mountain Peak.

The alpine fell fields lie above timberline and their vegetation consists of creeping shrubs, flowering plants and grasses. Alpine willow, which grows in mats where the ground is moist, Sierra primrose and epilobium, paintbrush, polemonium and phlox are among the colorful adornments of these heights. All of them prosper in relatively exposed and rocky situations. There are more than 2,000 species of plants in the Owens-Mono region, and within these categories are variations almost without limit (DeDecker, 1962). No attempt can be made in the compass of this work to cover the botanical field in any depth.

There were people living long ago in the Owens Valley, possibly 3,000—certainly more than 1,000—years before the Christian era began. These early inhabitants possessed a distinct culture found also in the Pinto basin of southern California and made dart and spear points altogether different from those used by the Paiute Indians of this millenium. Very little is known of them otherwise, whether as the climate altered they died out or moved away, or notwithstanding the cultural gap they were indeed the ancestors of the much more recent groups. In the absence of any written language there is no history of these Pinto people, and we can make only a few deductions based on artifacts they have left behind.

Among such are the petroglyphs. Throughout the Owens Valley and the adjoining tableland there are acres of carvings at unnumbered sites; some are mere scratches, others are half an inch deep. Heizer and Baumhoff (1962) have assembled a listing and descriptions of 99 outstanding Great Basin petroglyph sites. They point out that most of them could quite reasonably have been associated with good hunting or game ambush spots, and they feel the glyphs themselves were most probably a ritual device to insure the success of the hunt. In some instances the rock art was religious, involving a magic significance. Many sites show long-continued use. Heizer and Baumhoff suggest that if hunt shamans were functioning at ambush sites they might have been the ones who pecked out the designs. In any case, the Indians of today can shed no light on either the origins or the meanings of these decorations.

Pinto sites are numerous along the north shore of Lake Owens above the highest strandlines. Others are scattered through the valley as far north as Montgomery Pass. At Little Lake, south of the Coso Range, one of the oldest open-site dwellings found in the West was excavated by archeologists from the Southwest Museum, who obtained a wide variety of artifacts including almost 500 spear points. There is geological evidence that in Pinto times the climate was wetter, the streams ran full, and trees grew abundantly everywhere.

It is difficult to separate the Indians that survive today into tribes since they consist of very loosely associated family groups. Those of the Owens Valley are regarded as the southernmost relatives of the Northern Paiutes, while others to the east and south seem rather to be a Shoshone offshoot; they have colonies at Bishop, Big Pine, Independence and Lone Pine. The bands that occupy the Mono Basin are naturally called Mono Indians, yet except for language they are not much different ethnically from their Paiute or Washo neighbors. All are Great Basin people with similar skills and occupations, their diets varying as the food availabilities differed, but all of them devoted primarily to the search for sustenance.

Into this particular world of the early American the first European intruded in 1830. While it is true that Father Garcés from Tubac, en route to San Gabriel, had crossed the Mojave Desert 54 years prior to that, as the first white man to really penetrate the Great Basin, he had not however come as far north as the Owens Valley. It seems probable that Peter Skene Ogden, on his sixth and final expedition southward from the Snake River region, must have been the first Caucasian to enter it, and we have to say "probable" because the journal that would have established his route was lost in the Columbia River. That accident was described by Ogden in a letter dated March 10, 1831, to John McLeod: ". . . unfortunately below the main fall of the Col. my own Boat was engulphed in a Whirlpool and 9 men drowned" (Cline, 1963). This and other surviving letters to friends indicate imprecisely the route Ogden took to the Gulf of California and back to Fort Vancouver, between late October 1829, and July 6, 1830.

From disconnected comments he made it is thought he came down past Walker Lake and reached the Inyos in January, then continued beyond Owens Lake to the Mojave Desert. The streams he encountered were destitute of beaver, but he persisted through harsh terrain, suffering from lack of food and water. Eventually the party reached "the South West Branch of the Rio Collarado" and followed it, perhaps to its mouth, but trapping did not improve so they turned northward. Their route very probably was by way of Tehachapi Pass and up the west side of the Sierra to the Pit River and Goose Lake, where they would have re-entered the Great Basin. In any case they returned to Fort Nez Percés with what furs they had obtained, but it was for Ogden a journey of great privation and continual frustration.

Turning now to the impressive record of Joseph R. Walker, a most intrepid mountain man of high attainments, we find he either led or guided three expeditions pertinent to this account: that of 1833–34, mounted by Capt. Bonneville; the 1843 journey with the Chiles party; and the rapid thrust he led with Theodore Talbot under Frémont's command late in 1845. In the course of each he passed through the Owens Valley.

After pushing down the trapped-out Humboldt River in 1833 and crossing the Sierra Nevada in October, Walker wintered in Monterey and then began his return trip to the Bear River. Not wishing to repeat his rugged transit of the mountains, he took his men south and around them, and in the process he discovered the pass that Frémont years later named after him. Quite soon the group found themselves in the Owens Valley "in a temperate climate, and among tolerable pasture," wrote Zenas Leonard, "which latter was equally as gratifying to our horses as the former was to our men." Beyond Owens Lake they attempted to swing east and north but this put them in very dry and barren country and they were most fortunate in extricating themselves and finding the Humboldt River route by which they had come west.

In the spring of 1843 Joseph Chiles organized a party for settlement in California. On the way west from Missouri they encountered Walker and hired him to guide them the rest of the way. After great hardship, near Owens Lake they buried much equipment in the sand, abandoned their wagons, and continued on foot (the women and children riding horses) to complete the journey by way of Walker Pass (Farquhar, 1966).

From the Walker Lake rendezvous, mentioned previously, the main body of Frémont's third expedition continued southward without him down the Owens Valley to the lake, where they found the equipment cache left by the Chiles-Walker party. Thence they went over Walker Pass. Frémont had not seen the Owens Valley, nor its river or lake, but he gave them the name of his aide—a certain Richard Owens of Ohio whom he described in his memoirs as "cool, brave, and of good judgment . . . a good shot . . . valuable throughout the campaign." Thus he became the title figure for this land, although he did not go through the valley and never saw the lake or river (Schumacher, 1962.).

Settlement of this Basin borderland came late. Mono appears for the first time in its history with a punitive foray against local Indians led by Lt. Tredwell Moore in May–June 1852. He found promising mineral deposits and gave out a brief account. Two years later Leroy Vining reached the scene looking for gold and camped beneath Tioga Pass on the creek that, like the town at the southwest end of Mono Lake, has been named Lee Vining after him. A large early gold rush materialized in the summer of 1859 after Carl Norst discovered the precious metal in Mono Gulch and word of the event spread around, but this play was short-lived. Monoville, at the foot of Conway grade, thrived for about a year, but then most of the miners left it for newer diggings in Bodie ten miles or so northeast.

To the northwest of Mono Lake a beautiful canyon extends high into the Sierra Nevada Mountains and nests a small lake from which Mill Creek descends. Here the Lundy mine flourished for a short period and gave its name to both the lake and the canyon. Mill and Lee Vining Creeks are now used as sources of water power by the local electric utility and serve domestic water needs; thereafter the flow that once emptied into Mono Lake is now diverted to the Owens River through a tunnel under the Mono Craters and becomes a part of the Los Angeles water supply. June, Gull, Silver and Grant Lakes make a connected loop that feeds into Rush Creek. These lie below Mono Pass, the old Indian trail which was used as a wagon road to the West in the days of the mines. It should be noted that there are two Mono Passes, this one at 10,600 feet entering Yosemite Park south of Mt. Gibbs from Bloody Canyon and Sardine Lakes, and the pass that leads from the Rock Creek drainage 40 miles south of Gibbs to Mono Creek and the San Joaquin's south fork. The latter is a hiker's pass, at 12,000 feet.

About the time that the mines were first active Mark Twain came down from Virginia City to see what they were all about. He visited the mining camp at Monoville, and included a description of Mono Lake and its islands in "Roughing It," first published in 1872. This merry account embroiders the truth, but it contains some very keen observations, and Mark Twain put this part of the world on the map for the reading public.

The imprint of human activity is evident in two kinds of scar upon this land: the modern highway that carves wide swaths across the Conway grade, and the very nearly obliterated signs of a long-vanished railroad. The rails and roadbed came first, of course. Bodie's best years were from 1877 to 1881, and as many as 8,000 people lived there at the height of its growth, notwithstanding its exposed windswept location and its arctic winters. To serve the mines and mills of the district the Bodie & Benton Railway, 33 miles long (later extended to 37) was built in 1881. Primarily it brought in timber to shore up the mine tunnels. Myrick (1962) observes that, as a railroad the Bodie & Benton was a paradox, for it began on a hilltop and ended in a forest, it never served Bodie and never reached Benton, and it had no rail connection with the outside world. Yet for half a century it was a financial success. A link to the Carson & Colorado was graded in 1882 but no rail was ever laid. Operations continued until 1917, when the road was abandoned. Life in Bodie had its ups and downs, fluctuating with the fortunes of the Standard Consolidated Mine, the "mainstay of Bodie," but this enterprise dwindled early in the century and today the ghost town, preserved and reconstructed to make a state historical park, is a heavily visited tourist attraction in the summer.

Much more important to the economic development of the Owens Valley was the narrow gauge line built in 1880–83 called the Carson & Colorado. It began at Mound House on the Virginia & Truckee Railroad, continued via Fort Churchill and the east side of Walker Lake to Montgomery Pass; thence the route entered California and caught up with the Owens River at Laws (near Bishop), following the river to and partly around Owens Lake. This 3-foot wide railroad, 293 miles in length, ended at the town of Hawley (Keeler) where ore from surrounding mines was transshipped. Branch lines or spurs were extended to some of the mines or mills along the route and several tramways came down to the right-of-way, including one at Hawley from the Cerro Gordo workings and one all the way from Saline Valley, carrying salt 14 miles from deposits east of the Inyos. Originally it was planned to continue the rails to the Panamint, Darwin and Coso mining districts but Darius O. Mills, a magnate who was heavily invested in the C & C, came to Hawley on an inspection tour and there dropped his famous remark to the effect that the railroad had been built either 300 miles too long or 300 years too soon (Myrick, 1962).

As its name implies, it was formed with the idea of connecting two rivers on opposite sides of the Great Basin, and it did accompany about 26 miles of the Carson, thereafter heading generally toward Las Vegas. However, the original intent was modified by circumstance and from the vicinity of Candelaria the road then veered southward toward the Owens and the active mining districts near its lake rather than the Colorado River. Mines and milling constituted the chief support of this facility though ranching and the mercantile trade of many communities, some growing and some as ephemeral as the mines that flared and died, swelled the traffic.

The earliest actual settlers were stockmen. Samuel Bishop brought in the first cattle in 1861—500 head plus 50 horses—and in that year Charles Putnam started a trading post at what is now Independence. Still, it was mining that provided impetus to the region's development and a market for the beef the ranchers raised. Coso silver was discovered in 1860, San Carlos came two years later, but it was the Cerro Gordo silver that brought real prosperity. In eight years production from the "Fat Hill" near the Inyo crest amounted to an estimated $17,000,000 including lead and zinc values. By 1876, with the ore running out, the smelter was shut down but for the four preceding years the 85-foot steamer *Bessie Brady* plied between Swansea and Cartago on Owens Lake, loaded with silver bullion. Swansea has disappeared, Cartago and Keeler (its name changed from Hawley) remain barely visible, a few structures persisting, and the lake itself is altogether gone.

Early relations with the Indians were good but as the mines developed and population pressures increased they deteriorated. The presence of domestic cattle was too much of a temptation to the hungry Paiutes, especially after a heavy winter, with scarce game and widespread deprivation. Warfare broke out in 1862; raids, ambush and retaliation, and pitched battles followed; then soldiers were brought in from Fort Churchill and Santa Monica. Camp Independence was established on the Fourth of July. Conditions thereafter gradually improved as 1000 Indian men, women and children were transported willingly to a reservation south of Bakersfield. Others received local employment as farm laborers.

The Civil War years were times of discovery and designation along the previously unexplored and unmapped Sierra Nevada. The Alabama Hills west of Lone Pine were so named by southern sympathizers after the Confederate raider *Alabama* sank the Union warship *Hatteras* in 1863. Then when the *Kearsarge* in turn sank the *Alabama*, northern sympathizers bestowed her name on their mining district, from which Kearsarge Peak, the mountain pass and the creek were similarly derived.

The Owens Valley and the lowlands to the north of it constitute a weak zone in the earth's crust. Underlying this zone are innumerable fault fractures, and crustal adjustments still occur here. The main east-facing scarp in the valley lies at the foot of the Alabama Hills; it is a vestige of the cataclysm that took place on March 26, 1872, when the village of Lone Pine was destroyed and 27 people were killed, 60 injured, out of a total population of fewer than 300. The Coast & Geodetic Survey Bulletin 609 entitled *Earthquake History of the United States* (1939) asserts that this shock was the greatest of the three outstanding earthquakes in California history (as of that publication's date), those of 1857 (Fort Tejon), 1872 and 1906 (San Francisco), and observes that in a settled region it would have had catastrophic results.

The first Europeans to record the High Sierra peaks were Captain Pedro Fages and Father Juan Crespi in March 1772, but their mention was most perfunctory: ". . . some high mountains to the southeast, very distant." Four years later Father Pedro Font, from a hill near the mouth of the Sacramento River, looked across the broad and treeless sweep to a sight he recorded as *"una gran sierra nevada"* about 40 leagues away, and placed it definitely on a map for the first time. Meanwhile almost simultaneously, Father Francisco Garcés, from Tehachapi, observed and described the same range (Farquhar, 1966). Thereafter for 30 years no exploration, nor even any expressed interest in the range, materialized and about all the Spanish missionaries did was poke about in small boats in the lower reaches of the various rivers: the San Joaquin, Kings, Merced, American and Feather. The first range crossings were made, as we have seen, by Jedediah Smith (1827) and J. R. Walker (1833), followed by emigrant trains in the '40s, Captain Frémont, and the Forty-niners. That year of the Gold Rush saw William Penn Abrams confirming what Joe Walker had seen in the Yosemite, "Walls a mile high" and the "Rock of Ages" (Half Dome). But in June 1864,

Professor W. H. Brewer and his party went up the south fork of the Kings River to make a professional reconnaissance, and it constituted a historic beginning.

The short-lived California State Geological Survey began with Josiah D. Whitney as its chief, and it was he who ordered the on-site examination of the high country. Among the members of Prof. Brewer's party were the youthful Clarence King and Richard L. Cotter, both very strong and eager, and on July 4 these two began a five-day trip along the Sierra crest, climbing Mt. Tyndall, from which summit they could see the whole panorama of great peaks. They took bearings, mapped and named Mt. Whitney (after Josiah D.) and Mt. Williamson,[8] the first and second highest mountains, respectively, in the range. In this immediate view were also Mts. Barnard, Russell, Muir and Langley, all of the magnitude of 14,000 feet. Some of these are very rugged and technical but others, like Whitney, require no skill on the part of a climber but only a great deal of stamina and wind.

The ultimate surveys waited upon the efforts of a Federal agency, since the California Legislature in a fit of economy abolished their State Geological Survey in 1865. Its personnel then scattered—Prof. Whitney to Harvard, Prof. Brewer to Yale. Important explorations were later conducted by Capt. George Wheeler of the U.S. Geological Survey, in 1875–79, when he led the "Survey West of the 100th Meridian," and by I. C. Russell of the same agency, who made extensive studies in 1883 and engaged in mapping glaciers in the Mt. Lyell-Mono Lake region. John Muir had established the existence of living glaciers (which Whitney had emphatically denied) and wrote vividly of the mountains he lived among and loved so well. His ecstatic descriptions include the assertion that "the Sierra should be called not the Nevada, or Snowy Range, but the Range of Light . . . the most divinely beautiful of all the mountain-chains I have ever seen."

The 20th century brought about an almost total alteration in the life and economy of the Owens Valley. The 1800s were characterized by discovery, exploitation of the mineral wealth, then settlement and agricultural development. As the sporadic prosperity characteristic of mining in those times gave way to a more stable life of crop- and stock-raising, a new force for the most drastic

[8] Mt. Williamson (14,364) was named by Clarence King for Maj. Robert S. Williamson of the Corps of Topographical Engineers, who had explored extensively for railroad routes south and east of the immediate region.

The Approach to Mount Whitney by Road to Whitney Portal
Where the Summit Trail Begins, West of Lone Pine, California

change was at work. In 1880 the population of Los Angeles totalled 11,000 people. By 1900 it had grown to more than 100,000 and during the following decade this figure tripled. The years from 1892 to 1904 were dry ones and the need for domestic and industrial water became increasingly acute.

The single likely source of additional potable water within economic reach seemed to be the Owens River, and so Mayor Fred Eaton and Water Superintendent William Mulholland began a feasability study. In 1905, as the city reservoirs were dropping by three million gallons a day, Los Angeles voted $1.5 million to buy land, and with it water rights, in the Valley. From then on the battle for the Owens water became increasingly bitter as more and more of it was diverted to the southland.

The city voted $23 million more in 1907 to build an aqueduct 233 miles long from Aberdeen to the San Fernando Valley: this was completed in 1913. Another severe drought began in 1921 and with a population by now of 600,000 the shortages mounted again. So the city began buying more land and water rights, this time north of the Aberdeen intake. Meanwhile the Valley folk became increasingly disturbed and angry. In 1924 during prolonged drought conditions there were incidents: 40 men blew up the aqueduct north of Lone Pine in May, and in November the Alabama Gates were seized and all water turned out for five days. In 1926 there were two more dynamitings, the following year 14, and the city sent armed guards to patrol their canal. Resistance collapsed soon afterward when banks in Bishop were audited and found short of over $2 million; their owners, ringleaders in the water war, were convicted of embezzlement. This brought an end to the hostilities and the city went on to buy much more land, eventually to extend the system far up into Mono County and to build Long Valley dam and the power plants in Owens River Gorge.

The aqueduct itself was an engineering masterpiece involving huge quantities of material, facilities for 5,000 workmen, and a railroad spur 120 miles long to move these men with their equipment and supplies. A 9-mile temporary track known as the Red Rock Railroad was built up a canyon of that name to serve the construction project and then was dismantled less than two years later. Altogether, the Southern Pacific's Mojave-Owenyo line connecting with the Carson & Colorado, started in May of 1908 and finished in October of 1910, extended 143 miles.

The counties receive some compensation for losses of revenue due to the abandonment of ranching property. A news item in

December 1969 stated that the Los Angeles water and power commissioners had authorized payment of $2.6 million in lieu of taxes on property owned by the Department of Water and Power to Inyo and Mono Counties, the former to receive slightly more than $2 million, the latter some $535,000.

Nevertheless a beautiful valley once filled with productive farms was despoiled and turned back to sagebrush. The people were forced to find other occupations or move out, and Owens Lake dwindled rapidly to nothing. Some were tricked into selling, others were forced by circumstances to do so; and even if the process was entirely legal—no land had been condemned, and many ranchers sold out at prices that made them financially secure—the rape of the Owens was deplorable in that mankind changed Arcadia into a desert.

War brought a strange new infusion, temporary and not at all creditable, to Owens Valley. About ten miles north of Lone Pine on March 13, 1942, the U.S. Government established a concentration camp for some 10,000 Americans of Japanese ancestry. The euphemism employed was "Detention Camp," further softened by the descriptive term "agrarian community." The Nisei uprooted and confined there enjoyed small gardens, modest accommodations, shrines and places of worship, but not their freedom. Manzanar was abandoned in mid-November 1945, and the mark of it is hardly visible today, except perhaps on the minds and spirits of those who experienced confinement there.[9]

The years since 1945 have produced further extraordinary changes in the Owens, even as the national scene has been transformed. Here as elsewhere the increased leisure time and affluence particularly of city people plus their restless mobility have combined to bring in new wealth and activities. Dorothy Cragen in Genny Schumacher's *Deepest Valley*, described it this way: "In the hopeless years when their ranches were drying up, some Owens Valley people began to realize they still had the richest bonanza of all—their magnificent mountain and desert scenery. Tourist business is double the value of ranching, mining, and lumbering put together. Service stations alone account for twice as many dollars as cattle . . ."

---

[9] Another detention camp in the Great Basin was located in the Sevier Desert near Delta, Utah, at a spo' known as Topaz. Called a "War Relocation Area," it held 8,232 internees at its peak in ₁943 and became the fourth largest community in the state. It contained administrative buildings, a hospital, schools and Army-style barracks, all bordered by barbed-wire fences with watch-towers and armed guards. Today only crumbling foundations, torn-up roads and rubble remain. Big red ants and huge anthills share the empty site with horned lizards. The bitter memories linger.

Nor is this new economy a limited, seasonal thing, for each time of the year has its special pull—outdoor recreation of one sort or another for campers, sportsmen, climbers, skiers, rockhounds, botanists, antiquarians, and just about everyone who knows and loves the world that surrounds us.

Mammoth Mountain has its huge skiing complex, riding country, Devil's Postpile, cool clear lakes. In the Owens below Bishop the topography favors the development of summer thermals—powerful columns of rising air ideal for sailplaning—and this area has become a renowned center for engineless flight. Pack trains move into the forest-clad hinterland, hunters and fishermen roam the hills and streams. Geologists, amateur and professional, come to study and marvel at such anomalous phenomena as the still prominent fault scarps made a century ago around Lone Pine and north to Bishop.

For those who would know more about this valley and gain some feeling for its special qualities there is Mary Austin's *Land of Little Rain*, an esthetic portrait by a poet creating in prose. She lived in many parts of this region at one time or another and became quite submerged in her surroundings, though she earned the dislike of many people.

Otherwise, one might go and see for himself the austere beauty of the arid flats, the imposing battlements that Ansel Adams has caught so vividly in photographs, and all that is high and remote and unpolluted, filled with the peace of undisturbed and unfrequented spaces.

CHAPTER X

The Death Valley System
Amargosa River and Lake Manly

The deep and narrow trough called Death Valley lies along the southwest border of Nevada but wholly within the state of California. It is of comparatively recent origin, having been formed during the Quaternary period between one and two million years ago, and is a fault basin or "graben" rather than a true valley cut by stream action. Erosion features of the adjacent unglaciated ranges are geologically youthful and at lower elevations they show unmistakably where Lake Manly reached at its greatest development. This Pleistocene body probably attained its peak in early Wisconsin times about 65,000 years ago simultaneously with the 100 or more Pluvial lakes of the Great Basin. It then received input from several directions through lake chains that disappeared thousands of years ago, as Manly itself did, but the rivers of the system indicate quite clearly the courses these waters took.

These were the Owens River, covered in the preceding chapter; the Mojave River, which will be considered in the next; and the Amargosa, of immediate concern and the only one that still brings any water to Death Valley. Its name derives from the Spanish *amargo* which means "bitter." It rises in Nevada along Pahute Mesa between Black Mountain and Tolicha Peak; thence it flows southwest to Beatty, southeast to Ash Meadows, and across the state line about 110 miles from its source. Once in California it changes direction again near Tecopa, describes a complete semicircle some 20 miles in diameter, and then continues northwest to the terminal valley. The total length of its wash is approximately 180 miles.

Along this j-shaped course a single lake of about 1,000 square miles formed in the Tecopa-Shoshone vicinity due to stream blockage in Pluvial times and reached a depth of 400 feet (Hubbs and Miller); it has been designated Lake Tecopa.[1] Many other lakes

---

[1] The lake and the town of Tecopa carry the name of an old Indian chief noted for his moderation and memorialized as a peacemaker. The town is on the Amargosa River north of the canyon that stream carved through the Kingston Range. Lake Tecopa formed up river from the canyon, and northeast of the town at the edge of its vestigial playa lies Resting Springs where Frémont and his party laid over briefly in 1844 while negotiating

developed in basins adjoining the Amargosa drainage but did not overflow to it; there are also two others that probably did. In Sarcobatus Flat west of the headwaters Lake Bonnie Claire rose and covered 60 square miles without exterior connection; three small surrounding lakes discharged into it. A tiny lake in Ash Meadows and a much larger one in Pahrump Valley spilled to the Death Valley system, but along the California-Nevada border southeastward, Lake Mesquite and Lake Ivanpah were entirely isolated. Three very small lakes appeared in Eldorado and Jean Dry Lake Valleys northeast of Lake Ivanpah.

Reference was made in the preceding chapter to the lakes in Searles and Panamint Valleys. These were somewhat larger than Lake Owens and much deeper: Searles, which spilled into Panamint, had a 353-square mile surface and a depth of 640 feet, while Panamint—long, narrow and four-fifths as large—was 930 feet deep! Most authorities believe that it probably overflowed at this maximum to Lake Manly through Wingate Pass (altitude 1,976) but the main supply lines were the Amargosa and Mojave Rivers feeding Manly for thousands of years. Brief seasonal flow still travels down the Amargosa but none at all arrives by way of the Mojave. The lakes that formed along that river will be examined in the next chapter.

The catchment area of the Amargosa is greater than that of the Mojave, yet today it contains the smallest water supply of the three in the Death Valley system. Near the riverhead the water is permanent and of good quality but elsewhere it grows saline; in the middle and lower portions it has been called appropriately an artery of salt running through the desert (Hubbs and Miller, 1948). At intervals it is fed by warm springs, some of them quite large; the most important are Saratoga Springs and the one named Devil's Hole in Ash Meadows,[2] both of which contain populations of pupfish.

The intermittent Amargosa has been the butt of many jokes. Its streambed is dry except during the vernal runoff, thus it has earned the name of the "underground" or "upside down" river. The late Senator Pat McCarran of Nevada prankishly conferred the title "Admiral of the Amargosa Fleet" on some of his special friends.

the Old Spanish Trail. The town marks a point on the Tonopah & Tidewater where the Tecopa Railroad, 9.5 miles long, branched off to the Noonday and Gunsight mines in the nearby hills; these produced lead, silver and some gold during the years the feeder line operated (1910–22). Currently an iron mine at Beck Spring in the Kingston Range is under contract to ship several million tons of ore to Japan and a mill of 2,000 tons daily capacity is part of the operation.

[2] Ash Meadows takes its name from the leatherleaf ash trees (Fraxinus velutina Torrey, also called velvet ash) that grow there. It did not derive from volcanic ash or similar material strewn about the area.

In 1925 a promoter by the name of C. C. Julian who hoped to lure investors into his Leadfield mining scheme distributed handbills showing steamships ascending the Amargosa to load ore at Titus Canyon (Kirk, 1965). Besides lacking water the river channel lies some 18 miles east of Leadfield.

It may be observed that there are many rivers in the Basin and Range province which behave in a fashion similar to the Amargosa, and their prototype is the Hassayampa[3] of central Arizona, a tributary of the Gila, which goes underground several miles above Wickenburg—the town is built right on top of its channel. The name comes from *haciampa*, an old Navajo word meaning "upside down," and it applies to the Mojave River as well as the Amargosa. Yet in spite of its harmless appearance and recessive nature such a river can go on the rampage with devastating effect, flooding when the snows of a heavy winter melt rapidly or after torrential summer thunderstorms. In 1969 following prolonged spring rains some highways were washed out, cars were swept away, and several people were drowned along the Amargosa.

Much has been made of the geophysical disparities existing in the Death Valley region: the highest and lowest points in the conterminous states being no more than 80 miles apart. The highest is the summit of Mt. Whitney (14,494) and it may be discerned in good weather from several nearby peaks (though not from the valley floor); and the lowest is not at Badwater, 17 miles south of Furnace Creek Ranch, but at two places somewhat west of there which surveyors found in 1951 to measure 282 feet below sea level (Kirk). These extremes of elevation are one kind of anomaly—another is the widespread desert flooding that occurs following abnormal snow melt in some years. In 1964 a six-mile stretch of standing water gathered in the lower valley and there are photographs showing a canoeist paddling from Badwater to Eagle Borax. Such a lake formed again in 1969 and 1972 quite briefly but in each case the waters soon evaporated. Hubbs and Miller observe that the surface waters of the Amargosa have apparently not reached Badwater within historic times, this being the final sink of the river; but if indeed they have not, it would seem they arrived by the underground route.

Effects of summer thunderstorms are to be seen all about, for the alluvial fans extending far beyond the mouths of the canyons carry unmistakable evidence of many an ancient deluge. The size

---

[3] There is a legend concerning the Hassayampa River, quoted by C. T. Snyder, who once lived there. They say that he who drinks of it tells the truth no more.

of the rocks moved down these quite gentle slopes and the prodigious distances they must have traveled imply a force and violence not readily grasped in terms of today's meteorological norms. The sheer volume of debris washed into the valley is stupendous.

Lake Manly at its maximum extended nearly 100 miles down the lower two-thirds of Death Valley, covered 618 square miles, and was served by an encompassing drainage basin at least 20 times as large. It reached a depth of about 600 feet and left heavy sediments; beach deposits and strandlines mark its former presence. Lacustrine features, however, are somewhat scattered and faint except for the prominent sand dunes distributed near Stovepipe Wells. These have been moved about and relocated by wind patterns hundreds of centuries old and lie concentrated where the lake attained its widest dimension: here at Mesquite Flat, about 15 miles from the northern end of the Pluvial sea, it was almost 11 miles across. But the terraces indicating ancient water levels are found elsewhere, are quite rare in occurrence and rather obscure due to heavy obliterating erosion. The clearest adorn a black basalt hill called Shoreline Butte near the southern end of the valley, while others may be discerned at Manly Terrace above Mushroom Rock and at a site on the Daylight Pass road. Along this highway there is a cut made through gravel composed of shingled water-rounded pebbles; this bar is shoreline in origin and marks the upper limit of Lake Manly's eastern margin.

The sediments laid down are impressive. In the lower valley the floor consists of vertically alternating clay beds and salty muds that have been measured and found to be as much as 7,500 feet deep. Flash floods have rearranged the salt zones, redissolving the sulfates, carbonates and chlorides of the desert pavement. The salty crust runs up to six feet thick and makes strange noises audible to one who listens at suitable times and places—these may sound like the slow beginning patter of raindrops on a metal roof. The power of growing salt crystals is uncanny, for as they expand they may heave up very large stones or split apart rocks and wooden objects.

To complete the Pleistocene lake profile we should mention the hypothetical Lake Rogers, supposed by some authorities to have occupied the northern portion of Death Valley. Kirk (1965) mentions white sediments called the Niter Beds, found at the northeast edge of Mesquite Flat, and identifies them as a remnant of Rogers, but Clements (1958) places that lake north of Ubehebe Crater some 30 miles away and describes a whitish lake bed covering several square miles in the middle of the valley. He believes Manly and Rogers were in part contemporaneous but not connected, and cites the presence of a mastodon tusk and fossils of an extinct horse in this bed as proof of the lake's existence. Our basic map (I-416) shows Lake Manly covering the site that Kirk has designated and it omits Lake Rogers altogether. C. T. Snyder, who collaborated in its preparation, comments "No shore line, no lake was our rule." (Personal correspondence).

It is not easy to imagine a lake the size of Manly ever having been situated in this, the hottest known and one of the driest places on earth. The average annual rainfall is 1.69 inches at Furnace Creek Ranch, and the summer temperatures are consistently the highest of any regularly recorded area in the world. Evaporation rates vary from 12 to 14 feet a year, thus it is a source of wonder that any living brook or standing water can remain permanently in the valley. The evidence that it must have done so in a number of localities is irrefutable, however, for proof exists in the presence of fish species that remain to us from the Pluvial development and by their nature reveal not only the continuity of the waters but also a linkage between river systems and associated lakes that flourished in those early times.[4] Moreover, the degree of differentiation between species and subspecies of the same genus is a likely indicator of the lapse of time since their habitats became disconnected.

The fish fauna of the permanent waters in Nevada's portion of the Amargosa basin was listed and described by LaRivers (1962), who found the following species: Amargosa speckle dace *(Rhinichthys osculus nevadensis)*, two kinds of poolfish *(Empetrichthys)*, and two of pupfish *(Cyprinodon)*. These are native, and there have been no introductions. Hubbs and Miller, in examining the entire Death Valley system, found 10 species belong to 5 different genera—24 kinds in all, including subspecies. Springs in the Pahrump, Tecopa and Ash Meadows basins contained populations of the kinds mentioned by LaRivers which showed only subspecific differentiation, with a single exception: this was the unique and remarkable pupfish from Devil's Hole *(C. diabolis)*. This they think may have become isolated in Prepluvial times.

---

[4] Fish are intimately confined to the waters they inhabit and so precisely reflect its changing hydrographic history, Hubbs and Miller (1948) have observed. Contrary to popular notion there is no reliable evidence that they are commonly—or ever were—dispersed through underground channels or in waterspouts, or by way of fish eggs clinging to the feet or wings of waterfowl. The native fishes of the Great Basin occur only in habitats they could reach through surface waters; thus their dispersal is closely linked to the history of water courses.

The pupfish, so named by Hubbs because they are frisky, measure .8 to 1.5 inches long when fully grown. They have miraculously adjusted from the enormous, very cold, freshwater lake of the Pluvial world to the tiny, warm and isolated springs and creeks where they now live, each of which has grown increasingly salty until, at least in ,the case of Salt Creek, their habitat is as much as six times as salty as the ocean. (Salt Creek is today almost 2% salt by volume). The species here is *C. salinus*, whereas that of the upper river is *C. nevadensis amargosa* and that of Saratoga Springs, located near the riverbed where it enters the Monument, is *C. nevadensis nevadensis*.

Devil's Hole in Ash Meadows is a detached section of the Death Valley National Monument lying across the state line in Nevada. It consists of a secluded, natural, water-filled fissure of great depth with a constant temperature of 92° F. throughout the year; fifty feet down this varies by no more than a single degree (Alvin McLane, personal contact). The pupfish here are no more than .8 inch long and number about 800 individuals in summer when the overhead sun reaches in and stimulates the growth of algae that provide their main source of food; but in winter the population drops to about 200.

This species *(C. diabolis)* is found in no other location and has become endangered due to the pumping of groundwater for agricultural needs in the surrounding basin; this has lowered the water table and partially exposed the rocky shelf on which these fish breed. Should the water level drop below this ledge (now about half uncovered) it is feared the species would face extinction. Efforts to transfer some of the fish and establish a breeding colony elsewhere have thus far failed and experiments aimed at providing an artificial breeding platform below the ledge have not achieved the desired end. Heavy pumping, which began in 1967, was stopped in September 1971, but the recharge rate of the aquifer is very slow and the water level in the fissure has not risen noticeably (Dr. James Deacon, correspondence). The Devil's Hole pupfish are particularly interesting to geneticists because they show adaptive changes matching alterations in their environment and have speeded up the evolutionary process in ways not fully understood. The research potential here seems considerable, hence the need to preserve these tiny creatures through habitat protection.

Also living in Death Valley waters are various insects, snails and shrimp. They, along with the pupfish, have adjusted to warm and salty environments. The snail, *Asiminea infirma*, occurs today at

SHORELINE BUTTE, DEATH VALLEY, WITH STRANDLINES REMAINING
FROM LAKE MANLY, CLEARLY VISIBLE ABOVE THE DESERT FLOOR

SALT CREEK, DEATH VALLEY, HOME OF THE PUPFISH *Cyprinodon salinus*
These waters are six times as salty as the ocean.

Badwater, where it lives among the roots of the iodine bush and in neighboring situations. It is the only soft-bodied invertebrate that can tolerate a salt-saturated solution—though Badwater is by no means salt-saturated; brackish springs keep feeding it, and the presence of pickleweed, *Allenrolfea*, negates such a condition (Dr. Frits Went, personal contact). The shrimp, *Eulimnadia texanus*, is translucent and only a quarter of an inch long. It has a seasonal life and dies when the habitat dries up in summer, but fertilized eggs within the individual hatch out when the winter rains arrive, maintaining the species. The brine shrimp *Artemia salina* found in Mono and Great Salt Lakes is a different variety.

The animal life of this region is rich and diverse. Birds include the resident mountain chickadee, Clark's nutcracker and common crow. Among the visitors are snipe, coot and green-winged teal, and the white pelican stops over, perhaps on its way to Pyramid Lake. More than 230 kinds of birds have been recorded. Bats, lizards, the spotted toad and the kangaroo rat inhabit the valley, and two snakes (infrequently encountered) are indigenous—the sidewinder and the red racer. There are predators like the coyote, bobcat and kit fox who live upon the rats and occasionally on the local Panamint chipmunks. Also native to the desert scrub is the so-called ringtail cat *(Bassariscus astutus)*, which is not properly a cat but a member of the raccoon family. Bighorn sheep still exist in the remote highlands but they are in jeopardy because they depend on a natural water supply undisturbed by human beings or livestock, including the prolific and competitive wild burros brought along and turned loose long ago by man.

The valley's plant life is extensive and varied. Over 600 species have so far been identified and of these 21 occur nowhere else. Among the exclusives are the goldencarpet, the Panamint daisy, and the napkin-ring bush. Watercress grows in the mountain springs and streams. Six kinds of lily, ten ferns and two orchids grow here, as well as the typical desert shrubbery of arrowweed, shadscale, mesquite, creosote bush and the halophytes. One rather special and widespread plant is the desert holly, handsomest of the saltbushes, with silvery leaves that do not shed. Very little of the vegetation is cactus but some fine stands of it may be seen in Titus Canyon. Although there are 15 cactus varieties in all, only two are really common: the beavertail can be eaten in an emergency and bears magenta flowers; the cottontop has yellow blossoms and edible seeds which the Indians extracted from protective woolly tufts and spines.

Cactus thorns made them convenient tools, useful in basketry and weaving.

Wildflowers often bloom in great quantity through the valley as early as January or February, with the best displays developing by March 1 in good years. When conditions are ideal the bloom is spectacular. Carpets of yellow, purple, red, white and orange adorn the washes and alluvial fans. Primrose, lupine, paintbrush, poppy and mallow predominate, and the varieties may total over 100 in optimum seasons, among which 1973 was outstanding.

The abundance of wildflower blossoms depends almost entirely on the amount of rainfall during a two- or three-weeks' period in late November and early December of the previous year, according to Dr. Frits Went, who says, "Given a sufficient original rain of at least 25 mm. (approximately 1 inch) 80% or more of germinated desert annuals will survive and produce seeds." Otherwise, he says, they will remain dormant until another season.

There are half a dozen separate recognized horizons in the Death Valley subculture and they have been revealed at a number of open sites in the immediate valley region and along the Amargosa River. The earliest to be identified, a Paleo-Indian tradition known as Death Valley I, has been dated at about 9,400 B.P. (Jennings, 1964) and related to the Desert Archaic, although the diagnostic trait—the flat milling stone—is lacking in early Death Valley stages. Hunting points and scraping tools have constituted the most important surface-collected items, dating from the Anathermal. At Manly Terrace simple artifacts deeply imbedded in the desert pavement were uncovered and thought to be contemporaneous with the last high stages of the lake.

As climatic conditions altered, groups appeared and disappeared. The last of the pre-white cultures was that of the Desert Shoshone, who left arrowheads, pottery and basket fragments and made strange "rock maps" that have not been deciphered. Julian Steward, quoted by Heizer (1964), observed that the Death Valley Shoshone visited sites three to five miles from the nearest spring and often maintained camps for days at a time 10 or even 20 miles from water. He set forth that remoteness from present water is no proof that a site dates from the Pluvial period.

Probable descendents of the prehistoric Desert Shoshone are the Panamint Indians of today. Of these, only a few families remain. Living near the valley center, they move out in summer to more elevated, cooler quarters. In total there are perhaps one-fourth as many as when the white men first arrived—goldseekers ignorant of their own whereabouts, and badly organized.

The Bennett-Arcane party arrived at Furnace Creek Wash on Christmas Day 1849. All other, previous expeditions had passed Death Valley by. More demoralized than endangered, they dallied around for nearly a month and were then led out of their predicament by two healthy young bachelors, William Lewis Manly and John Rogers, who have been honored in the naming of the Pluvial lakes. At the time of this first visit the label "Death Valley" was bestowed by an unknown member of the group who, on departing, glanced back and pronounced the name as a malediction. (Only one death had occurred, however, and that one may have been natural). This concept of a hostile environment has been extended in other names given to features around the valley: Funeral Mountains, Devil's Cornfield, Hell's Gate and Dante's View, Coffin and Starvation Canyons, and similar lugubriously designated locales and features. Yet Death Valley is far from moribund and teems with life forms, as we have enumerated here, in addition to half a million visitors a year and a substantial number of permanent residents.

During the 1850s and '60s the region was visited by explorers, prospectors and survey teams, yet it was not until 1873 that any appreciable quantity of people came to stay. That was the year of the silver strike at Panamint City and the almost simultaneous discovery of borax at Furnace Creek. For a time mining flourished, but the silver ore proved too difficult to handle economically with the methods then employed, and so Panamint City folded; meanwhile the borax did very well. It was first observed in "cottonball" form—soft, fluffy masses—along the marshes of the sink. Chemically, borax is a hydrated compound of sodium oxide and boric acid,[5] and it has many industrial uses including functions in soap and glass making, water softening and the manufacture of welding fluxes and pottery glazes. Possessing some medical properties, it also has pharmaceutical applications.

William T. Coleman established the Harmony Borax Works in 1881 in the valley bottom, but high summer temperatures made the process unreliable and he soon moved to a site outside its confines near Shoshone. Here the famous 20-mule teams with their colossal wagons were developed; however, such transportation was in use

---

[5] In borax ($Na_2B_4O_7 \cdot 10\ H_2O$) the sodium oxide and boric acid are chemically combined, whereas the water is not and can be driven off at relatively low heat; but the other components are separated with difficulty.

for only five years. Colemanite, named after this promoter, is a hydrous calcium borate in crystalline form, and for a time Coleman mined rich deposits of it at his Ryan mine. Then in 1888 he suffered heavy losses and had to sell the property. Yet today Colemanite is being mined and processed at a plant not far from Death Valley Junction. Coleman is also remembered as a leader of the vigilance committees of San Francisco's 1850s.

A copper strike southeast of Dante's View was reported in 1904, and another below Ubehebe Peak resulted in some activity. Gold, silver, lead and asbestos showings attracted investors and miners to the district but few situations developed into going enterprises. Keane Wonder, Chloride City, Rhyolite and Bullfrog, Harrisburg, Skidoo—all were evanescent settlements where hope substantially exceeded results. Transportation became a problem where mining actually brought forth sustained production, and after mule teams and impractical steam tractors were tried the age of railroads dawned.

The lives of the several rail lines in this part of the world were stormy ones and most were very brief, for their entire history spans only 35 years. In 1905 the Tonopah & Tidewater began building northward from the Santa Fe line at Ludlow and reached Beatty (then called Gold Center) late in 1907. Other roads, varying from promotions with no real development to regularly scheduled facilities, included the Tonopah & Greenwater, the Tecopa Railroad, the Bonnie Claire & Ubehebe, the Bullfrog & Goldfield and the Las Vegas & Tonopah. The single railroad to materialize in the immediate Death Valley vicinity was the one that carried its name. Yet the Death Valley Railroad Company, established in 1914, was a wholly-owned subsidiary of the T & T, all in turn part of Borax Consolidated, Ltd. This was the English concern that controlled the principal mines. For 17 years it carried ore from the Biddy McCarty and Widow mines to Death Valley Junction. These were all narrow-gauge freight haulers of tenuous existence dependent largely on the health of the mines they reached, and the last of them expired in 1940 when the T & T finally ceased activity.

Today the sightseer and camper have taken over, the valley is part of the National Park System, and the riches it contains may be observed but not exploited. Los Angeles, with its millions, lies only 310 miles away and Las Vegas is no more than 140 miles off. Good highways provide accessibility. At all seasons of the year people come flocking to the scene, so it is no easy matter to maintain the quality of this fragile environment. Scientists who have made this unique area their laboratory for a wide variety of studies include Dr. Carl L. Hubbs of the Scripps Institution of Oceanography and his son-in-law Dr. Robert R. Miller, working mostly with the fish life; Dr. Frits Went and Dr. Nellie Stark of the Desert Research Institute, University of Nevada, devoting their efforts to observation of the desert biota and the interaction of plants, animals and environment; and a host of geologists, hydrologists, atmospheric physicists, zoologists and toilers in many other disciplines.

It seems appropriate to detail here a little of Dr. Went's work. Over a period of several years he has conducted a broad range of studies from mobile laboratories and trailers in the valley's northern end. These have included work with root fungi (*mycorrhiza*), observations of soil temperatures and humidity, transpiration, photosynthesis, germination and distribution of plant species. He has considered the role of ants and rodents in seed gathering, which results in scattering and spreading a plant occurrence, and the unusual establishment of the creosote bush "growing as if they were all intentionally planted at regular intervals." Here he developed the theory that the blue haze commonly seen in desert regions at certain times of the year is the result of emanations from the sagebrush cover. He has introduced and tested new plant species, among them the tamarugo, which is a form of mesquite native to the Atacama Desert of northern Chile; this plant requires no water in liquid state but draws what it needs from the atmosphere, and in this respect is unique. The tamarugo, Dr. Went believes, could be utilized for sheep forage in very dry parts of the Great Basin.

Dr. Nellie Stark found that sagebrush and extreme desert plants can cut their water loss by transpiration more than any plants from moist climates, and their very low water requirements under drought conditions can be met by internal dew formed down under the soil.

The meteorological profile continues to be extended and analysed as microclimatic data are gathered from weather stations distributed throughout the valley. Great weather differences are apparent, varying with altitude, natural features, and the haphazard impact of thunderstorms. Because of uncommon and extreme conditions an almost ideal desert situation exists for many kinds of scientific research. Scientists, tourists, campers all enjoy a peaceful coexistence these days here, and Death Valley offers proof to all that it is very much alive.

CHAPTER XI

The Death Valley System
Mojave River and Lakes

"East away from the Sierra, south from Panamint and Amargosa, east and south many an uncountable mile, is the country of lost borders."

With these lines Mary Austin began her desert epic, *The Land of Little Rain*, in which she expressed a deep emotional response to her surroundings. The statement identifies geographically as well as esthetically the southern Great Basin, for when borders are lost or ill-defined as they are here, the miles may not be counted with any exactitude and the limits of our province must be stated somewhat arbitrarily.

Where the funnel shape of the Basin points south toward Baja California it embraces the broad Mojave Desert,[1] the Salton Trough, and adjacent depressions of which several were once joined to the Colorado drainage. The way the waters behave today is conveniently useful in establishing boundaries, so we include the disrupted portions of the Colorado because they are hydrologically isolated and in addition are just as typical of the Basin as are some of its more northerly regions. The general desert aspect with its widespread aridity, here particularly intense, provides a very obvious continuity reinforcing our selection of limits. Covering an area of some 15,000 square miles, a washboard of ranges and minor intervening valleys averaging 2,000 feet above sea level, the Mojave Desert has a mean annual rainfall of no more than five inches and midday summer temperatures anywhere from 70° F. to 130° F. (N.B.—Mountain locations are somewhat cooler and wetter).

We are treating the Death Valley system and come now to the third and shortest of its major permanent streams, the Mojave River. Rising on the northern slopes of the San Bernardino Range in southern California, it follows a winding course northward and then eastward onto the desert, where it sinks into the sands. Its length, which varies seasonally, is somewhat over 100 miles. In the head-

---

[1] In this work we use the spelling Mojave for the California river, desert and town; Mohave for the Arizona mountains, county and lake.

waters above 3,000 feet the river and its tributaries are mostly perennial but the lower extent lies in desert and is intermittent or underground. Fenneman (1931) writes of the Mojave's special quality:

> . . . descending from the mountains and pursuing its stealthy course, hiding most of the time beneath its gravel bed and coming to light only where forced to do so by the impervious rock. Like the Humboldt it guides transcontinental railroads. It is lost at last in soda lakes.

During the final Pluvial spread the Mojave brought water all the way to Lake Manly and filled three large valleys besides, en route: here were Lakes Harper, Manix and Mojave.[2] These fluctuated greatly in surface area and level, and probably disappeared altogether at times; today, except after heavy rains, they are entirely dry. Lake Harper occupied some 86 square miles of a desert depression northwest of Barstow at one stage, and reached a depth of 130 feet. Manix, largest of the three, backed up from the Cady Mountains and spread widely to sumps now known as Coyote Lake ,and Troy Lake even though they are dry except after unusual precipitation. Blackwelder and Ellsworth (1936) put the maxima at 157 square miles, 380 feet deep, and they describe three separate Lake Manix stages. Eventually it drained through Afton Canyon, east of which the Mojave River watercourse expanded into its third and smallest lake: Mojave, stretching north and south from the town of Baker where playas called Silver Lake and Soda Lake today mark parts of its bed. Thence the flow passed 20 miles northwest into Lake Manly and in the process cut through a barrier of granite 11 feet thick at Mojave's outlet.

Fossil fish identified as *Siphateles mohavensis* (a chub) have been found in the beds of Lake Manix and authorities postulate that this species inhabited all the lakes of the Mojave system inasmuch as the river contains living specimens "retaining lacustrine adaptations and hence maladjusted to their present environment" (Hubbs and Miller, 1948). This variety is now the only surviving fish in the Mojave basin.

In the western extension of the Mojave Desert there are three enclosed valleys that received enough drainage to form Pluvial lakes. Two of them, in Fremont and Cuddeback Valleys, were relatively

[2] The LaJolla radiocarbon laboratory of the University of California, San Diego, has determined from faunal evidence that the last main stage of Lake Manix occurred ca. 19,500 B.P.; that of Lake Mojave was ca. 9,640 B.P.; and the final recession of Lake LeConte came just prior to the historic period—a development that began ca. 1,580 B.P. (a Colorado River incursion).

DRY CHANNEL OF THE MOJAVE RIVER WITH DESERT WILLOWS
U. S. Geological Survey, 1919 photo: D. G. Thompson, no. 388.

SODA LAKE, A PLAYA REMAINING FROM PLEISTOCENE LAKE MOJAVE,
SOUTH OF BAKER, CALIFORNIA

small but Antelope Valley's Lake Thompson was quite substantial—
215 square miles—and at peak spilled northward into Fremont. Its
site immediately west of Edwards Air Force Base is marked by
Rosamond and Rogers dry lakes. As far as we know these independent enclosures were not connected with the Mojave River system
in Pluvial times, though Hubbs and Miller suggest a topographical
basis for some earlier relationship, but they contain no fish that
might support such a contention, either fossil or living.

There were other short-lived Pluvial lakes, some hardly more
than shallow widenings of the Mojave progression. Little Mojave
Lake in Cronise Valley and a possible lake of far earlier times in
Lucerne Valley east of Victorville, of which no shoreline features
survive, complete this list. We pass along to the Pinto Basin and
the section south of it known as the Salton Trough. These are
separated by low mountain ranges in and east of the Joshua Tree
National Monument.

The Pinto Basin lies within the Monument itself, surrounded by
the Eagle, Pinto and Coxcomb Mountains. Thousands of years before
any human occupation it supported a large lake, but since the
shoreline indicators have mostly been erased the thought is that
it rose and fell quite early in the epoch. Long after Lake Pinto
disappeared a river scoured its upper terraces, and a primitive
people are known to have camped along its banks (although the
proof is rather scanty). No connection with the Colorado River has
been indicated—the basin seems devoid of fish—but a low alluvial
saddle 12 miles west of Blythe could have permitted a Pluvial
discharge from the Colorado to enter Chuckwalla Valley, into which
the Pinto River emptied (Hubbs and Miller).

South of here beyond intervening ranges lies a wide, elongated
depression known as the Cahuilla Valley or Salton Sink. Here Lake
LeConte rose at least twice, fed principally by overflows from the
Colorado, the mouth of which is located 80 or 90 miles away. A
clear-cut beach line runs from above Indio to below the Mexican
border and the ancient lake extended south another 20 miles; Hubbs
and Miller put its maximum length at 105 miles, width 35 miles,
and depth 300 feet. LeConte was much more recent than Pinto
and came about through river diversion rather than the increased
precipitation and reduced evaporation normal to the Ice Age. Yet
a great antiquity is ascribed to the lake's main stage because shells
of the mollusk *Hydrobia protea* have been found locked in tufa
nodules (of known age) at least 18 feet deep in the valley floor.

VISIBLE SHORELINE OF ANCIENT LAKE LeCONTE
Along the foot of the Santa Rosa Mountains, west of Salton Sea.

DETAIL OF SUBLACUSTRINE ROCKS
REMAINING FROM PLEISTOCENE LAKE LeCONTE, WEST OF SALTON SEA

The strictly marine fossils of the basin are all much earlier than the Pleistocene. Thus one may assume that the lake had many lives and that the last high stage—which wiped out much evidence of earlier ones—was quite recent.

Indian occupation of the basin before this last rise is established by the presence of travertine deposits over flooded pictographs and by ichthyological evidence—principally charred fishbones constituting a kitchen midden. The varieties of fish, related to Colorado River species, confirm the status of LeConte as an intermittently disrupted river adjunct *(ibid.)*.

Clark dry lake, near the northern end of the Anza-Borrego Desert State Park some 20 miles west of Salton City, lies in a self-contained basin showing signs of ancient waters: dunes and sediments at elevations verifying a depth of 50 to 60 feet. Although no terraces remain visible, the lake probably existed into Postpluvial times, judging by abundant Indian sites in its vicinity.

In northeastern Baja California south of the Salton Trough an ephemeral lake of considerable size called Laguna Salada sometimes appears. It is supplied by flood waters entering its southeastern end from the Rio Hardy, an arm of the Colorado River, and has filled at least six times in the past century. There are strand lines here that indicate the presence of a Pleistocene lake but evidence of its antiquity is lacking. This basin and lake have been named for James Ohio Pattie, who was an early scientist-explorer and the first American (1826) to reach the Gulf of California overland. Streams enter from the rugged Sierra Juárez to the west but quickly disappear in the playa alluvium; none supports fish life, but there is a detached pool at the edge of the flat that contains *Cyprinodon macularius*. Laguna Salada in Mexico represents the extreme southern tip of the Great Basin and is without any exterior discharge. On occasion when the basin was flooded various fish types were swept in from the river but they died off when the lake dried up. The fish fauna and hydrographic relations of the Pattie and LeConte basins are similar *(ibid.)*. Across the Sierra de los Cucapah that encloses the basin on the east lies Cerro Prieto, described in Chapter I, with its field of geothermal steam.

The march of the desert through southern California is characterized by sand hills and cinder cones, lava flows, gleaming white playas with clouds of blowing dust and whirling columns that dodge capriciously across the flats—an endless succession of ranges and basins. The long lean spines of the mountains repeat themselves

The Northwest Corner of Laguna Salada, Baja California
Here springs contain forms of pupfish persisting from Pleistocene times.

rhythmically and the widely scattered peaks make striking accents upon the horizon. Old Baldy and San Gorgonio raise landmark summits clad with snow through part of the year; the San Jacinto Range stands guard at the northern end of the Salton trench. On lower ramparts bleached grays and browns change sharply to reds and blacks where volcanic material has emerged, and the lonely washes turn briefly white when springtime brings evanescent moisture to the roots of growing things.

Names on the land can be eloquent: the Cottonwood, Coxcomb and Hexie Mountains; the Chuckwalla, Eagle, Chocolate and Orocopia (full of gold) Ranges; Sunflower Springs, Sidewinder Well (at least two) and Hot Mineral Spa reflect the ambience. Here is the archetype of the Lower Sonoran life zone, too sizzling and dry even for sagebrush. Instead we find the creosote bush, the desert catalpa *(Chilopsis)* and many kinds of cactus. Generally the flora and fauna differ little from varieties found in Death Valley though some are more plentifully distributed—great stands of *Yucca brevifolia* and *Y. schidigera*, in point, are scattered across the bajadas and valleys, most especially in Joshua Tree National Monument— hence the name. The century plant, *Agave deserti*, and the Spanish bayonet, *Y. baccata*, are common to several areas.

Mehringer (1967) lists six biotic communities for this region: lower Mojave (500 to 4,000 feet a.s.l.), higher Mojave (4,000 to 6,000), juniper-pinyon woodland (6,000 to 7,200), Ponderosa pine-white fir (7,200 to 9,020), bristlecone pine (9,020 to 11,500) and alpine (above 11,500). The lower Mojave supports the creosote bush community with bursage, hop sage and saltbush very plentiful. At higher elevations the same are found together with ephedra, winterfat *(Eurotia lanata)* and box-thorn *(Lycium)*. Around springs and in draws, cottonwood, willow, salt grass, mesquite, arrow weed and catclaw *(Acacia greggii)* are present. During Pleistocene history a diverse biota developed and the northern elements extended into these desert regions, only to become isolated eventually in the higher mountain reaches.

In the creosote bush community bats and rodents, the desert jackrabbit and the desert cottontail are abundant; kit fox, badger, coyote and bobcat are widespread but other carnivorous or herbivorous mammals are seldom encountered at this level. Birds include the rock wren, cactus wren, raven, horned lark and Gambel's quail, with others migrant in large numbers seasonally. Many kinds of lizards reside in this populous zone, as do snakes: the sidewinder, whipsnake, gopher snake and speckled rattlesnake. Occasionally the desert tortoise[3] and Gila monster are seen. At higher elevations and in aquatic situations different species appear. Birds are most common and varied in the fir-pine community. Relatively few endemic species are encountered, which is to say that most components of desert life-societies usually find their main distributions in other regions.

The oldest human fossils found in the Western Hemisphere are believed to be the Los Angeles Man, radiocarbon dated at ca. 23,600 years, and the Laguna Beach skull with an age of 17,150 (± 1,470). There is little supporting evidence for these finds and no information has been uncovered relating to cultures prevailing when these ancients were alive. We can suppose they were Paleo-Indians subsisting on available game, but proof is lacking. We must come down much closer to the present before we can describe the lifeways of the earlier people.

Projectile points used in peripheral big game hunting have not been dated older than 13,000 years (Krieger, 1964). Anthropologists think that before these points came into use, fire-hardened wooden spears may have been employed as weapons. The distinctive Clovis and Folsom points, among the oldest ever found, have proved that long-extinct animals—the mammoth, bison *antiquus*, camelops, etc.—were taken by ancient man, utilizing such traits. Jennings and Norbeck (1964) put the horticultural beginning at ca. 3,000 B.P. when the Pleistocene big game species were long gone from the Great Basin. A diagnostic element is the milling stone but this was used well before grain began to be cultivated—manos probably appeared at least 10,000 years ago.

The Early Horizon culture of the southern Great Basin lavished its principal attention on stone as a medium; it flourished until about 4,000 B.P. The Middle Horizon, 4,000 to 1,700 B.P., centered upon bone; and the Late Horizon had shell as its prized material

[3] The California Division of Highways recently was faced with an ecological problem during the construction of an expressway in the southern Great Basin. Several hundred desert tortoises were inhabiting an area to be crossed by the project and fences were planned to keep them off the pavement. But research showed they could climb or burrow under most obstacles in search of food, so relocation of these animals was ordered. The Department of Fish and Game handled their removal to a distant section of the Navy's China Lake Station in the Mojave Desert, and four tortoises were equipped with electric beepers. Like the Himalayan snow partridges and tule elk previously mentioned in this work, these beasts were monitored following their release, and Navy personnel found them to be settling in, burrowing to hibernate, and altogether accepting their new home.

(Heizer, 1964). Ornaments came increasingly into use as the culture developed, bone and shell being more easily worked than stone. Using 300 A.D. as the beginning of the Late Horizon, which then continued to the latter part of the 18th century and the opening of the historic period, we find that many cultural modifications appeared, such as the introduction of decorated pottery from the Pueblo. About 1,150 A.D. the Southern Paiute displaced the earlier inhabitants of the southeastern Great Basin and used brown un-decorated pots, mostly of a conical shape. The Shoshone also used pots, which were flat-bottomed. Neither grouping was agricultural in habit, though some Southern Paiutes learned rudimentary farming.

The Lake Manix complex is manifest in many chopper-scraper sites, most of which have been surface-collected and do not meet the minimum standards of control that archeologists require (a buried or unbroken stratum of occurrence that is identifiable. Index fossils and association with extinct animal remains are desirable attributes). Near the apex of an alluvial cone known as Calico Hill, overlooking a playa where Lake Manix once pushed northward, a chipping site has long been known. Here in November 1970, the late Dr. L. S. B. Leakey held a press conference and indicated the presence there of an ancient hearth. One way of identifying a hearthstone is by analysis of its contained iron particles. These become aligned with the earth's magnetic field where the stone has been exposed to heat while those not heated remain unaligned. If stones are found in a circle with characteristic alignment of iron particles a hearth may be assumed. Dr. Leakey asserted the existence of such a structure at Calico Hill on the basis of a single analysis and claimed an age of at least 50,000 years for it. In addition to the putative hearth material, artifacts consisting of flaked stone tools and rock cores were found in the vicinity but no fossils of organic origin turned up. This "discovery" was greeted with considerable skepticism by many professionals familiar with the area.

Also located on the Lake Manix periphery is Newberry Cave, within which atlatl material and sloth remains were found (G. A. Smith, 1957). Projectile points of many types occur throughout the Sonoran Desert region and among them the Pinto Basin point first reported in 1935 has since been found to be widespread and abundant. Very different from it are the Silver Lake and Lake Mojave points although they belong to the same horizon (the precise age of which has yet to be established). These points have been described by Davis (1966) as "very crude (and) appearing as if made by artisans who had the idea but not the proper technical knowledge for making a chipped stone tip for a dart." A series of Mojave Desert complexes is represented along and above beaches visible on the slopes of the Lake Manix bolson; here a number of large crude artifacts of unknown age have been recovered (Harrington and Simpson, 1961).

The surface-collected complexes that include the Pinto Basin, Silver Lake, Mojave and Amargosa are grouped as the San Dieguito sequence, but of the various occurrences in the Great Basin only one is considered of first-rate importance. This is the Stahl site at Little Lake where, in a buried and sealed context, a large assemblage of projectile points and knives belonging to both the Pinto and Silver Lake types in full association was excavated (Jennings, 1968); also, evidence of a village of seven houses was uncovered here. Another site outside the Great Basin has been designated the type locality by Claude N. Warren (1967). It lies in San Diego County on the San Dieguito River at the base of the western slope of the coastal range and is known as the C. W. Harris site. A radiocarbon date of 9,000 B.P. was obtained there and Warren suggests an age of 9,000 to 10,000 years for the complex as a whole. He postulates a generalized hunting tradition different from and earlier than the Desert culture and suggests that the desert expression of the San Dieguito is associated with high stands of the Pleistocene lakes.

The Mojave Desert conforms to no political boundaries. Two hundred miles at its widest, it extends from Tehachapi Summit well into the southern tip of Nevada. North and south, the limits are not easily drawn since it tends to merge with the contiguous Colorado and Amargosa Deserts. California's San Bernardino County is the largest county in the United States and it includes the major portion of the Mojave Desert, whereas in Nevada, Clark County's Eldorado Mountains provide the eastern terminal rampart. Culturally speaking the Mojave is, as Heizer (1964) asserts, an extension of the Great Basin toward the Pacific.

There are two Nevada sites quite important to the Desert culture lying just outside the Basin's boundary to the east, and they deserve mention because they emphasize elements of its tradition. These are Gypsum Cave northeast of Las Vegas and Etna Cave south of Caliente. Gypsum Cave yielded artifacts and prehistoric animal remains thought at first to be in association: dung and hair of the giant sloth, *Nothrotherium*, deposited in some quantity, and fragments of camelops and horse. A radiocarbon date of 10,500 B.P. was obtained from the dung but not from the atlatl shaft found in ostensible juxtaposition. However, some years later the shaft was dated and found to be much more recent, thus intrusive into the dung. No atlatl shaft older than 3,000 years has yet been authenticated (Jennings, correspondence). In addition to these items Gypsum Cave contained campfire charcoal and chipped stone implements, a smoothed stick, a cane torch, and hunting points. Etna Cave yielded horse dung in association with cultural material, artifacts of flint and textiles, and a series of stick figurines representing game animals. Their age has been radiocarbon dated at 3,750 (±330) years (Fowler, 1973).

Northwest of Las Vegas lies Tule Springs. Here a vast site discovered in 1933 was subjected to massive digging and intensive study but with quite disappointing results. In 1962 a construction camp was built and interdisciplinary field work undertaken on the scale of a military operation. More than 200,000 tons of overburden was removed and two miles of bulldozer trenching averaging 15 feet in depth gave access to the stratigraphic history. Large quantities of animal bones were exposed and modest archeological information was obtained. A few scrapers, some charcoal, and a bone tool radiocarbon dated between 11,000 and 13,000 turned up; also brought to light were Pinto points, knives, choppers, drills and gravers from 2,000 to 4,000 years old (Tuohy, 1965). But the results, considering all the effort and expense, were skimpy.

Modern Indian distribution is relatively stable and we encounter in order southward from Owens Valley the Northern Paiute, Shoshone, Southern Paiute, Serrano and Cahuilla groups. The Chemahuevi, virtually indistinguishable from the Southern Paiute, occupy hilly country between the Serrano and the Colorado River. There are reservations scattered around the desert peripherally from Panamint to Yuma and most of them are located in more agreeable situations than the open Mojave. Among these the Torres-Martinez overlooks Salton Sea; Morongo, north of Banning, enjoys the proximity of San Gorgonio Peak (11,485) and the San Bernardino National Forest; Agua Caliente adjoins the San Jacinto Wilderness Area.

The historic period in the Great Basin dawned in 1774, marked by the expedition of Juan Bautista de Anza. For 200 years the northward progress of the Spanish empire had been blocked by this desert barrier; then, following the expulsion of the Jesuits from New Spain in 1767, the Franciscan Fathers began extending their chain of missions along the coast of Alta California. Eventually there were 21 of them, spaced no more than 60 miles apart,[4] and they

---

[4] Sixty miles was the distance regarded as one day's ride on horseback. W. H. Hudson, in his charming little book, *The Famous Missions of California* (1901), quotes the French traveler DeMofras as stating that the distance from mission to mission nowhere exceeded 18 leagues (54 miles) and was often very much less.

reached from San Diego to San Francisco Solano in Sonoma Valley. These missions could not be supported by the Indian populations, whose way of life included neither agriculture nor the use of domestic animals, and who already were the victims of a very meager biotic resource. Furthermore, the sea routes were exposed and hazardous, hence the solution to this logistical problem seemed to lie in an overland route.

It was to establish such an access that Anza set forth from Tubac, south of Tucson, on the 8th of January 1774, with a party of 34 men, 140 horses and 65 head of cattle. The trail 250 miles down the Gila River was familiar but beyond the Colorado nothing was known of the country or its perils. Fr. Junipero Serra, directing a Spanish exploration, had ridden up Las Vegas Wash in 1770 but had turned back before entering the Basin, and others had probed for routes but failed. Yet Anza managed to complete his journey with a minimum of difficulty in a little over two months and thus created the "land bridge" that was needed. Though this route did not remain open very long, it greatly stimulated the colonization of Alta California (Pourade, 1971), and the Basin was thus breached by Europeans for the first time.

This attempt having been eminently successful, Anza was encouraged to undertake a larger expedition the following year, in the course of which he conducted 240 people, including entire families, along almost the same trail. Among them were Fr. Francisco Hermenegildo Tomás Garcés and his diarist, Fr. Pedro Font. Between them the first chronicles of the desert, containing many vivid impressions of the southwest, were put in writing. Garcés left the second Anza force at Yuma and struck out north on his own. He traveled 200 miles up the Colorado River to the vicinity of Needles, turned west, and on March 7, 1776, entered the Great Basin. He marched straight across the Mojave Desert and about at Soda Lake came upon the river, which he followed to the west and south, and used the trail across the mountains the Indians had taken when trading for shell with coastal tribes. He is believed to have cut west below Cajon Pass, and soon he was within reach of San Gabriel Mission in the valley just south of today's city of Pasadena.

Garcés possessed the essential qualities of an explorer: insatiable curiosity and a relentless drive, plus unerring instinct in choosing routes. His restlessness took him north through the central valley to Tulare Lake and the Kern River, whereupon he doubled back to his original footsteps on the Mojave River by way of Tehachapi

Pass. On May 25th he left the Basin about where he had entered it and put in his diary that he thought the Mojave "a very risky" way to go. Five years later he was to die at the hands of the Yuma Indians, who rose and wiped out their Franciscan Mission along with the small settlement nearby on the Colorado. Anza himself died in 1788, and the virtual closing of his route occurred as a result of the Yuma massacre in July 1781 (Pourade).

There is no record of further entry or exploration of the southern Great Basin during the next 45 years, though it seems quite likely that small parties of Mexicans could have worked stretches of what ultimately became the Old Spanish Trail. The Basin received no attention from what we complacently call the Civilized World. The myths of Cibola inevitably became recognized as wishful figments and the needs of the missions were somehow met otherwise. American independence, fought for and achieved, demanded full attention elsewhere, even though President Jefferson's Louisiana Purchase extended the new country's territory to the Rockies and published accounts of the expedition under Meriwether Lewis and William Clark captured America's fancy.

In 1811 John Jacob Astor founded his trading post at the mouth of the Columbia and five of his trappers penetrated the northeast corner of the Great Basin, where they spent the following winter. Still, this province remained unknown and unexplored for another 14 years. Mexico had thrown out the Spanish (their "Act of Independence" was signed September 28, 1821) and a year later Alta California became organized under a new regime that was anxious to establish trade with the Americans. Horses from the East, blankets from the West, were among the staples needed; word of this reached the mountain men, who were then active between South Pass and the Columbia. Gen. Ashley sold out to the Smith-Jackson-Sublette syndicate and returned to Missouri, and the new group's partners despatched Jedediah with 18 men southwest over what would become known as the Old Spanish Trail. We are not precisely aware of his route—much of his rough diary has been lost—but we know he passed swiftly down the Wasatch Range to the Virgin and Colorado Rivers, crossed about where Needles stands, and then traversed the Mojave Desert to El Cajon Pass. They reached the San Gabriel Mission on November 26, 1826.

Having returned to the Bear Lake rendezvous the following year, Smith repeated his journey through the southwest, only to find the Mojave Indians turned very hostile, and at the Colorado River they set upon his party without warning; half his men were killed and most of his livestock and supplies were taken. Smith survived this and many other violent adventures, only to be ambushed and killed at age 32 by Comanches at Cimarron Crossing.

When Peter Skene Ogden came down the Owens River in 1830 seeking beaver he crossed the Mojave and Colorado Deserts to the outskirts of Yuma and then turned north. He soon re-entered the Mojave and traversed its full width, leaving by way of Tehachapi Pass. Antonio Armijo undertook in 1829 to begin the trade the Mexicans had wanted with American centers far to the east. He is reputed to have been the first white man to look upon the Amargosa River, having crossed the desert intent upon reaching markets in New Mexico. In the opposite direction came William Wolfskill and George C. Yount during the winter of 1830–31, with a score of armed men and appropriate equipment. California-bound, they traveled the entire length of the Old Spanish Trail from Santa Fe to San Bernardino, becoming the first persons ever to do so. Strictly as an emigrant route it was first employed by the Workman-Rowland party, late in 1841 (Hafen, 1954).

With all these early forays, few lingered or found more than hazardous passage to more promising situations across ranges or rivers elsewhere. Then came Frémont. He crossed Oak Creek Pass south of Tehachapi on April 20, 1844, and on the 28th reached "a large creek of salty and brackish water"—which must have been the Amargosa River. His party spent the night of the 30th at Resting Springs, an oasis east of Tecopa, and continued thence to Las Vegas Spring (Cline, 1963). His journey then led him out of the Basin via the Muddy and Virgin Rivers. It was Frémont who named the "Mohahve River" (sic) which Garcés had called the "Arroyo de los Mártires" and Jed Smith had named "The Inconstant River." Spaniards referred to it as the "Río de las Animas," but Frémont's nomenclature stuck (Peirson, 1970).

He made other penetrations of the southern Basin. The following year he sent most of his party under Walker down the Owens and they went out over Walker Pass. In 1849 he crossed Salton Trough headed west; and again in 1853 he traversed this part of the province "near the 37th Parallel."

Exploration of the Mojave Desert consisted at first mainly of pathfinding, of solving the transit problems with maximum speed and safety. To this day it remains for the most part a bridge country sparingly endowed with services for the traveler and quintessentially dry. The Spanish had passed through, bent upon looting the New

World for crown and church, had plundered the land and plucked the souls of the natives, but in California they missed their mark—the gold beneath their feet that yielded at last to the picks and pans of the Forty-niners. Not extravagantly so, however, in the Mojave.

The California southland's hostile environment and thinly-scattered resources were not strongly attractive to mid-nineteenth century adventurers. There was little incentive to linger. Unassisted agriculture was not possible and irrigation water could be developed in only a few areas. The Mormons came in 1851 to found San Bernardino but they were recalled to Salt Lake City in 1857. For years, Victorville was known as Mormon Crossing. W. F. Holcomb settled on the Mojave River's Deep Creek fork in 1860 (Peirson, 1970), but there was little that could be called lasting inhabitation in the middle decades. A few mines flared, a few towns bloomed and withered, and the most persistent enterprises evolved around the non-metallics rather than gold and silver: the unglamorous quarries with their limestone, granite, borax, gypsum and salt figured more substantially in the region's development.

Railroads brought great change, and the early written history of the Mojave is largely the story of its railroad-building. Five major lines crossed or penetrated the southern deserts and at least a dozen more were contiguous and variously active. Of the five, two have disappeared: the Las Vegas & Tonopah, which connected Goldfield with the Salt Lake Route at Las Vegas, and the Tonopah & Tidewater, running from Beatty to Ludlow on the Santa Fe.

The most important ones were of course the Southern Pacific, the Santa Fe and the Union Pacific, three which over the years contributed so much to Los Angeles and the southland. The record is filled with their ups and downs; litigation, receiverships, mergers and maneuvers, details of which would be inappropriate here. First of these into the Mojave was the Southern Pacific, by way of Tehachapi Pass and thence to Los Angeles (1876) via a tunnel under the San Fernando Mountains. Trunkline rivalry had much to do with the routings and speed of construction in those days and the SP, which had taken control of the CP in 1868, forged its second transcontinental link in 1877: across the Colorado Desert by way of Salton Trough to Yuma. Known as the Sunset Route, it continues east beyond that point to El Paso and New Orleans (Myrick, 1963).

In 1866 the Atlantic & Pacific Railroad had been chartered by Act of Congress to build westward from St. Louis across the country. After many vicissitudes it was taken over by the Santa Fe and surveyed as far as Needles on the Colorado River. Hoping to block this approach and maintain its southern California monopoly, the SP branched out across the Mojave Desert from the foot of the Tehachapi; the right-of-way they chose crossed the sites of two ancient lakes, Thompson and Manix, and passed just south of Lake Harper's outlet where that body once spilled into the Mojave System about at Barstow. Other towns along this stretch are Boron, Daggett and Ludlow. Needles, 242 miles from the point of beginning, was reached on Patriot's Day 1883, beating by some months the A & P, which had not then reached—much less bridged—the Colorado River. In the end, after much corporate fencing, the Santa Fe took over operation of the Needles-Tehachapi section and this became part of its main line, with access to San Francisco (ibid.).

The third and last of the transcontinental rails to invade the southern Great Basin was Union Pacific's Los Angeles & Salt Lake Railroad, commonly known as the Salt Lake Route. It started out as a pooling of resources, the gathering together of small lines in northern Utah, and wound up in a southwestward extension, first toward Pioche with its rich discoveries, then to the City of the Angels. The first train went through all the way in February 1905. Storms caused great damage in the early days, particularly in Meadow Valley Wash (a tributary of the Colorado) and in Afton Canyon where the downstream arm of Lake Manix had formed and where lately the Mojave River resurged after summer cloudbursts or springtime flooding. This kind of rampage occurred notably in 1907, 1910 and 1938 with prolonged suspensions of service due to loss of structures and roadbeds. Today however, with redesigned facilities, such hazards are minimal.

Of the two that are gone, the Las Vegas & Tonopah never made money and lasted only 11 years. The first train to reach Goldfield, on October 26, 1907, covered the 197 miles from Las Vegas in a not impressive eight hours. It was economically unsound in concept and ceased operations in 1918. The other one, the T & T, was better planned and situated. Construction began late in 1905 and proceeded rapidly northward from Ludlow on the Santa Fe. Broadwell, Soda and Silver Lakes, playas in the Mojave drainage, were traversed or skirted; the site of Lake Tecopa in the Amargosa watercourse was likewise convenient. The mileage to Gold Center (Beatty) totaled 169, and Goldfield, 78 miles beyond, was reached over the B & G tracks. Connections with larger roads at Ludlow and Crucero helped keep the T & T going until 1940.

A baker's dozen of lesser lines wrote brief paragraphs in the Mojave story. Some never got off the ground; some, like the Carrara

Marble Company's electric cable railway or the Epsom Salts Railroad, a monorail, were short-lived curiosities. Others enjoyed longer lives and lengths, and proved more useful. Two or three may still be operating.

Trona, on Searles dry lake, was at last report still being served by the Trona Railway, standard gauge dating from 1914. Its *raison d'etre* was to haul the lake's deposit of hydrous sodium carbonate. John W. Searles ran mule trains there in 1862. At Amboy, half way from Barstow to Needles, the California Salt Company was operating at least until quite recently a short narrow-gauge line from Bristol dry lake to a mill beside the Santa Fe main right-of-way. Its payload included gypsum as well as salt. Thirdly, the Mojave Northern ran from Leon on the river just north of Victorville to mines and quarries in nearby hills. It was built to carry gold and silver ore but now handles limestone for the Portland Cement Company that owns it.

The Tecopa Railroad operated 9½ miles of standard track from 1910, hauling copper ore from the Gunsight mine to a mill on the T & T. Resting Springs, on the Old Spanish Trail, lies just north of this run and Tecopa Hot Springs surfaces a mile or two north of the junction. The operation was dormant after 1922 and was scrapped some years later. The Calico Railroad and the Borate & Daggett were narrow gauge silver-ore and borax carriers, respectively, active in the last century near the site of Pleistocene Lake Manix. A tourist restoration called the "Calico & Odessa" operates here, in a district from which silver worth in excess of $13,000,000 was taken.

There was the Ludlow & Southern which handled gold ore from the Bagdad mine eight miles from that town; the Nevada Southern which ran from Giffs to Barnwell but never did enter Nevada; and the Lida Valley which never went anywhere. Miscellaneous spurs and branch lines running mostly to mines and quarries existed but hardly merit attention.

As the 20th century dawned an extraordinary drama began in which many agencies, including the sp Railroad, played leading roles. This was the creation of the Salton Sea and the temporary stream capture by the Colorado of one of its long disrupted adjuncts. In 1901 the California Development Co., promoters of Imperial Valley, started to divert water from the river at a cut opposite Yuma in great volume—at an annual rate of some 400,000 acre feet—through their Imperial Canal. This precipitated a chain of events that ruined the company and came close to destroying the valley itself. The spring floods of 1905 were very heavy and at first brought down silt which blocked the canal entirely, then smashed through the new Mexican cut and raged on down into Salton Trough.

Much of the Salton Sink lies below sea level and its lowest point is comparable in this respect to Badwater in Death Valley. The lands which the California Development Co. had promoted in Imperial Valley were of this order and they had been receiving unpumped water from the Colorado brought in by gravity. The efforts to control the 1905 flood were inadequate and it soon became an unbridled force, the instrument of a disaster that wiped out structures and ruined farmlands. At once the Salton sump began filling. A considerable part of the Colorado's flow was pouring into the valley, forming rapids that grew into cataracts. These cut back 1,000 feet a day and tore up the bordering land. The new lake in the sink rose a daily average of seven inches and the salt works there were soon covered 60 feet deep. Indeed it was like the fable of the Sorcerer's Apprentice, materialized.

Into this situation the Southern Pacific had been immediately drawn. Their tracks ran beside the Salton Sink and were repeatedly flooded; the company completely relocated them five times. Furthermore the railroad had signed an agreement to buy out the California Development Co. and had thus assumed the risk and responsibility. It behooved them to find the means, technical and financial, to harness the flood. Should a channel at or below sea level be created—and this was well on the way to happening—the profile of Lake LeConte would recur, the right-of-way would be lost, and a huge estate would become entirely submerged. This was the very real threat.

On February 10, 1907, the victory was finally won and the innundation controlled, although by then the Salton Sea extended over 400 square miles, and $3 million had been spent to close the break. The story of this fantastic struggle has been well told elsewhere (e.g., Hosmer, 1969). Today the Imperial Valley constitutes the Great Basin's richest agricultural territory, embracing a million acres or more of irrigated fields and pastures and the metropolitan districts of El Centro, Brawley, Calexico, Holtville and Imperial in California, together with Mexicali in Mexico. Here are grown a profusion of fruits and grains, garden truck, cotton, feed crops, dates and dairy products. It extends from the Salton Sea down to and across the border, much of it below sea level and all of it naturally arid.

Its entire development has occurred since the turn of the century.

Dams have since been built on the Colorado River and a new canal, the All-American, is engineered to prevent any repetition of the 1905 calamity. The Salton Sea has remained as a semipermanent feature of the landscape, of high value as a recreational resource. But the *net* evaporation loss is more than five feet per year and the Sea is already more than four times as briny as the ocean. This worries state officials, who foresee a possible end to the abundant fish life it supports. They assert that agricultural waste waters are carrying in more than 10,000 tons of salt a day and that to build salt extraction plants, dikes and exchange channels would cost hundreds of millions.

During World War II the Sea was used by the Navy for various purposes and a population of barnacles, now multiplied to stupendous quantity, was then introduced. These and other characteristic marine plankters are believed to have been carried in the bilges of seaplanes, often pumped out here, or on buoys and boats hauled in from the ocean.

The ever-increasing thirst of the Los Angeles megalopolis motivated a colossal engineering project designed to import Colorado River water, beginning in 1933. The resulting aqueduct, which runs 241 miles to Lake Mathews, involves 92 miles of tunnel and five pumping stations handling 1,100,000 acre feet a year at a velocity of 1,600 c.f.s. Parker Dam, serving it at the river, was completed in 1938 and backs up Lake Havasu from which this water is diverted. Downstream lies the Imperial Dam, which similarly diverts the water supplying the All-American Canal. Both these giant facilities came into full operation by 1940.

Here then, in the southern funnel of the Great Basin, the desert waters so meagerly furnished by Nature have been supplemented hugely by man in order to provide a basis for his occupancy and livelihood. These were the first of many vast schemes that the State of California, bursting at its population limits, has envisioned for present and future needs. Some of them have been brought to completion; others are still on the drawing boards or lie in the minds of imaginative engineers. Not all of the planning that has been developed for the future is wholly practical, and perhaps much of it may never really be needed.

THE 1905 FLOOD, FLOWING 13,000 C.F.S., THAT CREATED THE SALTON SEA
U. S. Geological Survey, 1905 photo: W. C. Mendenhall, no. 576.

SOUTHERN TIP OF THE IMPERIAL VALLEY
Seen from Cerro Juarez in Baja California, Mexico.

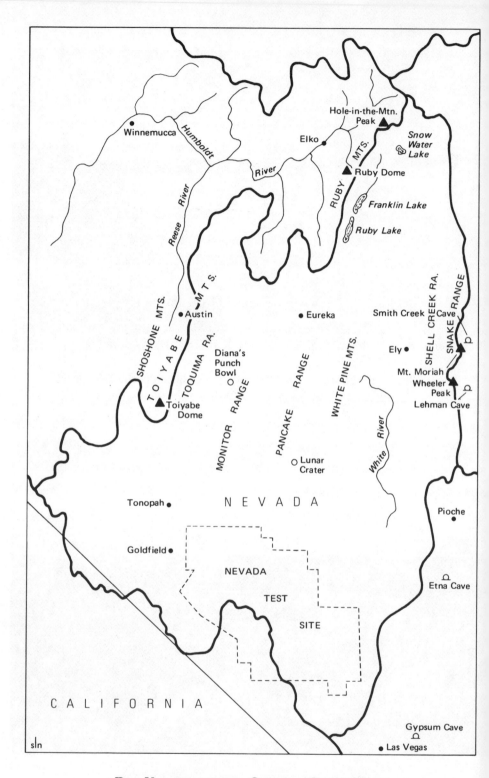

DRY VALLEYS OF THE CENTRAL GREAT BASIN

CHAPTER XII

The Central Great Basin
Isolated Lakes

We have considered the northwestern and southern regions of the Great Basin and now come to the central section with its entirely isolated lakes. To the north lies the Humboldt River drainage, a part of the Lahontan network, and to the east that of Lake Bonneville. Southeast, the Colorado River basin provides a boundary. West and southwest, the components of the Death Valley system discussed in preceding chapters mark the limits of this central congeries where almost half of all the Great Basin's Pleistocene lakes were gathered.

This middle ground is composed mostly of undrained and wholly enclosed valleys, by no means uniform in characteristics; nor were the lakes which materialized within them alike in shape, size or degree of isolation. Along the California-Nevada state line between Walker Lake and Pahute Mesa over two dozen of these small valleys show signs of the Pluvial occupancy. They are separated one from another by low and almost barren ridges and each contains its own playa. Many of these are grouped by Hubbs and Miller under the heading "Area of Sterile Basins," for although a few flowing springs lie widely scattered, there are no surviving fish and but few fossils that might indicate ancient populations.

There were four lakes in Soda Spring Valley: Acme, Luning, Mina and Rhodes. Huntoon and Garfield Flats, Teel's Marsh[1] and Columbus Salt Marsh filled with water. Clayton Valley, Gold Flat, Kawich and Ralston Valleys, Stonewall and Sarcobatus Flats—these are some of the loci which Hubbs and Miller group together, all being fishless, and they reach to basins which were structurally connected with the Lake Railroad system, the Death Valley system,

---

[1] Teel's Salt Marsh was the locale in 1861 of a scheme to raise camels (Hazeltine, et al., 1960). They were employed to carry salt, soda and hay to the mining camps. The arrival of a camel train at Austin in 1863 is described in Thompson and West. Originally the War Department bought these animals for Army operations in the Southwest. Mack and Sawyer (1965) put the 1870 census at 70, saying they were a common sight in Austin and Virginia City in those times; they also mention a man in southern Nevada who about that time raised ostriches for their plumes and as beasts of burden, unsuccessfully. Hazeltine states that in 1879 one Theodore Glancy was raising ostriches "in the Bismarck Range between Bodie and Carson City."

and the Pluvial White River; however, no hydrological interchange now exists.

Lake Clayton formed just east of Silverpeak and left a playa 17 miles long by 5½ wide; its surface area was twice as big but it had no great depth. Here in this location 100 miles north of Death Valley one-fourth of all the lithium mined in the United States is produced, from 45 wells running 300 to 1,700 feet deep. Lithium carbonate is pumped from the lakebed to evaporation ponds and upgraded from 300 p.p.m. to 5,000 p.p.m., then shipped off to processing plants. This element weighs one-thirtieth as much as lead and can store eight times as much electricity, so it is used in storage batteries and as a radiation shield. Its affinity for carbon is strong, and its ability to absorb CO_2 was dramatically shown during the Apollo XIII crisis, when it may have helped to save the lives of the astronauts. Lithium has many scientific and industrial uses, including medical and thermonuclear applications.

Fish Lake Valley lies adjacent to the Area of Sterile Basins. It is the site of Lake White Mountains (185 square miles, depth unknown) which Hardman thinks discharged to Columbus Salt Marsh across an intervening saddle. Hubbs and Miller have noted terraces below Gap Springs, located here, and report two forms of chub, *Siphateles*, in Fish Lake Valley waters. Alluvium washed from foothills of the White Mountains at the southwest valley limits show lacustrine modifications, and a broad playa occupies the opposite end.

Nye County, Nevada is shaped like an upright sledgehammer and occupies the center of the southern half of the state. It is the third largest county in the United States and, covering more than 18,000 square miles, is larger than Massachusetts, Rhode Island, Connecticut and Delaware together. Its population is less than 6,000 or about .3 persons per square mile, and it lies entirely within the Great Basin—if we include the disrupted White River Valley. That stream drains south from the White Pine Mountains through Preston, Lund and Sunnyside and some of its flow may have, within historic times, reached the Colorado River.

This large and almost uninhabited county typifies the central Basin, graced as it is with many spectacular mountain ranges and sweeping landscapes majestic in scale. The southern extension of the Shoshone, Toiyabe, Toquima and Monitor Mountains succeed one another across the wide head, with long and relatively narrow valleys between that give contrast and sharpen the scenic impact. This is most impressive when clouds move across and render the peaks elusive and dramatic. Southward toward the deserts where the ridges are lower and land forms gentler, dryness intensifies.

Two very large lakes formed in this hammerhead of Nye County, Toiyabe (250 square miles) in Big Smoky Valley, and Railroad (525) in the valley of that name. The first extended north of Round Mountain well up into Lander County, about to the base of Toiyabe Peak (10,793) which rises ten miles south of Austin. Big Smoky is one of the longest valleys in the Great Basin, roughly 120 miles, and Lake Toiyabe covered over a third of this distance. At the valley's lower end a considerably smaller lake, Tonopah, appeared. Both have left isolated playas, and scientists have speculated as to exterior associations inasmuch as Lake Toiyabe's location has springs containing two species of fish, one being a *Rhinichthys* virtually indistinguishable from a Lahontan type. Lake Tonopah, however, left no fish.

The lake in Railroad Valley[2] merits special attention for its great size, and also because it may have disappeared quite recently. It was almost as big as Death Valley's Lake Manly and attained a maximum depth of 315 feet. Its site lies between the Pancake and Grant Ranges and is traversed by U.S. Highway 6 which passes through the settlements of Currant and Warm Springs. Very high peaks overlook this valley—Troy, Duckwater and Currant Mountains are all well over 11,000 feet. Although the dry lakebed does not now ever fill, streams enter and there are living springs with fish populations along the lower slopes of the Grant Range, particularly at Timber Mountain. Chub species have been identified by Hubbs and Miller as *Crenichthys nevadae* (related to a Death Valley fish, *Empetrichthys*) and *Siphateles obesus* (now synonymized with *Gila bicolor obesa*), a variety characteristic of the Lahontan system and found also in waters north and west of it. In total, eight subspecies of chub, each occupying its own spring or group of springs in the Lake Railroad system, are recognized. Names on the map include Willow, Butterfield and Blue Eagle Springs and substantial wet areas reserved for migratory birds, as well as drier refuges for game—including antelope—have been set aside in the general vicinity. Ten miles south of the highway at Black Rock Summit a gaping

[2] How Railroad Valley got its name is something of a mystery, since it lay sixty miles over the Pancake and Fish Creek Ranges from the nearest rail, at Eureka, at the time it became known as such. Decades later the Nevada Northern, still no closer than 45 miles, was spiked. The late Robert A. Allen, then Nevada's State Highway Engineer, quoted a theory in his *Origin of Place Names, Nevada* (1941). He told of a franchise granted in 1871 for a railroad in five surrounding counties and said "surveying may have been done in this valley." He also said a natural gravel bar resembling a roadbed might have suggested the name. Other than this, information seems to be lacking.

bowl quaintly named Lunar Crater indicates the volcanic activity that has taken place here very recently.

There is an unsubstantiated Indian legend supporting the theory that Lake Railroad may have dried up within the last 200 years. Hubbs and Miller recount the story of an Indian named Morey Jack, aged 93, well-known and well regarded, who many years ago mentioned to the man in charge at the Railroad Valley Wildlife Refuge that "his father told him of having heard *his* father telling of swimming in the now perennially dry bed of Railroad Lake." One wishes that Jedediah Smith could have left a more precise account of his 1827 route, or that an eyewitness description existed to support this idea of a living remnant.[3]

A lake contemporaneous with Railroad sprang up in Reveille Valley east of the range of that name. At full development of 50 square miles it drained northward over a low alluvial rise and into Lake Railroad. Bodies of water similar in size formed in Coal and Pennoyer Valleys, south and southeast, but they do not appear to have had any outside connection.

The White River basin adjacent to the east—with its extensions: Pahroc, Pahranagat and Coyote Spring Valleys—drained to the Colorado River in Pluvial times but is now disrupted. The lakes alongside, other than a minor one in Cave Valley, did not contribute to that flow. Dry Lake Valley held two small isolated lakes, Bristol and Delamar, which Hardman has identified; he also established the drainage of Lakes Mormon, East and Corn Creek, which spilled in series to Las Vegas Wash. Unconnected lakes occupied Indian Springs Valley (62 square miles), Yucca and Frenchman Flats (both very small) and Emigrant Valley. Deeply indenting the Great Basin where it swings east are the valleys of the Virgin and Muddy Rivers and Meadow Valley Wash, all belonging to the Colorado River system. These delineate our province.

North of Railroad Valley and beyond the head of the White River, within the state of Nevada, lie many high troughs that held lakes predating the appearance of the human race. For the most part they clustered in what is now White Pine County, from well below

---

[3] A similar legend relates to Lake LeConte, covered in the preceding chapter. Hubbs and Miller, while admitting such legends are generally unreliable, repeat the Cahuilla Indian story of fish very plentiful at one time and the lake then drying little by little "five life spans ago." That particular legend is detailed and plausible, they say, and is supported by concrete evidence: residual colonies of pupfish, *C. macularius*, are present in isolated springs above and below the LeConte beach line and quantities of charred fishbones have turned up in relatively recent Indian occupation sites. The main stage of LeConte is thought to have ended 1,000 years ago but recent studies indicate it existed into the 18th century A.D. (See footnote 2 of Chapter XI).

Ely northward, almost up to Wells in Elko County, and west into Eureka County. East of this region it was all Lake Bonneville, whose vast expanse lapped along the Utah border and pushed into Nevada from above Montello down to White Horse Pass. This sea was contained by the Goose Creek Mountains, the Toana Range and the Goshute Mountains, and further south rise the Deep Creek Mountains and the Snake Range. All of these constitute the Bonneville divide and present a very easily discerned and massive demarcation.

The dozen or more lakes west of this barrier lay in separate valleys with small glaciers decorating some of the ridges between them. Just one of these persists today beneath the summit of Wheeler Peak in the Snake Range; however, this living remnant is mostly buried in loose till and the visible portion looks more like a very modest snowfield. It is the only known living ice glacier in the Great Basin. Below the cirque that cradles it, a long and very fine example of rock glacier winds north toward the head of Lehman Creek.

Spring Valley lies compressed between the Snake Range and the Schell Creek Range immediately to the west and here a very long and narrow Pluvial lake materialized. From end to end it stretched at least 60 miles and it averaged 5½ miles wide; its greatest depth came to 265 feet. It was the subject of an intensive study by C. T. Snyder and W. B. Langbein (1962), who reconstructed from the geological evidence the hydrologic regimen needed to maintain such a lake and compared it with today's climatic conditions. The valley now receives 8 inches of precipitation annually on the floor, and up to 30 inches high in the surrounding mountains; its rate of evaporation is estimated at 44 inches per year. Langbein and Snyder speculate upon the changes of climate that could bring Lake Spring back into existence. The most likely combination of adjustments among those possible, they suggest, is a 30-percent decrease in evaporation rates and an 8-inch increase in annual precipitation.

The lake in Spring Valley occupied one-fifth of the total basin and did not overflow. It could not have done so, the Snyder-Langbein study shows, because the level where this could have happened would imply a depth of over 500 feet and an area filling 36 percent of the basin, or 580 square miles. There is no indication of any such development.

Today the valley loses water entirely by evapotranspiration since there is no surface export and no known groundwater movement to adjacent basins. It is ideal for this study by reason of its situation:

midway between the Uintah-Wasatch and Sierra Nevada boundaries of the Great Basin, of which it is typical in all aspects. The general altitude of its floor is 5,535 feet. Shore features of the ancient lake may be seen widely below the 5,780 contour. Hubbs and Miller collected two species of fish (a dace and a sucker) in Spring Creek, which flows into the north end of the valley, and they report other native fish present in minor springs along the foot of the Snake Range.

In driving from Ely, Nevada, to Delta, Utah, on U.S. Highway 6 one crosses Spring Valley about at its mid-point where the playa is quite narrow. Alluvial fans project from the canyons on either hand and a clear view of the landscape for 50 miles or more may be had to north and south. This highway comes down from Connors Pass (7,723), crosses the valley and swings north some miles to exit eastward at Sacramento Pass (7,154). Dominating the entire panorama is Wheeler Peak (13,061), for it is the second highest mountain in Nevada and much of the year it is ornamented with a cape of snow. On the opposite side of Sacramento Pass, balancing Wheeler Peak, rises Mt. Moriah (12,050).

The remaining lakes that came into being between Bonneville and the drainage of the modern Humboldt River were packed quite uniformly within the Elko-White Pine area of east central Nevada. In total they amounted to about 3,000 square miles of water and ranged in size from Goshute Valley's Lake Waring (478) down to minor gatherings at Egan Creek and South Steptoe Valleys no more than 10 square miles each. There is even doubt that the latter formed at all; we have examined South Steptoe basin and do not find any signs of a Pluvial lake. Both these small bodies would have spilled into Steptoe Valley where a lake, estimated by Hardman to have been almost as big as Waring, built up between the present towns of McGill and Currie. At peaking there was some discharge between the two, Hardman concluded.[4]

Elko County's Clover and Independence Valleys maintained a single large lake, as did Ruby Valley in which Lake Franklin took shape. Remnants of the latter persist today in Ruby Lake, Ruby Marsh and Franklin Lake, all receiving runoff from the Ruby Mountains that rise abruptly just to the west. Snow Water Lake in Clover Valley and Goshute Lake in Steptoe fill up in a normal season and are relicts of the extensive Pleistocene development. They are fed by snowfields in the East Humboldt and Cherry Creek Ranges.

---

[4] Carl L. Hubbs, revisiting the site of Lake Steptoe recently, deduced that it was actually much smaller and never spilled to Lake Waring.

Lakes Newark, Hubbs and Gale were substantial, though not as large as Waring, Steptoe and Franklin. Gale in Butte Valley had a Pluvial connection with Franklin and Clover. Lake Antelope, north of Spring Valley, and Lake Jakes complete the cluster. The latter rose in a valley named for its first settler, known only as "Dutch Jake," and is served by Illipah Creek, now stocked with trout. Here there are no native fish, however, nor in Antelope Valley's live spring water. These and their companion lakes maintained hydrographic integrity even though Lake Bonneville approached within ten miles in some places.

Bighorn sheep were present in the Ruby Mountains up to historic times and Zenas Leonard, clerk with the 1833 Walker party, recorded the incidence. Early trappers and explorers saw elk, red fox, wolves and wolverine, in addition to animals common today (*Nevada Wildlife*, 1965). The mountain lion, bobcat, antelope, deer and small mammals persist, their habitats more commonly in the higher country where feed and cover obtain rather than in the open and relatively barren flats. The Bureau of Land Management, Ely District, lists 225 varieties of birds now found, 25 of them rare; also two shrews, 14 kinds of bat, weasels, mink, skunk, porcupine, badger, fox, coyote and ground squirrels. There are 34 kinds of rodent, 5 types of rabbit or hare. Elk, though not abundant, are still present in the Schell Creek Range, and Spring Valley is a favorable location for antelope. Game birds include the indigenous dove and exotics—introduced species—such as pheasant, chukar and Hungarian partridge.

The U.S. Fish and Wildlife Service (usfws) manages a number of areas within the region we are treating. At Ruby Marsh, most of the wetlands are reserved, but near the south end a public hunting ground has been designated, and fishing is unrestricted. Camping facilities were installed by the b.l.m. and a fish hatchery by the State of Nevada. In Railroad Valley the usfws manages one extensive reservation, and at Lower Pahranagat Lake (which is artificial) another. Similar activities are conducted by the Nevada Fish & Game Commission at Hiko and Sunnyside where the Key Pitman and Wayne E. Kirch wildlife preserves utilize prepared water resources.

These last together with the Pahranagat refuge lie in the disrupted White River basin. Encompassing several mountain ranges and valleys of southern Nevada, the Desert National Wildlife Range set aside mainly to protect the bighorn sheep overlaps the Energy

Research and Development Administration's Nevada Proving Ground and occupies large sections of Clark and Lincoln counties.

There is ample evidence that man was early on this scene. The nearby archeological discoveries at Danger Cave, to be covered in some detail in the next chapter, indicate a cultural continuum going back at least 10,000 years. This central region was investigated professionally by parties led by M. R. Harrington and S. M. Wheeler between 1925 and 1936. Kachina Cave in Snake Creek Valley was excavated by these people and three sites in Smith Creek Canyon where field work was undertaken in those decades have been studied much more thoroughly in quite recent times. Groups from the University of Alberta tested deposits in Smith Creek Cave, Council Hall Cave and Amy's Shelter with good results—evidence of a Lake Mojave Period occupancy, implying the presence of man at Smith Creek Cave 8,000 years or more ago, was obtained; maize was present, indicating a Puebloid pattern.

Smith Creek lies just north of Mt. Moriah and flows eastward into Snake Valley south of Gandy, Utah. The caves, which lie close to the mouth of the canyon, have yielded many bones, including those of horse and the giant condor, *Teratornis*. A layer of bristlecone pine needles was found just below the Lake Mojave Period living floor which must have blown in from a tree very close to the cave. Since these pines do not now grow below the 11,000-foot level on Mount Moriah one may assume that a much colder climate existed when the deposit, situated at about 6,500 feet, was covered over; this seems to indicate a totally different climatic pattern (Bryan, 1972).

Bronco Charlie Cave, named for a Shoshone Indian who lived in it for some time, is situated in Deadman's Canyon in the Ruby Mountains west of Lake Franklin's site. It contains pictographs assumed to be aboriginal, and when excavated in 1972 yielded cultural material, foodstuffs and environmental data. Elko series projectile points, elsewhere determined to be as old as 8,500 years, were found but absolute dating was unclear (Casjens, 1973).

In 1966, under a grant from the Desert Research Institute, 20 sites in this part of the Great Basin for which records existed were restudied and 86 previously unreported sites were identified and described (Fowler, 1968 a). Also, a very significant cave in Newark Valley was excavated as one phase of the same program (Fowler, 1968 b). Three-fourths of these sites were "chipping stations" yielding flakes and implements but no other cultural material; eleven were open campsites containing hearth and midden deposits, and six were rockshelters. The results of this survey tended to substantiate the existence here of the Desert Archaic over several millenia, followed by a brief (ca. 900 A.D. to 1200-1300) interlude of horticultural and village life west to the Utah-Nevada border. A subsequent reversion to the earlier traits then took place. This late shift in the basic lifeway could have been brought about by an alternation of climate such as a winter rainfall type replacing one of predominantly summer rain, or in any case a change to inadequate summer precipitation.

Newark Cave is a small wave-cut cavern at 6,150 feet a.s.l. on, the side of Buck Mountain east of Newark Valley. It faces northwest, lies above the highest of a series of terraces formed by the Pluvial lake and measures about 30 feet across the mouth, 30 feet in depth. It was filled by cultural deposits to within a few feet of its ceiling and from this accumulation a quantity of artifacts including projectile points and implements was obtained. Eight firehearths and three pits were uncovered. Though not especially rich, this inventory did coincide with essentials of the Desert Archaic in most respects. However, lake-associated flora and fauna were absent, indicating that occupation followed the disappearance of Lake Newark. A suite of radiocarbon dates shows that use of the cave lasted from about 5,000 B.P. to ca. 1100 A.D., probably on an intermittent basis (Fowler, 1968 b).

Toquima Cave was used by a hunting-gathering population for about 3,500 years prior to the historic period; it lies south of U.S. Highway 50 at the northern end of the Toquima Range. Many other caves have been found throughout the central region, not all of them showing signs of human occupation. Northumberland Cave in northern Nye County south of Wildcat Peak, and Whipple Cave, a huge grotto located 60 miles south of Ely, were never inhabited (Mack and Sawyer, 1965). Goshute Cave, northeast of Ely, has been used by Indians for an indeterminate period, but Lehman (otherwise called Baker) Cave lacked any natural entrance and so could hardly have been known to prehistoric man. It was discovered in 1878 when Abe Lehman's horse broke through a thin partition; thereafter its interconnected underground chambers were gradually explored, and in 1922 it became a National Monument under the jurisdiction of the National Park Service.

Bordering closely on the Great Basin are many interesting sites in Lincoln County, Nevada. Beaver Dam Wash, tributary to the Virgin River, was the scene of a 1970 study conducted by Don

D. Fowler covering 25 sites, the principal occupation of which appeared to be by carriers of the Virgin Branch Anasazi tradition dating ca. A.D. 700-1300. The O'Malley Rockshelter in Clover Valley was also excavated in 1970 and evidence was uncovered there of occupation by carriers of three cultural traditions: Desert Archaic, dating from ca. 9,500 B.P. to ca. 1000 A.D.; Puebloan, from 1000 to 1300 A.D.; and Shoshonean, 1300 to 1890. These occurred in a cave depth of over 20 feet.

From the many archeological indicators obtained at these eastern Nevada sites we can infer the continuity of the Desert Archaic involving the hunting and gathering lifeway. Animal trails and drinking springs were adorned with rock drawings in many places throughout the region. These fall into two categories: petroglyphs carved into the rock surface, and pictographs, which are painted on the rock.[5] Although there are many repeated, recognizable configurations, no language can be deduced and only general meanings given the recurring figures. Students of rock art have tabulated some of these as follows: dot and circle, rain, man, quadruped, snake, fertility, ladder, rake. Sometimes an animal is depicted so well one knows it for a goat or antelope. There are even some symbols that suggest a camel, although this species (Camelops hesternus) disappeared from the Great Basin at least 7,000 years ago. Dating rock art is most uncertain. Rarely, a phenomenon such as an overlay of desert varnish or, as mentioned in Chapter XI, a travertine deposit of known date formed over flooded pictographs will establish great age for some example. But generally the twin mysteries of "what and when" remain unsolved.

A notable petroglyph discovery was made in the Snake Range in 1935 but the nature and location of the slabs were not revealed until 1970 lest theft and vandalism should result in their destruction. Meanwhile these were studied professionally, photographed, and about 80 of them moved to a safe storage. The site was at 7,000 feet in a pinyon grove on U.S. Forest Service land and was found by a rancher tending stock. The carvings included significant examples of five styles typical of Great Basin rock art: Representational (human beings and animals); Curvilinear (abstract—curves and spirals); Rectilinear (boxes, cross-hatching); Scratched; and Pit & Groove. This last is believed to have been the earliest of the forms

[5] A petroglyph site of interest is located at Hickison Summit (6,564) above Stoneberger Creek in the northern end of Monitor Valley. Here just off U.S. Highway 50 the B.L.M. has developed a recreation area with tables, shelters, etc., and fenced the rock drawings against vandalism. A heavy growth of cedar and juniper suggests this may have been a game ambush spot in ancient times.

and has been dated as far back as 5,000 to 6,000 years ago, whereas the Representational is thought to have originated during the Christian era. Some of these Snake Range drawings could possibly have been executed in early Medithermal times when a cooler and probably wetter climate would have afforded more favorable living conditions.

This find is unique not only for the number and variety of the unmolested specimens but for the unusual site itself—in high wooded country. Most Nevada petroglyphs are found in open spaces; they appear on blocks of basalt or large boulders located in mountain passes, at the edge of valleys, and beside springs. But these were carved on thin stone slabs, far from any stream source or channel, in a pinyon grove facing south toward an open hillside, above a small gully. Two seeps now dry may have been intermittent game attractions when the artists worked out their inventions. Quartz crystals, which are plentiful in the vicinity, probably provided the material for their engraving tools, with which the designs were pecked out.

The region east and north of Nye County has belonged traditionally to the Shoshone for many centuries; these people tended to concentrate in the Deep Creek and northern Railroad Valley areas. Contact with the white man was somewhat limited here, nevertheless the Shoshone suffered from his diseases and his habit of upsetting the ecology. During the 1850s an epidemic of cholera decimated the Great Basin Indians and starvation was prevalent among them. Game animals had been driven off and the food supply, normally quite precarious, dwindled to a point where mere survival became difficult.

During the years of the Civil War there were occasional hostilities along the Humboldt River and across the route of the Overland Stages (Forbes, 1967). This reflected an unrest that was general among Indians during this time. No reservations had been formally created, though in 1859 the Utah Superintendency had set up reserves in Ruby and Deep Creek Valleys; then came changes in personnel and a dearth of funds, and the "farms" were allowed to disappear. Mac Eh Temoke, Chief of the Ruby Valley Shoshone, went to Washington in 1863 to negotiate a treaty. It resulted in certain Indian lands being ceded to the Government but not in any discernible improvement in the Indians' condition.

Forbes points out that, unlike the eastern tribes, the Nevada Indians could not be considered reservation people anyway, that even today only about half of them at most have ever lived on reserved land with any horticultural potential. Moreover, of those who have done so, large numbers have found it necessary to leave seasonally in order to maintain a minimum level of subsistence. We must bear in mind that these people inherit no agricultural tradition, dislike farming, and generally lack the necessary skills. Many of those who attempt it inevitably fail.

Today there are Shoshone populations at Reno, Austin, Eureka, Duckwater, Fallon, Schurz, Elko and Ely. As mentioned in Chapter VIII, their principal concentration is at Owyhee, just beyond the Great Basin boundary, and some of them enjoy (if that is the word) the privileges of Yomba and Te-Moak Reservations. The Deep Creek Valley straddles the Utah-Nevada state line east of Cherry Creek and there the Goshute Shoshone occupy a reservation remote from disturbing influences. Their numbers have increased, and though for various reasons their lot in life is far from ideal one must conclude it has improved. The hope is it will continue to do so.

The rapid progress of Jedediah Smith in early June 1827, was recounted very tersely in a letter to Gen. William Clark. He crossed the Sierra Nevada in eight days (May 20–28) and arrived at the southwest corner of Great Salt Lake June 17; he described the country he had crossed as "completely barren and destitute of game," so we may assume he traveled over the more arid stretches of the central region. Certainly he was the first white man to make the Great Basin transit, but he established no route and 18 years were to elapse before any reconnaissance was undertaken here. The 1830s did not constitute a time of discovery. The Walker and Bartleson-Bidwell parties skirted these valleys on the north, and it was not until 1845 that the inquisitive John C. Frémont, detaching himself from the main body of his Third Expeditionary force at the Ruby Mountains, came this way. He mapped the country as he whipped south through Diamond and Big Smoky Valleys, but his was a very swift and limited observation, and it added very little to the public knowledge of this *terra incognita*.

Thereafter, the land from Walker Lake to the Utah deserts lay undisturbed while emigrants and Forty-niners passed it by, either to the north along the Humboldt River or far to the south. Its mineral wealth was not to be sought or exploited until the 1860s, and the forbidding qualities of a rugged terrain and perennial drought repelled permanent settlers. But one man was to change all this—in 1859 the Army sent Capt. James H. Simpson of the

Topographical Engineers on an expedition to find wagon roads across this territory. His party left Camp Floyd, Utah, on May 3 and reached Genoa six weeks later; his return journey began after a fortnight's rest and ended August 5 at point of beginning. This survey followed roughly the line taken by U.S. Highway 50 today and it shortened the journey from the East to San Francisco by more than 250 miles. In consequence of this it was adopted at once by the Overland Mail, the Pony Express and the trans-continental telegraph.

The geologist attached to this expedition was a perceptive mining engineer named Henry Engelmann, and he has been credited with being the first to recognize Lake Lahontan's earlier existence. In his report he wrote: ". . . this compound serrated mountain-system has been partially covered with lakes and large inland seas (some of the more southern and lower portions perhaps by the ocean) . . . within the present era." He had a fine grasp of the nature of the province, as he stated that the name "Great Basin gives a wrong impression of its hypsometrical condition." He understood it to be an inverted basin, and of its drainage he wrote: "It is divided into many systems disconnected with each other, and all the streams originating there are lost within its limits."

The Pony Express, activated in 1860, was short-lived but spectacular and captured the imagination of people everywhere with its concept of succeeding against almost insurmountable hazards: the empty deserts, the high mountains, and especially the hostile Indians. A rigid 10-day schedule was maintained over the 1,966 miles from St. Joseph, Missouri, to San Francisco during the year and a half it operated. For an evaluation of performance we might offer the standard maximum of riding 60 miles in a day in contrast to the 65 to 100 miles covered at full gallop by these young men; they stopped only to change mounts, at stations that were about 25 miles apart, and their horses were expected to average 20 miles an hour.

The service lost quite a few station tenders and at least one rider to Indian predators, also $1.5 million on their operations, even though they charged $5 in gold per half ounce of mail carried the full distance. In October 1861, the transmission of the first telegraph message between the same terminal cities proclaimed the start of a faster, cheaper service and this delivered the *coup de grace* to its horseback competitor. Pony Express stations were utilized thereafter by the regular overland mail, which continued in existence until supplanted in turn by railroad mail in 1869.

That was the year Lt. George M. Wheeler of the Engineers Corps, U.S. Army, made the first north-south traverse of the central Great Basin. He started from Halleck Station on the Central Pacific, and during the first of his two expeditions beginning that May and lasting five months he covered a wide territory, especially down the Utah-Nevada border. Of significance in this account was the presence on his staff of Grove K. Gilbert, then in the midst of his first experience in the West. On this tour of duty he devised his configuration of Lake Bonneville, a classic that remains accepted. The Wheeler excursion in fact constituted the first "professional exploring" undertaken in the Great Basin interior (Goetzmann, 1966). Lt. Wheeler was sent out again in 1871 and that year covered an even greater territory, somewhat to the west, including Death Valley during a grueling summer. His work was presented in the u.s.g.s. report, *Beyond the 100th Meridian,* 1879.

The 'Sixties were years of exploitation, especially of mineral wealth, and this gave impetus to an opening up and sparse settlement of the central Basin—though more often than not the ultimate result that followed "boom and bust" would be a ghost town. Basalt, Silver Peak, Candelaria and Gold Point were small-to-medium strikes involving gold and silver in the southwestern districts close to California. Silverpeak, beside the bed of Pluvial Lake Clayton, is still important for lithium production. Tybo and Tempiute, in the middle of the central region, produced lead, zinc and silver, while mines in Railroad Valley (Troy and Willow Creek) and in Reveille Valley recovered gold, silver, lead and other values.

The Belmont silver strike of 1865 drew many adventurers but never really boomed, though right across the Toquimas in Big Smoky Valley gold in some quantity was discovered later at Manhattan (1905) and Round Mountain (1906). Belmont became the Nye County seat in 1867 but today there is little left of it. Rhyolite and Bullfrog (1904) in the Amargosa River basin brought substantial development including rail connections, yet actual discovery was in total relatively small (Nev. Bureau of Mines, 1964). Besides these a great many lesser deposits were located and consequent interest aroused; for in spite of the lack of water a widespread belt of mineralization proved attractive to hordes of prospectors.

To the northeast Eureka, Hamilton and Ely strikes provoked much excitement as rumors spread and adventurers came flocking. Though a very rich deposit, Hamilton's ore lasted only a short while (1868–70) but in that time the population swelled to 10,000 as the new county of White Pine was organized. A fine courthouse was built that remained a landmark for many years after the town had been finally abandoned. The Eureka properties, located in 1864, also resulted in a separate county designation and great local expansion that was stimulated by a newly developed process of smelting the high grade silver-lead ores. In the 1870s there was great activity here, and eventually as many as seven smelters operated simultaneously; the mines were extensive and lasted well into the 20th century. Today the smelters are gone, leaving only their sprawling piles of dark slag, and the town is quieter. Yet substantial deposits of rich ore remain, awaiting the solution to serious underground water problems that have frustrated efforts to recover them. Various companies have tackled the situation and hope persists for a resumption of Eureka's former prosperity.

The history of the Ely district—which began in 1867 with a gold and silver discovery, spreading to Osceola (1872) and Taylor (1873), both of which were quite profitable—has been considerably brighter than that of most Great Basin mining centers. Although the precious metal concentrations were soon exhausted, copper claims were filed there prior to the turn of the century and the first open-pit operation began in 1908. Since then enormous tonnages of displaced overburden and of ore removed have transformed the landscape; monumental waste piles and immense craters mark the countryside at Ruth and Kimberly a few miles west of Ely. Here, over a billion dollars worth of the red metal has been mined in half a century and this is far in excess of what the Comstock Lode produced.[6] Today this enterprise is quite active though subject to economic fluctuation.

To handle the region's ores, freight and public transportation, it was inevitable that railroads would be proposed. Several were actually built. By 1869 the CP had been extended across the northern width of the Great Basin and the two feeder lines mentioned in Chapter VIII, the Nevada Central and the Eureka & Palisade, were connected with it. A plan to extend the latter from Eureka to Ely was considered and discarded, and instead a new line directly northward from Ely was incorporated June 1, 1905, as the Nevada Northern. It began as a standard gauge road to accept rolling stock directly from the transcontinental route and its primary purpose was to export copper, hauling ore mined at Kimberly to the smelter

[6] The Ruth-Ely-Robinson mining district has yielded more than twice as much ore value as the Virginia City mines, mostly in copper but with gold, silver, lead, zinc and molybdenum too—in total, well over $1 billion. Elsewhere, four areas have exceeded $100 million: Yerington, Tonopah, Goldfield and Pioche. The Nevada Bureau of Mines lists 344 districts, with production data for each.

at McGill and blister copper thence to the junction. Because the smelting processes required great quantities of water and nearby sources had been pre-empted by the town of Ely, it was necessary to locate the facility 30 miles away where a plentiful supply from Duck Creek was available (Myrick, 1962).

McGill marks the southern end of Lake Steptoe's position and the Nevada Northern runs the length of its dry bed to Currie, thence down the Goshute Valley in which Pluvial Lake Waring appeared. The wide flat bolsons where these long-vanished waters covered almost a thousand square miles provided ideal reaches for laying rail. No tunnels or difficult grades were required over the 140 miles from Ely to Cobre (copper in Spanish), so named by a mining engineer fresh from Mexico. Here the Southern Pacific connection is made; and 20 miles south of there at Shafter, named for a Spanish-American War general, the Western Pacific Railroad crosses.

In contrast to the ease of construction across the valleys north of Ely the difficulty and expense of extending a line 10 miles west to the Veteran pit at Kimberly was prodigious. Grades were very steep and tunnels were necessary in Robinson Canyon, and ore trains did not begin to shuttle from mine to smelter until April 1908, though regular passenger service out of Ely northward had been inaugurated (after two days of wild celebration) on October 1, 1906. In its heyday, Pullmans and specials ran frequently, children were brought daily from McGill to school in Ely, and the SP's Overland Limited was regularly met at Cobre. But over the years passenger service was reduced due to lack of patronage and in 1941 it was discontinued entirely. Diesel power supplanted steam; yet the Nevada Northern remains operating today, last of the Nevada short lines and a wholly successful going concern.

Pioche lies just beyond the Basin near the Utah line, in the Colorado River drainage. There a Mormon missionary to the Indians found silver in 1863, and the following year the Church colonized at Panaca. This district's best mining production has come from lead-zinc-silver locations and here also the mining promise resulted in great agitation for railroad-building. The Salt Lake Route mentioned earlier was directed toward Pioche but went over mountains to the south and ran down through Meadow Valley Wash. Then a branch line was put north from it at Caliente, as far as the mines. Over the years the district has been a large producer.

Tonopah and Goldfield, with heavy values in gold and silver, were of a similar magnitude to Pioche and at first were boom towns enjoying great activity. Then came dismal slumps; but both are still county seats and have lately shown some modest growth, particularly Tonopah. Their lives as railroad centers were relatively brief, as noted elsewhere in this account, but their oasis characteristics have been maintained.

The only Nevada oil to be found thus far in commercial quantity has come from Railroad Valley, although companies have drilled more than 200 dry holes in many other parts of the state. This uniquely successful (but exceedingly limited) focus known as the Eagle Springs field began with a discovery well 65 miles southwest of Ely, drilled in June 1954. These small producing wells all lie within Nye County, 14 of them, and at least seven have yielded over 100,000 barrels each. Still, the total cumulative field production in 21 years has totalled no more than 2.9 million barrels. This figure stands in some contrast to the Texas daily allowable of 3.3 million barrels *per day*.

The central section of the Great Basin still remains largely unpopulated. Ely, with fewer than 5,000 people, McGill and East Ely together about the same, and Tonopah with less than half that figure are the only towns of even moderate size. A few settlements and occupied crossroads, along with widely scattered and isolated ranching spreads constitute the entire pattern of habitation. Yet many sightseeing visitors come to this part of the desert to look at the Lunar Crater, Diana's Punchbowl, ghost towns or just the unblemished and endless scenery. Sportsmen are drawn to the hunting and fishing opportunities, mountaineers to the high wild areas of the Snake Range, the Toiyabes and the Ruby Peaks; campers, hikers, rock hounds, skiers—outdoorsmen of every persuasion—visit and linger. The Wheeler Peak area has been approved in some quarters for National Park status but local opinion strongly opposes such a change: the people of White Pine County, at least the majority of them, prefer to keep the wilderness setting and discourage any tourist inundation, however that might improve the economy. There is no marketable timber, even though the Humboldt and Toiyabe National Forests cover many a square mile of central and eastern Nevada, and the grazing resource runs thin in most places. Thus in the final analysis the year-around cash flow depends to a great degree upon the payrolls of the mines and what the tourist passing through may leave behind.

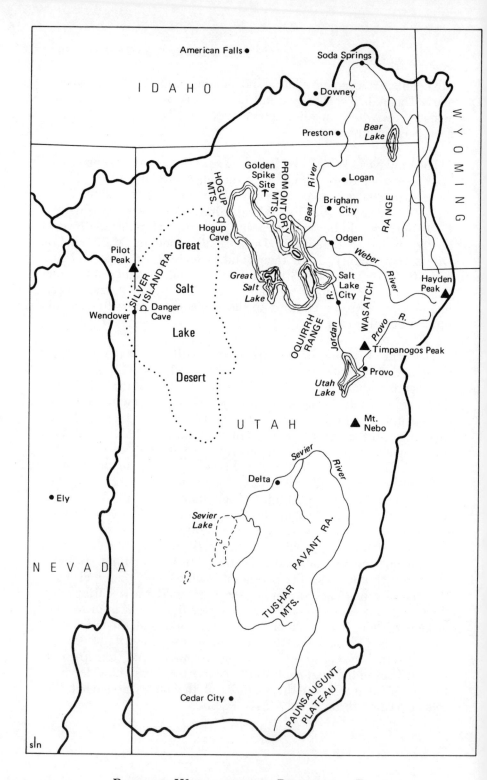

REMNANT WATERS OF THE BONNEVILLE BASIN

CHAPTER XIII

The Bonneville System
Tributary Rivers and Lakes

Almost all the northeastern wing of the Great Basin was involved in the Lake Bonneville system throughout the Wisconsin stage. The Basin's boundaries enclose small portions of Idaho and Wyoming as well as the northwestern half of Utah, and most of this area drains into the sump where the largest single accumulation in the province formed. In this chapter we will consider the outlying portions of the system and its bordering unassociated waters, leaving to the next chapter Bonneville with its modern relict, Great Salt Lake.

The principal crest line of the Wasatch Range trends diagonally across Utah from the indented corner where Wyoming intrudes to a point near the southwestern extremity of the state and it divides the Great Basin from the Green River-Colorado River drainage. The two Utah areas are about equal in size. The physiographic changes that have taken place since the Pluvial phase subsided are limited to a few minor lava flows, isostatic rebound resulting from removal of the enormous weight of Lake Bonneville, and the widespread postglacial desiccation of the Holocene epoch. Wind erosion has affected the distribution and deposition of soils and salines but the streams and small creeks flow much as before.

At present three rivers fed by many tributaries flow down into Great Salt Lake from the northern extension of the Wasatch Mountains. These are the Bear, the Weber and the Jordan. In the central part of the range the Provo River feeds Utah Lake (which is drained by the Jordan), while to the south the Sevier River collects water all along the many plateaus and further reaches of the Wasatch and describes a hairpin course leading to the desert terminus known as Sevier Lake. Near its mouth it is joined by the Beaver, draining generally northwest from the Tushar Mountains by way of Milford. Additionally, there are a few detached runnels which did not, at least in the late Pleistocene, have any connection with Lake Bonneville. These we will treat regionally, as they may seem important.

There was a small lake in southwest Utah near the north end

of Pine Valley, west of the Wah Wah Mountains. It was named Lake Pine by Hubbs and Miller (1948) who point out that many of the outlying portions of the general drainage, especially near the Utah-Nevada state line, are now isolated minor basins. Snyder (Map I–416) names it Lake Wah Wah, which seems more definitive, and depicts an oval shape of no great depth about seven miles in diameter. Gilbert thought it was once a filled trough connecting the Snake Valley arm of Lake Bonneville with its Escalante Desert arm, but evidence does not appear to support that opinion. Only a small playa remains.

Little Salt Lake, near Parowan in the valley so named, is presumed to have fetched a higher Pluvial level and probably to have discharged when completely full through Hieroglyph Canyon to the Escalante Desert arm; presence of an endemic Bonneville fish type confirms this interpretation (Hubbs and Miller). However, fish data are lacking in the evaluation of other lakes and playas within or near the southern boundary of the Bonneville drainage basin. A number of these were mapped by Jones (1940) as Pluvial without supporting evidence and none of them is shown on Map I–416.

The water most important to the region being examined here, southwest Utah, is carried by the Sevier River, which furnishes an extended segment of the Wasatch front. This stream rises on the Markagunt and Paunsaugunt Plateaus, which are tipped northward and are drained in that direction by the East Fork and the Main Fork of the Sevier. The channels merge at Junction, Utah, where there is a reservoir, and the river then continues between high ranges to Gunnison. At that point it is joined by the San Pitch River and another, very large reservoir is formed. Thereafter the Sevier reverses its direction west and south to emerge in the desert 140 miles from its source.[1] The Sevier Lake Playa lies 50 or 60 miles beyond this hairpin bend. When first mapped in 1872 it had a water surface of 188 square miles and a saline content of only 9 per cent; but today it exists as a substantial body of water only after prolonged and heavy runoff, inasmuch as the normal flow is retained upstream and utilized for agriculture. In hot, dry summers the lake may disappear entirely.

The natural hydrographic relationships of the Great Basin and the Green River-Colorado River drainage have been violated in several places by intentional transfers established for human needs. A typical example is in Grass Valley, extreme southwestern Utah,

[1] An extensive sand dune area occupies the northern end of the Sevier Desert between Lynndyl and Jericho, west of the Gilson Range.

where a tunnel carries water from the head of the Santa Clara River, a tributary of the Colorado by way of the Virgin River, across a divide to Pinto Creek in the Great Basin.[2] Hubbs and Miller point out that in this way fish may be transported from a system where they have been indigenous to one where they were previously unknown. Other similar transfers in or out of the Bonneville basin exist, some being of natural origin. For instance, near Kanarraville a large alluvial cone lies astride the water parting and its stream is utilized alternately on either side. In the past it presumably wandered during times of heavy flow and carried its fish population from one basin to another. This phenomenon helps to explain the presence of species in some areas where they could not otherwise be accounted for.

The physiographic features of this region, which lies below what might be thought of as the waistline of Old Lake Bonneville, are impressive. At either end of this line, which roughly coincides with the 40th parallel of latitude, tall sentinels rise overlooking the scene: on the east Mt. Nebo (11,928), apex of the Wasatch, and on the west Haystack Peak (12,101), standing out in the Deep Creek Range. Wheeler Peak (13,061) and Mt. Moriah (12,067) lie south of Haystack within Nevada, while many summits comparable to Nebo adjoin it along the eastern crest. Two worth mentioning belong to the Tushar chain northwest of Beaver, Utah, Delano Peak and Mt. Belknap, both well over 12,000 feet.

At the western edge of the Markagunt Plateau on the slopes below Brian Head (11,307) the gaudy and colossal erosion pattern called Cedar Breaks faces the Great Basin desert. Set aside as a National Monument, this brilliantly-colored natural amphitheatre 2,000 feet deep and framed by dark contrasting evergreens drains down through Coal Creek Canyon to Quichipa Dry Lake below Cedar City. Just beyond the boundary of the Basin at this point lie the two National Parks, Zion and Bryce, cut by the Deep Creek fork of the Virgin River and the headwaters of the Paria River, respectively, both of which are tributary to the Colorado (Ridd, 1963).

Not very far north of the great bend of the Sevier lies Utah Lake, a natural fresh-water body 130 square miles or more in area whose basin was once filled deeply and widely with the integral Bonneville development. Like other remnant lakes receiving irrigation runoff it has grown brackish over the years and also has been

---

[2] Another water transfer into the Great Basin, and a substantial one, is that from the upper Duchesne River via aqueducts to Strawberry, Hayes and Sevier Bridge reservoirs.

subject to industrial pollution. Its normal outlet is the Jordan River, which flows north through Salt Lake Valley between the Wasatch and Oquirrh Mountains, but that flow in these days is minimal due to diversion, and at some seasons the Jordan becomes virtually stagnant. Salt Lake Valley is full of Bonneville reminders: wave-cut terraces and deltas belonging to various lake stages, quite frequent near canyons on the east side especially. Set back from Utah Lake's shoreline are a number of cities including Provo, third largest in the state and seat of Brigham Young University. Several mountains exceeding 11,000 feet lie close at hand, among them Mt. Timpanogos and Provo Peak.

Hayden Peak (12,475) rises 56 miles northeast of Provo and is important for two reasons: it is the westernmost of the high Uinta peaks, located only a few miles from the junction of that range with the Wasatch mountains; and it is the point of origin for three of Utah's main interior streams. The Uintas, barely impinging on the Great Basin, constitute the only important mountain system in the conterminous states running directly east and west and contain the highest summits in Utah. On the north slope of Hayden Peak are Amethyst and McPheters Lakes in which the Bear River is born. Just to the west of them springs the Weber River, while somewhat to the southwest the Provo River has its source in Lost Lake. The Bear and the Weber flow down into Great Salt Lake, the former by a much longer and more devious course, and each has substantial tributaries among which the Ogden, part of the Weber system, and the Malad draining south from Idaho to meet the Bear near its mouth, are noteworthy.

Bear Lake straddles the Idaho-Utah border very close to the Wyoming line and is approximately the same size as Utah Lake. Its namesake river does not flow in or out of it naturally but passes by several miles to the northeast. Canals have been dug to obtain input from the river and outflow downstream, however, and the lake is maintained at a fairly constant level to serve as a reservoir in multiple use. Bones of the mammoth have been found nearby, and the lake has a most interesting Pleistocene history.

In order to reach this vicinity the Bear River, longest of the three which nominally support Great Salt Lake, passes into Wyoming down a valley compressed between the latter's Bear River Divide and Tump Range and Utah's northern Wasatch extension. After crossing and recrossing state lines it doubles back west and south at Soda Springs, Idaho, with a configuration very like that of the Sevier to enter Great Salt Lake near Brigham City. Although describing a course some 500 meander miles long, its mouth is no more than 90 miles from its source. This drainage forms the northeastern corner of the Great Basin itself.

At some time in the past, probably not a great many thousand years ago, the Bear became temporarily blocked below the lake. One may observe wave-cut terraces 25 or 30 feet above the present lake surface at the south and southeastern extremities. Budge (1950) notes that there are few well-developed water level marks on the surrounding hills, and cites this as reason to think the ancient Lake Bear did not last as long as Bonneville. He puts the present level at 5,294, which is 26 feet below the most prominent beach mark and only 75 feet below the highest one.

Bear Lake is now approximately 200 feet at deepest, near the center of the eastern shore about a mile out, and its average depth is only 30 or 40 feet. In size (21 miles long by 6 to 8 miles wide) and in altitude it is comparable to Lake Tahoe, though it lacks the profound deeps and crystal clarity of the latter and its shores are almost wholly developed. Since it had an earlier, larger form one may ask: how did that come about, and why was it short-lived?

Mansfield (1927) thinks that near the close of the glacial period alluvial material in the north end of Bear Valley dammed off the entering waters, causing the formation of the larger lake; in time, this dam would have been washed out. But Budge quotes William Peterson, a former professor at Utah State University, Logan, who suggested that a glacier moving out of Georgetown Canyon in the Preuss Range had blocked the river. Then when the waters of the lake reached a rather high stage the river cut a new channel to the west and re-entered the old streambed farther north. After the glacier receded the river resumed its old channel. In both hypotheses a temporary obstruction is assumed and defended; either one would account for the Pluvial lake. The fishes here belong to the Bonneville fauna and show some local differentiation: they include the peaknose cisco (*Leucichthys gemmifer* Snyder), a relict unique to Bear Lake, considered a zoogeographical enigma.

Bear Lake Valley is a structural basin featured by the Bear Lake Fault, which runs north-south along the east side of the lake. A great crustal movement some 270 miles long called the Bannock Overthrust contributed at least a million years ago to the dropping of the valley floor, which then filled with water to form the original lake. The mountains now surrounding the drainage—Bear Lake Range to the west, Preuss Range to the northeast, Bear Lake Plateau to the southeast—are not remarkably high or impressive but provide, to the west especially, a pleasant rolling and wooded background for the cultivated lowlands.

Lake Thatcher, not a Pluvial body, was formed in a basin on the Bear River west of Soda Springs by a lava flow more than 34,000 years ago. The Bear had drained previously to the Snake by way of the Portneuf River but when blocked by the lava it spilled over a quartzite divide into Cache Valley and the Bonneville drainage well before the last lake rise to the Bonneville terrace (Morrison, 1966). Thus the Bear system is a disrupted portion of the Columbia drainage.

Extreme western Utah is dominated by the Great Salt Desert, of very considerable extent. From the northwest corner of the state where the Goose Creek, Grouse Creek and Raft River Mountains give rise to small ephemeral watercourses that once fed Lake Bonneville, it reaches southward past the Silver Island Range to a scattering of ridges, lava beds and dry washes that are characteristic of the basin and divide it from the Sevier Desert.[3] This section of Utah was never much favored with streams and there is little breadth to the zone of drainage. Along the Idaho border, from Nevada to the Malad River, there is almost no water: the creek beds seldom carry any, and the few springs or seeps are consumed at isolated ranches. Thousand Spring Creek drains a patch of Nevada and so does Deep Creek—the one that rises west of Haystack Peak and flows through the Goshute Indian Reservation. Otherwise, around the rim of this remote and untenanted expanse the several arroyos contribute little and measure no great distance.

In addition to what we have covered here there are salt flats and playas distributed throughout the desert section, subject to springtime flooding and wet after intensive rain such as the summer thunderstorms produce. There are also numerous small mountain lakes of no particular size or importance and, plausibly, many artificial reservoirs in the high country installed for better management of available resources.

A considerable prehistory of most of the Great Basin has been revealed through a series of archeological discoveries made during the last few decades in western Utah and these have led to recogni-

---

[3] Many land forms in the western Bonneville basin carry almost horizontal markings low on their slopes that are not strandlines at all but exposed sedimentary layers far older than the Pleistocene. Contrariwise, the strandlines themselves may have lost horizontal position, deformed by isostatic rebound occurring when the huge but transient earth load imposed by Lake Bonneville was removed. Crittenden (1961 *et seq.*) has discussed the process and calculated the strength and viscosity of the mantle. This readjustment, which has widely altered the original levels, continues at a very slow rate, it is believed.

tion of the Desert culture as a distinctive way of life. It was first defined by Prof. Jesse D. Jennings of the University of Utah, and the principal source of relevant material which he uncovered is so important to our knowledge of the subject that description in some detail seems warranted here. The site is known as Danger Cave and its location, facing the Great Salt Lake Desert, lies in the Silver Island Range (otherwise, the Desert Hills) a mile or more east of Wendover on the Utah-Nevada state line, squarely within the Great Basin.

Danger Cave became well-known after excavations by E. R. Smith in 1940–41, the promise of whose work was fulfilled by that of Jennings in 1949–53. The latter's findings and interpretations were published soon thereafter in a long definitive report (Danger Cave, 1957). The cavern itself is an arched grotto averaging 60 feet in width and 120 feet long in Paleozoic limestone dissolved along a fracture. The portal lies about 200 feet below the Stansbury strandline of Lake Bonneville, or 4,325 feet a.s.l. It slopes gently down inside from front to back and the significant floor is 13 feet below the mouth. Here was found a rich assortment of hearth material and cultural debris that shed light not only on the way of life of the ancients but also on their degree of antiquity. Radiocarbon dating indicates that it was first occupied between 11,000 and 10,500 years ago. Here man took shelter and built fires for warmth, and at some time in the remote past he learned to use them for cooking.

The receding shores of Lake Bonneville were probably then still close at hand, thinly covering the now dry and gleaming salt flats; and the ranges which stand out across today's landscape were islands or peninsulas jutting into the farflung waters. In that early day *Homo sapiens* lacked such things as pottery, knowledge of agriculture and the use of domestic animals. As described by Jennings, he "moved across the land completely parasitic upon its normal fauna and flora. He modified the landscape for neither shelter nor food." He moved occasionally, not as a nomad, and the search for sustenance required most of his time and energy. He lacked material possessions and had no skill or taste for warfare.

An array of artifacts turned up in Danger Cave, all relating to the traits of this culture—the hallmarks of which were the basket and flat milling stone (Jennings). Over 1,000 hand or grinding stones and another 2,000 chipped stone pieces consisting of hunting points and various implements were found. A wealth of textile and cordage items, leather goods (including a moccasin), worked bone, wooden shafts, skewers and pegs, arrows, fire drills, shell fragments, quids and coprolites were among the diversified ethnic treasure left in this special place. Mainly these were forms altered for or through human use by people for whom they acquired significance. They constitute evidence revealing the cave dwellers' habits, traditions, intentions and environmental conditions. From a study of this evidence we can conclude that the climate was arid even as today throughout the occupancy, that food was scarce and hard to come by, and also that human ingenuity had developed to cope with rough conditions.

The provenience of an artifact is the precise spot where it was found and is expressed in terms of a site plan (usually a grid) and a level, or horizon. Ideally the alterations in a culture can be traced chronologically from one horizon to another. The various traits represented by the artifacts help to determine the culture. For example, hunting points show that the people who lost or discarded them were engaged in pursuing large animals, baskets indicate seed and nut gathering, snares show an interest in smaller animals, and quids (which are the by-products of mastication) mean that foods such as the edible rhyzomes and leaves of the desert bulrush (*Scirpus americanus*) were available. Further determination of diet can be achieved by analysis of coprolites—fossilized fecal material of human or animal origin. Jennings (1957) found pickleweed seeds in laboratory samples that were scored and abraded. He concluded these had been carefully gathered by ancient man, parched and milled, and probably used in a gruel (those with horny skins had survived milling and the digestive process). Yet there was otherwise little to indicate techniques of cooking in the Danger Cave specimens.

The artifacts were collected from five major layers, between which were considerable time gaps; these could indicate some climatic aberration. The higher strata, representing more recent occupations, carried pottery sherds. Wooden objects were made of mountain mahogany, serviceberry and greasewood. Miscellaneous clay pieces included possible effigies or figurines. Iron oxide lumps used as coloring material, mostly red but also a few yellow, were recovered. The cave produced 637 examples of cordage made from a wide range of vegetable fibres such as hemp, cedar, flax and common sagebrush; their uses included string bags, snares and nets, the latter a correlate of small animal trapping.

Also from the upper levels came 148 pieces of identifiable basketry, made with various techniques of both twining and coiling, a total of 14 kinds of manufacture recognized. Baskets and bags were necessary to the gathering and storing of seeds, nuts and other food items, also to the cooking process. Grains were winnowed

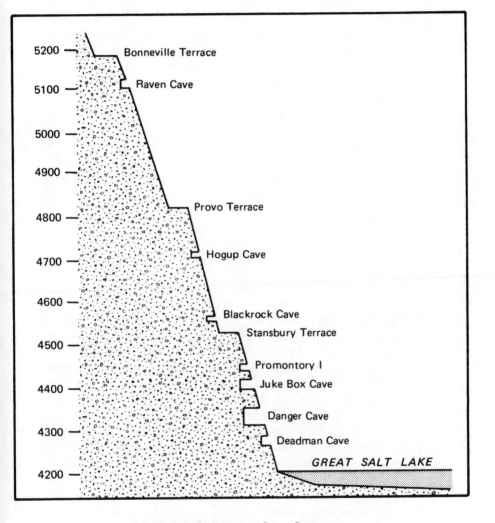

5200 — Bonneville Terrace

5100 — Raven Cave

5000 —

4900 —

4800 — Provo Terrace

4700 — Hogup Cave

4600 —

Blackrock Cave

4500 — Stansbury Terrace

Promontory I

4400 — Juke Box Cave

Danger Cave

4300 — Deadman Cave

GREAT SALT LAKE

4200 —

RELATIVE LEVELS OF CAVE SITES
AND PRINCIPAL LAKE BONNEVILLE TERRACES

and parched in baskets and cooking was accomplished by shaking live coals with the food so as not to scorch the container, or by dropping in heated rocks. Shapes varied according to use: conical ones carried the gathered harvest, flat ones were employed in winnowing, tightly woven jug-shaped and pitch-covered types were for liquids.

Cave sites may shed light on climatic alterations, not only through stratigraphic gaps but by the cultural evidence as well. The early big-game hunting lifeway characterized by the use of chipped stone points gave way to one of gathering and trapping as the large game animals disappeared. Previous to about 6,000 B.P. the Pleistocene fauna in the subarctic included early species of caribou and musk ox, bison *(B. antiquus figginsi)* and mammoth; in warmer and drier regions species included the camel, ground sloth, tapir, sabre cat, dire wolf and indigenous horse.[4] After that date there appear to be no acceptable finds, so, as of then these animals are considered to have become extinct in the Great Basin. They may have been hunted out of existence but many authorities feel that climatic change and consequent loss of food sources must have been the major factor in their disappearance.

No extinct species were recovered from Danger Cave, though many western caves of comparable age have shown man to be contemporaneous with and hunting the horse and camel, the dire wolf and giant sloth. Jennings observes that it is reasonable to assume therefore that these animals were missing from western Utah by the time of earliest occupancy and that a differential rate of extinction could have been possible.

It would be wrong to assign a single date to a given site even though we can make educated guesses about its earliest use, based on sophisticated techniques. Most sites were frequented over long periods, some for thousands of years, or enjoyed intermittent use. As the lakes rose and fell, caves at shoreline would have been flooded and abandoned at times and much evidence of earlier inhabitation destroyed. Thus it is the "dry" site that produces the richest cultural remains, organic materials surviving, and may be dated more precisely. Many sites were used only at certain seasons, perhaps for

---

[4] The Pleistocene mammalia of northern Utah represented a broad spectrum, as shown by fossils on display at the Utah Museum of Natural History. One of these is the skeleton of a peccary *(Platygonus compressus)* which was a warmth-loving animal—living forms occur from Texas to Argentina—and another is the skull of a giant musk ox *(Symbos cavifrons)* which was much larger than today's variety in the far north. Existence of the pig could indicate an earlier, much warmer climatic stage for the Utah-Idaho region; whereas presence of the cold-loving musk ox (the skull came from a gravel pit north of Salt Lake City) indicates considerably colder times during Lake Bonneville's flourishing.

as little as one or two months out of the year. Others served mainly for burials, and some were principally cache sites used for storing implements and food. A few combined these different uses.

The question is often raised as to why so many artifacts were discarded in these places, as if the autochthonous people had been clumsy or careless with their things. Jennings points out that the production of Danger Cave consisted almost entirely of fragments showing heavy use—in other words, worn out. These people were frugal and treasured their artifacts as long as they were serviceable. As for hunting points, found in great profusion and of many distinct types and styles, these may have become dulled or broken, he observes, and tossed aside after brief employment in favor of easily prepared replacements. He doubts any appreciable amount of material was really lost.

Other sites in the vicinity of Danger Cave were explored at about the same time (Raven Cave, Jukebox Cave) but their cultural offerings were meager. Elsewhere, adjacent to Lake Bonneville's shores and somewhat earlier, a number of locations were dug and cultural evidence comparable in some degree with the Wendover findings was produced. Deadman Cave and Black Rock Cave belonged to the Protoarchaic stage, and Indian Caves along the Promontory Range (Steward, 1937) contained quantities of diagnostic material suggesting a subculture.

A particularly rich Desert culture site was uncovered on the south-western flank of Hogup Mountain about 60 miles northeast of Danger Cave. Here under the direction of C. Melvin Aikens the excavation of Hogup Cave took place during the summers of 1967 and 1968, and his extensive report was published in 1970. This is another large cavern in limestone, situated midway between Lake Bonneville's Provo and Stansbury terraces at an elevation of 4,700 feet and facing the northern tip of Great Salt Lake Desert. Artifacts from the site totalled nearly 10,000 items. Materials consisted of pottery and clay, chipped and ground stone, bone, hide, cordage and fiber, textiles, and wood. Sixteen separate strata were identified in deposits 14 feet thick and a series of 23 radiocarbon determinations were made from organic substances found within them. Dating of charcoal in Stratum 1 on bedrock indicated an occupation 8,500 years ago ($\pm$160) and the successive layers formed a sequence ranging to 1450 A.D. ($\pm$80). Further ethnological evidence suggested an occupation into historic times (ca. 1850 A.D.).

The archeological data from Hogup Cave paralleled and augmented that which Jennings had obtained in Danger Cave and confirmed many Desert culture assumptions. Projectile points were found to have a similar longevity. But a dramatic shifting in floral and faunal frequency was observed, and an "early" and a "late" Archaic were defined. Though this shift might have resulted from climatic change, the author points out that it could have been due to an influx of new people with different "exploitive patterns"— which is to say that newcomers might have possessed quite special tastes and skills, and also might have lacked some of the more familiar ones.

There was also an apparent gap of 1,600 years between Strata 7 and 8 which Aikens thought might have arisen from inadequate sampling, and this hiatus in dates (bracketed, incidentally, by a much larger one at Danger Cave) involves the period from 6,200 B.P. to 4,600 B.P. This falls squarely within the Altithermal age postulated by Antevs. Three deposits yielded dates prior to this 1,600-year gap, one at its end, and these four fall within the allotted Altithermal time. Aikens feels that neither the Hogup nor the Danger sequences show any pronounced cultural changes until about 3,200 B.P. and that no simple relationship between climatic change and cultural change can be assumed on an area-wide basis. The local environments were far more affected by the progressive drying of Lake Bonneville than they were by temperature and moisture fluctuations within the Neothermal time spans.

At Hogup Cave pottery sherds of six types were found in layers 9 to 16 dated from ca. 3,200 B.P. down to the present. They included Great Salt Lake Gray, Knolls Gray and Shoshoni ware—types found also in Danger Cave; the first two belong to the Fremont tradition. Pottery traits constitute a departure from the Desert Archaic. Aikens thinks that the Fremont, widespread along the eastern fringe of the Great Basin, is closely related to the High Plains culture, from which he believes the traits were carried distantly westward. The Indian Caves in the Promontory Mountains, referred to above, are assumed by some authorities to manifest a separate Promontory culture; but Aikens questions the validity of this concept and points out that important ties between the Fremont-Promontory unit and the northern and western Plains are very clear.

An attribute of the Fremont is bison-hunting. In later strata, evidence of it disappears, replaced by Shoshonean patterns having the small game-gathering indicators and thus showing a reversion to much earlier traits. It may be observed here that the bison were common north of Great Salt Lake until quite recently, and that the mountain sheep has also disappeared in historical times. Other than these, the entire range of plant and animal species noted in the Wendover caves can still be found in the region.

At this point a further look at the Fremont seems in order. It was a late development and involved among other things the cultivation of maize; it is thought that about 20 varieties were recognized and grown. The Desert culture, non-agricultural, obtained over a wide area east of the Great Basin boundary, and in Utah it was replaced: by the Fremont east of the Wasatch, by the Sevier-Fremont west of that divide. The latter was more strongly influenced by the Anasazi than by the Fremont proper. At some point (probably during the 13th century, A.D.) the Fremont seems to have disappeared and the traits of the Desert culture were then resumed.

The Anasazi were Pueblo Indians and are commonly associated with the Four Corners area and the cliff houses of the Mesa Verde. Their tradition is widely spread in the southwest and though it undoubtedly is reflected in the Fremont, many anomalous traits are at variance with the assumption that the latter is a hybrid manifestation of it. Aikens proposed that the basis was primarily western Plains, with the Anasazi a superficial overlay. A quite recent work by Elsasser and Heizer (1966) links northern California to the Fremont-Promontory and underscores a continuity from the western High Plains all the way to the Pacific Ocean.

To summarize: the Desert lifeway persisted without significant change in the Great Basin for thousands of years. Sophisticated attributes like metallurgy, political development, or a calendrical system were never attained. Its most interesting aspect is stability, as Jennings has shown, and this characteristic pervades the archeological evidence. Material traits were added but essentially the orientation was toward Nature—the securing of food from the environment and an adaptation to very harsh conditions. Most of the traits were integral and consistent right down to the historical period when white incursion disrupted the Indians' basis of existence.

In the 1770s when white men first appeared on the scene the tribal distribution was fairly stable, geographically. Utes occupied the plateau province, the shores of Utah Lake, and the Sevier River basin. West of the Wasatch Front, broadly, Shoshone and Goshute bands moved about their desert territories. Southern Paiutes were established in Beaver and Iron Counties, southwestern Utah. All these people lacked knowledge of their autochthonous predecessors, though old legends persisted and the Desert culture they maintained suggested some link. The question of ancestral relationships remains in limbo.

Perhaps the most dramatic change in the lifeway of the Indian was generated by the horse, extinct in the western hemisphere for more than 6,000 years but reintroduced by the Spanish. Many tribes soon found there were better uses for this animal than eating him and some of them developed an incomparable horsemanship, so expert in fact that military men have called the Sioux the greatest cavalry the world has ever seen. Crows, Comanches, Kiowas, Arapahoes, Cheyennes—all the Plains Indians developed superb equestrian skills and grew to depend upon the horse in hunting and warfare. Mounted Indians generally acquired more material wealth while those without horses grew more timid and impoverished (Malouf, 1966).

During the 18th century and almost to the middle of the 19th, the slave trade proved very profitable to the more aggressive tribes, particularly the mounted Utes. Malouf observes that in 1839 the Paiutes who lived in the region of the Sevier River were hunted by the Utes in the spring when the Paiutes were weak and helpless, after a long and hungry winter. They were taken to Santa Fe and sold as slaves or traded for horses. Some American trappers appear to have been involved in this industry also, and the Navajos too raided Southern Paiute areas for slaves, whom they sold mostly to the Mexicans.

Among the Great Basin Indians, only the Bannocks seem to have attained high equestrian distinction, although the Northern Shoshone acquired horses and made good use of them. Anthropologists have commonly assigned the Bannocks to a territory in southern Idaho, but O. C. Stewart (1966) believes they were true Northern Paiutes from Oregon who, having obtained horses early from the Shoshone, returned to live and hunt with them instead of remaining to fish the Snake and gather food otherwise. The Bannocks, he says, traveled with the Shoshone, shared the same camps, and controlled no territory distinct from the Shoshonean. In 1964, he wrote, they were still multilingual, nearly all of them speaking Northern Paiute and Shoshone as well as English.

Some northern Great Basin bands were given names as if to indicate that, like the Bannocks, they were permanent groups. One example was the Tosawitch, or "White Knives," who roved about the inverted T-corner area where Idaho and Oregon join Nevada.

Their name derived from a special kind of flint which they found in the mountains north of Stony Point, across the valley from Battle Mountain. The Tosawitch were apparently Shoshonean people, though mixed bands were sometimes encountered along the Humboldt River with Utes and Bannocks present. They worked the white flinty material to make knives used in dressing food (Malouf).

Linguistically, the Paiute and Shoshone are closely related and both groups share typological similarities to the Desert culture. They have always been politically disunited, moving in family bands of a dozen or two individuals usually related bilaterally but often joined by friends or acquaintances. The band was a very flexible unit formed to meet social needs and acquire food more efficiently, and it remained more or less aloof to other bands; but on occasion the members might engage in wife-stealing forays against outsiders.

We have referred already to the two tribal divisions called Paiute: the Northern or Paviotso, and the Southern, who are more closely related to the Utes. The Yahuskin were localized Oregon bands of Northern Paiute stock, as were the Mono Indians east of Yosemite Valley; whereas the Chemehuevi were a people virtually indistinguishable from the Southern Paiute occupying southeastern California, especially riparian to the Colorado River. The Goshutes were localized Shoshone living in the desert country west and northwest of Utah Lake, central to the broad strip of Shoshone territory that ran diagonally like a bar sinister from Bear Lake southwest to Death Valley, crossing the entire breadth of the Great Basin.

Six months after Garcés broke into the Mojave, two other Franciscan friars tried the Basin's Utah rim. They had journeyed with a retinue from Santa Fe and, guided by Indians, had crossed the Green River near Jensen in hopes of reaching Monterey. Their purpose was to establish a route to the northern coastal missions, and like de Anza and Garcés they too had no knowledge of landmarks, distances or obstacles ahead. Fathers Francisco Atanasio Domínguez and Francisco Sylvestre Vélez de Escalante entered the Great Basin on the 21st of September 1776, near Utah Lake and encountered friendly Timpanogos Utes who told them about a great body of salty water lying a little to the north. But the season being advanced, the fathers passed up a chance to see it and kept to their main purpose, hoping rather for a stream of fresh water that might sustain them and their livestock along the way.

The legendary San Buenaventura River was in their minds, luring them even as it would so many others (Morgan, 1943). Accompanying them and ready to map that waterway was Don Bernardo Meira y Pacheco of Santa Fe, a retired militia captain with skill in cartography; his record filled with quaint references endures. They skirted the Basin from Deseret to Milford, were frustrated by the exiguous nature and random wanderings of the Sevier and lesser waters. Somewhere northwest of where Cedar City is today, with dwindling supplies and hopes, they gave up the quest and turned back to Santa Fe. Their adventure had been chancy—they were lucky to survive.

Thirty-five years were to elapse before the Great Basin was again disturbed by white contact. Meanwhile Lewis and Clark ascended the Missouri River (1804–06) far to the north; John Colter and others trapped on the Yellowstone. Then in 1811 Wilson Price Hunt came west to set up a trading post for Astor at the mouth of the Columbia. At Henry's Fort in eastern Idaho he detached four trappers, later joined by a fifth,[5] to search for beaver some distance to the south. In the course of their wanderings they reached the Bear River Valley and thus became the first Anglo-Americans to enter the Great Basin, but they left no chronicles of this experience and it is known mainly through Robert Stuart's journal. Stuart himself reached the Bear but not Great Salt Lake. In 1813 the Arze-Garcia party broke trail from the Green River to the Sevier and so provided another access to the desert Basin, but as yet there had been no penetration. No concept of it, no knowledge of what it might contain, had ever been given to the world.

The Bear River country figured significantly thereafter in the developing history of the Far West. It provided a favorable purlieu where trappers could foregather, make winter quarters and stage expeditions. Peter Skene Ogden recorded in his 1824–26 journal that Michel Bourdon discovered and trapped the Bear in 1819; Donald McKenzie visited it later that year and named it. Here the first big rendezvous was held and for 20 years the custom of holding an annual convergence was carried out. In the 1820s trappers were very active between South Pass and the Columbia. William Ashley formed a partnership with Andrew Henry in 1822 and brought scores of young men from the East to work the watersheds for beaver. The annual meetings, held in the fall, attracted widespread interest; one of them, conducted in 1825, drew 3,200 people, of whom 2,500 were Indians (Malouf, 1966). The resident Bear River tribe in those days was the very numerous Wyoming Shoshone.

---

[5] The five trappers were Joseph Miller, Jacob Reznor, Edward Robinson, John Hoback and Martin Gass. Robbed of horses and equipment by Arapahoes, they passed a difficult winter and were rescued the following August by a party under Robert Stuart (Cline, 1963).

William Sublette had established himself in Cache Valley, and in 1826 he and Jedediah Smith, with David E. Jackson, bought out Ashley, who then returned wealthy to Missouri and ran successfully for Congress. Smith's travels that year and the next have been detailed already, but it should be added that he gave much time and energy to exploring Utah and, more than anyone else, was responsible for opening up the Great Basin. His transit of it in 1827 was a shining achievement.

There has been some dispute as to who discovered Great Salt Lake. In 1811, an edition of Guthrie's *New System of Geography* was published containing a map of North America that showed a considerable lake with no outlet, about where Great Salt Lake belonged. This bore the caption "Lake, etc., laid down according to Mr. Lawrence who is said to have travelled through to California in 1790–91." However, nothing further is known of "Mr. Lawrence" (*Encyclopedia Britannica*, 14th Edition).

In 1824 Ashley's men were moving into northern Utah but the first white man to reach the lake's vicinity seems to have been Etienne Provost, an independent trapper out of Taos, New Mexico (Cline). Provost, after whom Utah's third largest city was named, entered nearby valleys in the fall of that year and may well have seen the lake, but he never mentioned it. Hence the honor of discovery has been bestowed upon the Ashley scout Jim Bridger, who explored the Bear River and shores of the lake early in 1825. Importantly, he told of his experience. Dale Morgan (1943) describes Bridger "floating down the river in a bullboat of buffalo hide" and imagining himself upon the shores of the Pacific, but other historians think he rode horseback to the scene.

Early in 1827 a caravan from St. Louis guided by Thomas Fitzpatrick brought west via South Pass a four-pounder (Bonney, 1960) and this field piece was the first wheeled vehicle to enter the Basin. From then on, many parties came through this gateway of the Rockies, pioneered by Fitzpatrick in 1824. Capt. Benjamin Louis Eulalie de Bonneville, on leave from the U.S. Army and greedy for the money he believed easy to obtain in furs, arrived with a noteworthy roster of supporters that included Joseph R. Walker. But by then the beaver were mostly trapped out and his years in the West (1831–36) were unprofitable. Disillusioned, he returned to his military career with little more than a wealth of memories and some considerable fame, thanks to Washington Irving.

Probably the most important of Bonneville's contributions was his ordering up of the Walker expedition. Forty-strong, they were sent out ostensibly to examine Great Salt Lake, but in fact what they accomplished was a thrust entirely to the California settlements then held by Mexico. They departed in July 1833, and actually did explore through Park Valley along the north shore and half way down the west side of the lake before turning toward the Humboldt and California. We have already described their further journeys and we owe Zenas Leonard, clerk of the company, a debt for having kept a very lively account of the enterprise.

The 1830s marked the end of the fur trade and the beginning of a national concern with the West. Irving's *Adventures of Captain Bonneville in the Rocky Mountains and Far West* (1837) caused a great stir; it included two maps that imparted some idea of the Great Basin to a wide audience for the first time (Goetzmann, 1959) and aroused keen interest. California still belonged to Mexico, but Oregon had for some years been joint territory of the United States and Britain (the boundary was not established at the 49th Parallel until 1846) and remained open to settlement. Access via South Pass involved crossing Wyoming to the Bear, thence north to Soda Springs and to the Snake at Fort Hall (established in 1834). The Oregon Trail followed that stream but at the Raft River confluence the California Trail split off, taking a more southerly course through the City of Rocks and eventually reaching the Humboldt. The first emigrant wagon train to come west was that of the Bartleson-Bidwell party in 1841,[6] then others soon followed along the northern corridors. Meanwhile the Workman-Rowland party, using the same route taken by Wolfskill in 1831, became the first emigrants to reach California over the Old Spanish Trail, also in 1841.

Lieut. John Charles Frémont was sent west in 1842 to explore the country and establish better routes. With 25 men he got as far as the Wind River Mountains that year and climbed a peak long believed to be the one that carries his name, second highest (13,730) in the range. But Orrin H. Bonney in *Guide to the Wyoming Mountains* identifies the summit from Frémont's own data as Mt. Woodrow Wilson (13,500 +) some miles to the north. (This writer, having climbed Fremont Peak and read the account, finds Bonney's contention reasonable.) The explorer then returned quickly to Missouri.

---

[6] The Bartleson-Bidwell party did not follow the California Trail but instead came down the Bear River and passed north of Great Salt Lake to Pilot Peak, thence through the Ruby Mountains (probably via Secret Pass) to reach the Humboldt River about 10 miles west of Elko. They abandoned a number of wagons and much material at Johnson Ranch Springs south of Oasis, Nevada.

The following June he set out upon a much more ambitious reconnaissance that required over a year and covered seven western states. Traveling west from Chouteau's Landing (now part of Kansas City) he passed down the Bear and reached Great Salt Lake early in September. The expedition's mapmaker, Preuss, describes in his diary the cloud of waterfowl that, as they approached the river-mouth, rose "with a sound like distant thunder." They had a collaps-ible rubber boat into which air was pumped to float it and with this they explored the island now called Fremont but designated "Disappointment Island" by him because it proved barren of game. They climbed the 800-foot apex to take bearings and make observa-tions.[7] For a time they had only seagulls to eat, being unable to shoot anything else, but five days later they reached Fort Hall and feasted on antelope (Preuss, 1958).

This, the second Frémont expedition, reached Fort Vancouver on November 7, 1843; Klamath Marsh December 10, and re-entered the Great Basin west of Summer Lake a few days later (Chapter II). We have already traced its progress through the Mojave Desert and across southern Nevada to the Virgin River in extreme south-western Utah. The party reached that point on May 6 and two days later headed into the mountains, arriving May 24 at Utah Lake. The Muddy, Virgin and Sevier Rivers had provided them with water, and the high Wasatch meadowlands the grass their livestock desperately needed. It was here at Utah Lake, where the Escalante-Domínguez *partida* had encamped 68 years earlier, that Frémont made his famous pronouncement regarding the nature of the province he had just encircled and the non-existence of the San Buenaventura River.

"The Columbia," he wrote, "is the only river which traverses the whole breadth of the country, breaking through all the ranges, and entering the sea . . . It is therefore the only line of com-munication between the Pacific and the interior of North America." There could be no Buenaventura, and all the land between the Wasatch Mountains and the Sierra Nevada was enclosed and drained internally, "truly a great basin."

It is difficult to understand how, in the light of 18th-century Spanish explorations, the circuits of Jedediah Smith and Joseph Walker, and the maps then available, anyone could have believed

---

[7] Frémont lost the cap to his telescope on this island and it was found there 20 years later by Jacob Miller, who was running stock. Though displayed in the Miller home for many years it has since disappeared.

the Buenaventura myth.[8] For at least 17 years the nature of the Sierra Nevada barrier had been known, so why did not Frémont recognize, or at least guess, the truth without stepping off some 2,000 miles? He did in the end acquaint the American people of western realities through his report to Congress following this reconnaissance, which had government backing; thousands of copies were printed and it was widely read. Most importantly, it stimulated the nationwide movement for expansion.

Frémont went east from Utah Lake to Pueblo, Bent's Fort and the Missouri River. In Washington there was much commotion and war with Mexico over the annexation of Texas seemed imminent. Congress quickly smoothed the way for a third western venture, and this time the party consisted of 62 men fully armed and equipped. With Walker and Kit Carson among them, they left Bent's Fort on the Arkansas the 16th of August 1845. Frémont carried secret instructions to be followed in case war did break out. Reaching Great Salt Lake in October, he chose to cross the salt flats directly; here he blazed a trail, for even the Indians had always avoided that stretch. Thence he traversed the Silver Island Mountains and drove through to feed and water at Pilot Peak which was used often as a landmark and was first named on a map by him. His further travels across the Great Basin have already been covered here.

Meanwhile the wagon trains were moving. In 1846 Capt. Lansford W. Hastings took a caravan across the gleaming flats and his route became known as the Hastings Cutoff; though dry and dangerous, it saved many a mile over the much-frequented Fort Hall roundabout. Extending roughly from Fort Bridger to Elko, this was no trek for the inexperienced and the somber truth dawned upon members of the Donner party that same year—but only after they had become irrevocably committed. Others before and after them negotiated the way successfully. Then by 1850 the Cutoff was superseded.

The major date in Utah history, marking the turning point between exploration and the beginning of settlement, was July 24, 1847. On that date the wagons of the Latter-day Saints came down Emigration Canyon and paused at its mouth just long enough, legend

[8] Goetzmann (1959) thinks that Frémont did not have access to the Gallatin map of 1836 or the Bonneville one dated 1837, either of which would have scotched the Buenaventura notion. Nor is it known if he had seen Smith's or Walker's accounts. Quite possibly he indulged in wishful thinking. Goetzmann (1966) calls Frémont a romantic stormy figure—more of an artist than a scientist—and suggests that he disintegrates upon close historical scrutiny, that his posture tells us more about the 1840s and 1850s than his actual achievements do.

says, for Brigham Young to intone "This is the Place."[9] The first Mormon group numbered only 156 people, but by the end of the summer nearly 2,000 had arrived. Thus began a colonization unique in American history.

The story of Great Salt Lake and further comment on events and developments in this northeastern lobe of the Great Basin will be treated in the chapter that follows.

---

[9] Brigham Young's traditional fiat is considered apocryphal by most historians, who insist it was invented many years later.

BONNEVILLE TERRACE AND OTHER STRANDLINES, NEAR DRAPER, UTAH
U. S. Geological Survey, 1925 photo: W. C. Alden, no. 1577.

THE WASATCH FRONT AT BIG COTTONWOOD CANYON
SHOWING THE BONNEVILLE SHORE LINE
U. S. Geological Survey, 1901 photo: G. K. Gilbert, no. 1797.

CHAPTER XIV

The Bonneville System
Great Salt Lake

By a wide margin, the largest Pluvial lake to form in the Great Basin was Bonneville. At maximum filling its surface measured just under 20,000 square miles—almost that of Lake Michigan today—and it covered the Escalante Valley, the Sevier Desert, Snake and White Valleys, the Great Salt Lake Desert, Cache Valley and many adjacent areas. It then reached into Nevada and Idaho in a number of places and was served by a drainage basin larger than New York or Pennsylvania and more than half the size of Utah—the figure is 53,325 square miles (Map I-416). Logically enough, its modern relict, Great Salt Lake, is the largest remnant water body in the Great Basin today. But even so, what we see is only a shrunken vestige one-fourteenth the size of its ancestor.

All around the Bonneville site throughout northwestern Utah the wavecut terraces that identify the lake's longer lasting stillstands are very evident. At least 17 distinct levels can be traced; the three most prominent ones are called the Bonneville, the Provo and the Stansbury shorelines. These, together with other lake-associated phenomena such as deltas and gravel bars, are widely displayed along the lower slopes of the ranges, promontories and islands in presentations that make the region one vast museum for geological study.

Long before Wisconsin time there were Tertiary lakes in the intermontane basins here, vouched for by exposed and subsurface indicators, and deep lakes were certainly formed during the early and middle Pleistocene successions. But evidence of them is nearly everywhere eroded away or buried beneath younger sediments. Only the record of inundations during the past 70,000 years or so is relatively well-recorded and accessible; these lake cycles, collectively known as Lake Bonneville, are of immediate concern to us here.

Opinions vary as to just when the peaking of the lake took place. Morrison (1966) suggests that the high water stage could have been attained as recently as 15,000 years ago, whereas Malde and Trimble

(1965) and others believe a date of 30,000 years B.P. to be more plausible; and Antevs (1948) puts it even earlier, ca. 62,000 B.P. The level reached was probably close to 5,120 (925 feet above the modern average[1]). The waters had then risen 30 feet above the Bonneville stillstand (Morrison) whereupon, abruptly, a most dramatic event took place: the lake burst through a soft barrier and soon developed an enormous flood which passed down the Snake and Columbia Rivers to the ocean.

The place where this happened is Red Rock Pass, five miles south of Downey, Idaho, and the crumbling cleft through which the waters poured is easily reached and examined today. Here layers of red sandstone lie exposed and the terrain at hand has been altered only by the slow erosion of unnumbered centuries. U.S. Highway 91 and the Union Pacific Railroad use the passage where the outflow excavated its channel some 320 feet down to a hard limestone threshold. There the elevation, vividly marked by the long Provo stillstand, is 4,800 feet.

Beyond the discharge point at Red Rock Pass there is a gentle valley sloping northward, occupied by Marsh Creek, which flows into the Portneuf River; it in turn is tributary to the Snake, which it joins above American Falls. Two major spillways were cut at this point by the great flood and boulders up to ten feet in diameter were moved many miles (Malde, 1960). Below Twin Falls a canyon 24 miles long, half a mile wide and 500 feet deep was excavated by cataract recession and within it gravel bars over 100 feet thick were deposited. High on the walls of Hell's Canyon far down the Snake the marks and sediments of this gigantic surge of waters are plainly visible today. Malde and Trimble (1965) estimate "a probably maximum discharge rate of about 15 million cubic feet per second—four or five times the average discharge of the Amazon River."

This peaking of Lake Bonneville and spillover was followed by a deep but short-lived recession, probably almost to dryness, Mor-

[1] The Bonneville shoreline, determined by Crittenden (1967) to be at 5,090 feet a.s.l. at Red Rock Pass, was not the highest level reached by the lake; Morrison believes that it rose "probably briefly 30 feet above it." The fact that terraces higher than 5,120 occur in many places, especially around the central basin, is explained by isostatic rebound—the doming up of the earth after the lake load (estimated in trillions of tons) was removed. The 5,090 figure for Red Rock Pass, at the lake's farthest reach, is taken by Crittenden as the datum representing zero uplift. Actual depth figures also varied as sediments built up and raised the lake bottom. Maximum lake developments of the Kansan and Illinoian glacial stages (700,000 to 300,000 years ago) did not reach as high as Bonneville's but their depths were comparable inasmuch as tue floors were several hundred feet lower than those of Wisconsin age.

OUTLET CHANNEL OF LAKE BONNEVILLE AT RED ROCK PASS
U. S. Geological Survey photo, ca. 1880: G. K. Gilbert, no. 3410.

PANORAMA SOUTH FROM RED ROCK PASS
U. S. Geological Survey, 1914 photo: R. W. Stone, no. 677.

rison believes. His study of the Graniteville soil formed at that time reinforces this conclusion. Then came three relatively small lake cycles with rises to 4,770, 4,470 and 4,410. The second of these is known as the Stansbury level and it probably was reached about 8,000 years ago. Morrison asserts that the lake basins during the Altithermal period were in general completely dry; the Midvale soil was then deposited. Several subsequent relatively shallow lake cycles bring the lacustrine history down to the present condition, with Great Salt Lake rising no higher than 65 feet above present levels throughout the past 4,000 years. Downtown Salt Lake City lies comfortably above that elevation.

One indication of a very dry interstadial following the Stansbury lake's decline is a deep and wide channel found below today's surface where the Jordan River then flowed to a destination that lay beyond—possible no more than a playa. Gvosdetsky and Hawkes (1953) have published a study of this drowned riverbed, which cuts through much older deposits.

First to recognize the extent of the ancient lakebed, interpret its nature, and publish his conclusions was Capt. Howard Stansbury of the Corps of Topographical Engineers.[2] He arrived from Fort Bridger in 1849 under orders to survey routes to and from Great Salt Lake Valley and circled the lake on land; the following year he and his men made a complete survey of it. One member of his staff was Lt. John W. Gunnison, whose name will figure again later in this account. He was given a special assignment to explore south of the lake and undertake a subsurface examination, inasmuch as Stansbury's orders included making "a correct survey of the lake itself, not neglecting soundings." In reference to this water Stansbury observed that "an elevation of but a few feet above the present level of the lake would flood the entire flat to a great distance, thus forming a vast inland sea." The altitude of its surface in 1850 was 4,201 (Morgan, 1947) about as it is today.

Stansbury's party had rough going in 1849 from the Malad River across Curlew and Park Valleys; their stock suffered from lack of feed and water, and they were fortunate to find a running stream at Pilot Peak on October 29 which saved the animals. Arriving at the stretch known later as the Hastings Cutoff in November, Stansbury wrote of this desert that "its extent, and perfectly level

---

[2] Dale Morgan (1947) states that it was Dr. James Blake, surgeon and geologist with the Stansbury expedition, who first realized the character of Great Salt Lake as the remnant of an earlier, much larger one. But Blake had left the Survey, misappropriated property, and brought a lawsuit against Stansbury, who understandably failed to mention him by name in his celebrated Report of 1852.

surface, would furnish a desirable space on which to measure a degree of the meridian, its only use of any value." But he was sufficiently imaginative in the course of his reconnaissance to grasp the idea of Lake Bonneville extending hundreds of miles, with mountaintops that appeared merely as islands, reaching to glacier-laden ranges and deeply covering all the desert he had just crossed. Thus his work anticipates the later more elaborate analyses of Clarence King and Grove K. Gilbert. I. C. Russell also recorded the general development of this region but it was Gilbert who set forth the classical description of Bonneville (1890) and provided its major levels with names. Since then much scientific attention has been given his concept and many new techniques have been devised and applied.

Among these we find the study of fossil soils, or paleopedology. One outstanding example of soil correlation (mentioned here in Chapter VI) is the relationship established by Morrison and Frye (1965) between the Sangamon soil of the midwestern United States and both the Cocoon soil of the Lahontan beds and the Dimple Dell soil of Bonneville in the Great Basin. These strata were simultaneously laid down in pre-Bonneville time. Pedology has distinct limitations, however, and sometimes the data it yields are inconclusive. For one thing, snail shells and wood can be radiocarbon dated only to about 32,000 B.P., at which point radiation ceases and the sample is considered "dead." For another, samples can become contaminated by the carbon content of surrounding air or water prior to testing. Morrison and Frye obtained a series of dates from a single bed of marl near Delta, Utah, with ranges covering at least 17,000 years; they call such results "inconsistent and at present baffling." But they go on to say that even if some recent stratigraphic studies shed doubt on the absolute synchroneity of lake and glacial fluctuations they do reveal large oscillations, of Lahontan in particular, that were previously unknown.

Although there is argument as to whether or not the Altithermal period (7,000–4,500 B.P.) was much hotter and drier than the preceding Anathermal, most authorities agree it was followed by a humid cycle that brought prolonged erosion during which new sediments were laid down. These are especially plentiful and easily examined in the side canyons of Salt Lake Valley, worked extensively by Gvosdetsky and Hawkes. Butterfield and Bingham Creeks descend from the Oquirrh Mountains on the west flank, while to the east along the Wasatch front Little Cottonwood, Big Cottonwood, Mill, Parleys, Emigration and City Creeks all run down to the Jordan. Here the deltas and wave-cut terraces marking the many stages of Lake Bonneville are clear.

Much of Lake Bonneville covered land now known as the Great Salt Lake Desert, familiar to all who have crossed it on Interstate Highway 80 or who rode the wp and sp passenger trains in daylight hours over its northern extension. This is the largest known example of the wet playa (Snyder, 1962) and is closed and undrained, with a water table near or at the surface which is retained by the bedrock. It has both the wet mud flats and bodies of evaporites classified particularly as crystal-body playa, neither moist-type nor dry. Water cannot escape except by evaporation or evapotranspiration. There is little plant life, for only the pickleweed (*Allenrolfia occidentalis*) or similar salt tolerant plants can survive. Outside the playa grow certain phreatophytes, well plants with less tolerance for salt, and beyond them are found the xerophytes where groundwater lies beneath reach, at great depth. Sagebrush, appearing even farther from the playa, is an index of good fertility, drainage and climate.

People unfamiliar with the salt flats are prone to conjecture about the hazards of driving or walking over them. The color is something of a clue to the state of the ground: during dry times a wet playa carries the salts upon its surface,[3] creating a white appearance, but in wet periods the salts are dissolved and carried down into the sediments, leaving a dark gray aspect. The experienced desert prowler will advise: if you are not certain, then follow the wheel tracks.

Thus in this sometimes frightening expanse of shimmering mirages and deceptive distances the playa dries out sufficiently in late summer to support heavy vehicles. Accordingly, the world's fastest racetrack has been laid out along the foot of the Silver Island Range. Here when conditions were suitable—surface, wind and light—many land speed world records have been set; recently these exceeded 600 m.p.h. Racing is usually conducted in August and September, whereas during other seasons of the year the track may become flooded and altogether unusable.

[3] The movement of salt across the Great Basin caused by strong prevailing westerly winds was prodigious. After the periodic desiccation of the lakebeds, exposed and dried salts were easily dispersed; thus when the lakes were reborn their waters stayed fresh for a long time. Great quantities of sodium chloride (NaCl) must have passed over the Basin's outcrops of silver ore, some small percentage of which penetrated the veins to create cerargyrite (AgCl) known to miners as horn silver (Gianella). The migration of salts across hundreds of miles throughout the Basin and beyond must have involved incalculably large amounts of these compounds.

Great Salt Lake is today a fluctuating and shallow concentration of saturated waters. Its highest level (4,211.6) and greatest area (ca. 2,400 square miles) attained in recorded history were measured in 1873 following a decade of unusually heavy precipitation. Since then the trend has been one of general decline with three or four intermediate peaks, and the historic low came in 1963 when the lake dropped to 4,191.35 and covered only 940 square miles. The maximum depth was then only 26 feet. Levels have altered by as much as 3.5 feet (1907) seasonally, but a foot or two in any one year is fairly normal. The average annual inflow (1931–60) has been measured at 2.45 million acre feet, of which 1.5 million is surface inflow (the three rivers mentioned plus springs, seeps and sewer outlets) and the remainder is contributed by direct precipitation and groundwater movement. At the levels prevailing today a million acre feet of inflow, net of evaporation, will produce a stage increase of 1.7 feet (Peck and Richardson, 1966).

In the 1870s when the salinity of the lake was first measured it averaged about 15 per cent, versus today's 27, a figure that varies with the point on the lake and depth at which the water is sampled. The u.s.g.s. has estimated a dissolved-mineral inflow of three to five million tons each year but this is minute compared to the five billion tons, approximately, of dissolved solids already present.[4] Salinity increases or decreases by 1.0 per cent for each foot of water level change, the total lake area by about 2.5 per cent, and the evaporation rate varies according to these changes. Bathers cannot sink nor fish survive in this water and the only life forms it contains are the larvae of two genera of flies *(Ephydra* and *Tipula)*, an insect (genus *Corixa*), a brine shrimp *(Artemia)* and several species of algae. Frémont noted beach deposits one to twenty feet wide and up to twelve inches deep made of oat size larvae; he referred to them as "worms," and said Joseph Walker told him of a similar phenomenon in salt lakes east of California.

In Bonneville times strong currents transported sand and gravel many miles to create spits, hooks, bars, beaches and similar deposits. Precambrian material was carried at least five miles southward from Farmington, the nearest source of such, to establish beds at North Salt Lake City. But in late years the natural lake circulation has been restricted or destroyed, especially where the northwest

---

[4] Somewhat more than three-fourths of this material is sodium chloride, or common salt; nine per cent is sodium sulfate, five per cent magnesium chloride, four per cent potassium chloride, four per cent magnesium sulfate, and one per cent a miscellany which includes lithium and bromine compounds.

arm has been partially blocked by the rock-filled railroad causeway built in 1959.

The dimensions of today's lake fluctuate somewhat but may be put roughly at 72 miles north-south by 22 miles wide. It consists of two distinct sections divided by the Promontory Mountains, Fremont Island and Antelope Island. The eastern basin is small and shallow, the western one much larger and deeper. Within the latter are several small islands, among which Gunnison, in the northwest arm, is most interesting. Here a large nesting colony of white pelicans gathers annually. This lonely uninhabited sanctuary lies 30 miles away from the marshes of the Bear River where these birds must forage for carp or shellfish, making the round trip daily during their spring occupancy. Dolphin Island lies offshore from Hogup Mountain, Carrington Island off the tip of Stansbury; both are barren and drab.[5]

The Mormon colonization of Utah brought large areas of land under cultivation for the first time, and to support this agricultural activity it became essential that adequate supplies of water be developed. Irrigation dates from the Mormon arrival[6] and all the best lands were pre-empted with astonishing speed. Within two years the Latter-day Saints spread 100 miles from Salt Lake City, down along the Wasatch to the Sevier and San Pete Valleys. Then within another two years they reached out as far as western Nevada and California. By the early 1860s they were almost everywhere in the Great Basin. Most important to the emigrant trains were the settlers of this faith who, residing beside the routes to the west, catered to the basic needs of these transients, while the latter in turn provided an economic blessing to the pioneers themselves. Generally, however, the forbidding nature of the region together with the theocratic character of local government discouraged outsiders from lingering in Utah.

Relations with the Indians were at first benign but the inevitable clash of cultures and interests became intensified as colonization

[5] The effect of a fluctuating level on the eight islands (inselbergs) in Great Salt Lake is interestingly shown by Cohenour and Thompson (1966), who demonstrate that at 4,210 they are all detached but at 4,191 all would be connected with the mainland and become peninsulas. The lake volume difference represented by this 19-foot drop—or rise—is 21.3 million a.f.

[6] Mormons first turned water on the land July 23, 1847 (Arrington, 1958) but it took them three years to learn the importance and effective use of irrigation. Under their Doctrine of Riparian Rights all water had to be returned to the stream. They developed a system of public ownership under which the "Principle of Stewardship" governed land use. It was accepted that "the Earth is the Lord's," and the Saints were His stewards.

progressed. The strongly-organized Utes and Navajos came increasingly into conflict with the settlers; so also did the Northern Shoshones, though to a lesser extent. But the Paiute and Goshute bands, being fewer in numbers, loosely organized and less aggressive, caused them little trouble. Forts were built in many places but at the outset were seldom used or needed.

Talk about a transcontinental railroad began in earnest after the annexation of California. A number of routes were advocated but inasmuch as the scope of such an enterprise lay beyond the financial reach of private business, the impetus had to come from Washington.[7] Surveys for a right-of-way across Colorado went forward in 1853 under John W. Gunnison, now a Captain, and he carried them to the eastern limits of the Great Basin in October. There he unwisely left his main force of about 60 men, and departed to explore the lower Sevier River. Included in his party of eight were Frederick Creutzfeldt, the German botanist who discovered the bristlecone pine, and John Bellows, who had accompanied Gunnison on the Stansbury expedition. On the morning of October 26 while they were preparing breakfast near the river six miles west of Deseret the entire group was butchered by a band of Pavant Utes seeking revenge against the nearest white men for a totally unrelated incident (Morgan, 1947).

There were other unpleasant happenings, the most gruesome of which was undoubtedly the Mountain Meadows Massacre in September 1857. Located 300 miles southwest of the capital, this small valley lying just north of the town of Central, Utah, was an important stop on the Old Spanish Trail. Here came a very large party of emigrants, about 140 in all, on their way to California, and a mixed group of Indians and white men ambushed them. Except for a number of children, all were killed and their property stolen. At that time the Mormons were bitterly resentful of the presence of United States troops asserting the national authority, and Judge John Cradlebaugh (the same who later became a Congressman from Nevada) attempted to bring the culprits to justice—an effort in which he was totally frustrated by widespread Mormon recalci-

[7] After the Treaty of Guadalupe-Hidalgo was signed (1848) there was constant discussion of a railroad to link California with the East and of what route it would take. Asa Whitney had proposed one to the northwest in 1844 when Oregon was beginning to be settled, and Col. J. J. Abert was urging, from 1849 on, a route at the 32nd Parallel—extreme southern Arizona and New Mexico (Goetzmann, 1966). One important survey was that of Capt. Gunnison, and after the 1853 massacre the work was continued under Lt. E. G. Beckwith, who crossed the Utah desert to Pilot Peak and surveyed down the Humboldt River. He designated Nobles and Madeline passes in the Susanville vicinity but these received no ultimate consideration.

trance. Juanita Brooks (1962) has researched this bit of history most faithfully and believes that John D. Lee was made the scapegoat for those who perpetrated the crime and benefited therefrom. Lee went to Arizona Territory after the incident and operated Lee's Ferry across the Colorado River for many years. In 1874 he was seized in southern Utah, brought to trial and eventually executed— the only man to be tried for the Mountain Meadows outrage.

Matters came to a head with the Indians by 1865 when the Black Hawk War, so-called, took place. (This campaign is not to be confused with the one similarly labeled in which Abraham Lincoln volunteered in Illinois, in 1832.) It was named for a Chief of the Utes, and it resulted in considerable bloodshed; the whites were forced out of central Utah, scores of them were killed, and thousands of head of horses and cattle were driven off. Hostilities were finally ended by a treaty signed in 1868.

One may well ask: what about the Indian here today? Where and how does he live? The requirements of white society make it very difficult for the modern Indian to become assimilated, since he is fundamentally clannish and beset by needs and yearnings that can hardly be satisfied in the kind of world that now surrounds him. Most Indians live apart, either in colonies handy to some work area or in reservations on some remote and traditional ground. Government has become more compassionate and understanding over the years but nonetheless the Indian's problems are deepseated and lie beyond any easy solutions.

Utah has a colony at Salt Lake City and a few relatively small reservations inside the Great Basin: the Goshute at Deep Creek, extending across the Nevada border; the Washakie, in Malad River Valley; Skull Valley, north of Dugway; and Kanosh, at the foot of the Pavant Range. Outside the Basin there are the Shivwits on the Santa Clara River, the much larger Uintah and Ouray, the Hill Creek Extension, and the enormous Navajo Reservation of northern Arizona that extends well into southeastern Utah. These last are peopled mainly by remnants of the plateau tribes. At Brigham City the Intermountain School operated by the Bureau of Indian Affairs receives about 2,000 Navajo boys and girls for vocational and standard high school education. Its facilities are modern and teaching quality high. Of all the Indian tribes, today the Navajo are much the most numerous.

The year was 1868 when the first steamer to navigate Great Salt Lake was built and launched by Gen. Patrick E. Connor for the purpose of transporting ties and telegraph poles needed mainly along the railroads. Connor, who became known as the "Father of Utah Mining," helped to establish the new Gentile city of Corinne and his ship, the *Kate Connor*, worked the lake from south to north and supplied the transcontinental line then nearing completion. That event, observed with the ceremony of the Golden Spike at Promontory, Utah, on May 10, 1869, signaled historical changes in the economy and society of the state.[8]

Brigham Young was incensed because the Union Pacific's route did not pass through his capital but instead came down Echo Canyon to Ogden and thence north of Great Salt Lake. To offset this snub the Mormon hierarchy went ahead on their own. First came the Utah Central Railroad, launched one week after the Promontory show, which ran south from Ogden to Salt Lake City. Then came the Utah Southern and Utah Northern, both organized in 1871; the Utah Western followed, and in 1880 the Utah Eastern was instituted to connect Coalville with Park City, 25 miles away (Bancroft, 1889). These five roads totaled 376 miles of track and were unique for having been constructed without Federal land grants or outside money. Mostly they served the mines.

Corinne briefly rivaled the Mormon capital, growing to be the Territory's second largest city by reason of its situation on both the Union Pacific and the river. Other steamers besides the *Kate Connor* ascended the Bear to transship cargoes of merchandise and ore at this railhead: the *Rosie Brown*, the *Pluribustah* and the *City of Corinne*. The latter carried three decks and was used mostly for transporting mineral; she was a sternwheeler 150 feet long and the most imposing boat ever to sail the lake. But as the Utah Northern reached into Idaho and, railroads took over the freighting traffic, the steamboat business failed and the town of Corinne itself swiftly dwindled, overtaken and surpassed by Ogden. Even the ship named after her became the *General Garfield*—converted to an excursion boat, she abandoned Corinne for a new home port, Lake Side, on the eastern shore below Farmington (Morgan, 1947).

The Utah Northern has a special interest for us because of its route through the Bonneville lakebed. Begun in mid-1871, it was running trains to Franklin, Idaho, by the middle of 1873 up the

---

[8] The Golden Spike ceremony took place just south of Promontory, Utah, at a spot sometimes called Promontory Summit. The site is located ca. 28 miles north of Promontory Point where many writers have erroneously placed it. There were actually four spikes used in the brief rites: two gold ones from California, a silver one from Nevada, and another from Arizona made of gold, silver and iron. The silver spike and one of the gold pair are in the Stanford University Museum but the other two have disappeared.

Bear River and through northern Cache Valley, which was once filled by a Bonneville arm. But later that year it succumbed to a financial panic—"Black Friday" on Sept. 19, 1873, marked the crash.[9] Reorganized four years later, it was pushed beyond to Banida and Oxford, then conveniently through Red Rock Pass, where track was laid in the summer of 1878. From there it went by way of Marsh Creek and the Portneuf River to the vicinity of Pocatello; eventually it reached well into Montana. Still operating, the facility has been part of the Union Pacific system for over 90 years (Beal, 1962).

A second direct route between Chicago and San Francisco came into being when the Western Pacific Railroad was completed early in the present century. The first rails were spiked at Salt Lake City on May 24, 1906, and the Nevada boundary was reached a year later (Myrick, 1962). These tracks connected with the D&RGW, which started at Denver in 1870 as a narrow gauge (36 inch) line with the unlikely target of Mexico City set forth in the prospectus. Its Utah portion was built in the name of the Rio Grande Western, then was merged with the parent road in 1908. By then all trackage had been converted to standard gauge. In 1883 the main line, 386 miles in length, was completed and a number of short branches gave access eventually to mining districts along the way such as the Bingham Canyon and Little Cottonwood (Alta) diggings.

The Utah & Pleasant Valley, privately financed and built, ran 50 miles (a part of it through Spanish Fork Canyon) and now is part of the D&RGW main line. Another unusual railroad was the Utah and Nevada, which commenced in 1872 as the Salt Lake, Sevier & Pioche but only went as far as Stockton, just south of Tooele. It was unique for having no bonded indebtedness of any kind; the UP took it over in 1883. Other short lines included the Sanpete Valley Railroad, the Summit County, and the American Fork (Bancroft).

Utah was first called *Deseret*, which in the Mormon vocabulary signifies "Land of the Working Bee," and it is still known as the Beehive State. That name is singularly appropriate, for its churchmen are about as industrious a group as one might encounter anywhere. Tithing and other support given the Church require

---

[9] There were at least two "Black Friday" panics a century ago: the one of reference here and an earlier debacle occasioned by the collapse of an attempt to corner the gold market on the part of Jay Gould and Jim Fisk, which took place on Sept. 24, 1869.

unremitting effort, thus the institution prospers and in turn provides material aid where needed, as well as spiritual benefits. Through its highly organized and widespread business activities, pursued with extraordinary acumen, the Church has brought employment and prosperity to many generations of Utah citizenry.

In this new land, far from inhabited centers, the emigrants had to develop an economy in addition to maintaining their social integrity. The land and its wealth was theirs to utilize, but when the Forty-niners came hurrying through with gold on their minds Brigham Young encouraged none to stay. Gold was a useless thing, profane, and gold mining would become "a destruction to the nation" he said. Gambling, an element in all mining, was forbidden under Mormon law, nevertheless mining did attract many people since coal, iron and other necessary metals lay at hand. Iron was discovered in 1849 and the first pig was cast three years later; prospecting began in earnest in 1863 and by 1870 a smelter was under construction. Whereas the mines of Nevada were proliferating long before the coming of the railroads, the opposite held true for Utah's development, and it was not until the 1870s that mineral deposits came under intensive exploitation in the Territory.

Following the inauguration of railroad service in 1869 dozens of boom towns sprang up, flourished, and then died. The Ophir mine in the Oquirrh Mountains, located in 1870 and provided with a stamp mill the next year, yielded quantities of silver, while other good producers in that general area included the Tintic, southwest of Utah Lake, and Park City, 40 miles northeast. Both districts are still active and producing. Park City grew to be a true bonanza, pouring out silver, lead, zinc, gold and copper worth hundreds of millions. Today the town is also widely known as a winter sports center. Just across the Wasatch Divide west of it lies Alta, another resort now devoted to skiing and avalanche study, but in 1873 the scene of a wild and populous mining camp. Its ore was very rich but limited in quantity.

Frisco, south of Sevier Lake and terminus of the Utah Southern Railroad, was the site of a very substantial discovery: the Horn Silver mine that may have yielded more than $60 million in metals and was the center of living for about 6,000 people at its peak (Roylance, 1965). A marker placed there recently reminds one of its vanished glory, reciting the figures. Yet now there is nothing left as, "boundless and bare, the lone and level sands stretch far away."

The leading metal of Utah's twentieth century is copper. Its principal source lies in Bingham Canyon above Salt Lake Valley where an open pit, considered to be the world's largest, has been excavated two miles in diameter and half a mile deep. Some have named this the greatest single mining project ever undertaken. Supporting that claim they quote these figures: since the pit was opened in the early 1900s two billion tons of rock and overburden have been moved and over 7,000,000 tons of metallic copper extracted. The dollar equivalent of this recovery undoubtedly exceeds that of all other mining in Utah's history.

What part has water played in determining Utah's socio-economic system? A look at the map and the data involved will immediately reveal its importance. Over 80 per cent of the state's more than one million people live in the five counties along the northern Wasatch Range (Cache, Weber, Davis, Salt Lake and Utah), yet these constitute less than six per cent of its total area. Moreover, since much of the terrain within them is mountainous and relatively uninhabitable, it can be asserted that four-fifths of Utah's population is actually living on less than two per cent of its land; furthermore, almost half this group is concentrated in three metropolitan areas: Provo, Ogden and Salt Lake City. All three lie within the Great Basin and enjoy an oasis-type environment: steppe with subhumid climate, and an abundant water supply from the nearby Wasatch Mountains. Water assuredly was the determinant in establishing the pattern of settlement, although as Stegner has observed the Mormon colony—unlike most other American frontiers—did not owe its existence to rivers. Water still dictates to a large extent the residential distributions we find today.

In their early time the Mormons were farmers rather than stockmen and put their land in crops rather than pasture. For the first half century of white occupation the most important industry in Utah was agriculture, but this picture has changed. While there is some acreage in wheat, sugar beets, alfalfa seed, potatoes and a number of fruits, only four per cent of the land is used for crop production. Hay, oats and barley are among the crops ranking highest in value but four-fifths of farm income derives from livestock: cattle, sheep and poultry (Roylance, 1965).

Many low-lying portions of the state are too salty for any kind of farming, even if irrigation water and suitable drainage could be provided. Some higher land beyond the reach of irrigation has been profitably managed by dry-farming it, a method that involves crop raising in alternate years, cultivating in fallow years, and conserving ground moisture with mulches, etc. Livestock is usually moved to the mountain slopes and high valleys in summer, with the desert rangeland serving in winter when snow is enough to satisfy the animals' water needs and not too deep to cover the browse or restrict movement. These ranges support large numbers of sheep as well as cattle (Martin and Corbin, 1936).

The extractive and processing industries have by far the widest economic impact, although the Federal government is today the largest employer in the state. The Department of Defense operates many installations and controls a few very large tracts such as the Wendover Bombing and Gunnery Range (ca. one million acres, currently inactive) and the Dugway Proving Grounds (larger than the state of Rhode Island); these lie in the western desert section. A considerable portion of the manufacturing business in Utah is defense-oriented.

Cultural activities, especially those fostered by the Mormon church, have achieved national distinction. Group efforts received the most encouragement, thus choral and orchestral music, drama and the dance all are favored; whereas the solo arts—painting and sculpture, writing, and single performance achievement in music and dancing—receive much less support, for the Church is a gregarious institution.

Three distinguished writers grew up in Utah and all fled the scene for what they believed to be more promising intellectual pastures. Each in his special way has depicted the western environment and background in history: Wallace Stegner, Dale L. Morgan and Bernard DeVoto all produced definitive works involving the Great Basin. DeVoto, who became a Harvard professor and historian of stature, was strongly critical of his early environment in Ogden but loved the West and was eloquent in support of conservation at a time when not many voices were speaking up for it; for such contributions he has been memorialized. Dale Morgan's monumental work entitled *The Great Salt Lake* is a panoramic portrait of the intermountain West with the lake as a focus and covers its history from early man (or what was then known about him) down to 1947, the date of publication. DeVoto died in 1955, Morgan in 1971, and Stegner remains among us, the most prolific of the trio and possessing high talent as a novelist.

Recreation, with the growth of affluence and leisure time, has assumed an ever-increasing importance in the economy. Thus far not much attenuated by the energy shortage, it exerts a powerful influence. Again we find the many interests and outlets of this field centered upon water and influenced by its distribution. Collected and stored water provides a playground for swimming, boating and fishing. As it falls in the form of snow it provides the basis for skiing and other winter sports. The hunter is concerned with springs and shores where his quarry tends to gather.[10] Gold-panners require streams; and the amateur archeologist is well aware of water as a center of attraction for prehistoric man, though none of it may remain at a once-inhabited site. Campers, hikers, botanists and bird-watchers all depend to some extent on water.

Great Salt Lake, unique in scenic quality, nevertheless has presented many challenging problems to the people of Utah. Being so broad and shallow, its fluctuations of both level and extent render the margins elusive. Its inevitable function as a drainage sump makes it the repository of much chemical jetsam from cities and fields, to an extent that has alarmed and disgusted the citizenry, who otherwise and rightly regard this body as a tremendous geographical asset. Here lies a knotty environmental problem.

Once the cynosure of visiting tourists and the setting of exotic water sports, the lake has languished in use as progressive drying moved it far from accustomed beaches and resort facilities. State Parks have been established at Willard Bay and the north end of Antelope Island but the goal of setting up a comprehensive lake park or reservation has not been achieved. Federal assistance has been sought and studies at that governmental level have been undertaken, yet no resolution of the problem has materialized. Resource management presents a very complicated and often controversial proposition owing to the multiplicity of functional entities overlapping and contending among the industrial, governmental and private sectors.

Early in 1959 Utah's Senator Moss asked the National Park Service to make a reconnaissance of the park potential and this was accomplished that summer. The study set forth a public interest, indicated some possibilities and defined many of the special problems. Admitting a substantial public concern and need, it also stated, "there is a lack of agreement as to how this should be accomplished

---

[10] Utah is crossed by several wildfowl flyways. These areas have been set aside for their protection: Bear River Migratory Bird Refuge west of Brigham City; Locomotive Springs National Wildlife Refuge at the northwest end of Great Salt Lake; Fish Springs National Wildlife Refuge at the south end of Great Salt Lake Desert; Clear Lake Migratory Wildfowl Refuge below Pavant Butte and not far from the site of the Gunnison Massacre. Near Indian Peak (9,784) in the Needles Range, a section of Pine Valley has been reserved as a game management area. Here a dry wash leads northward to the playa remaining from Lake Wah Wah.

and by what level of government . . . Today the lake is a 'dead sea' covering about 1,500 square miles (yet is) one of the outstanding physiographic features of the United States . . . Its level has dropped due to both dry weather and the diversion and impoundment of the waters that feed it. There is no co-ordinated plan for its development and utilization." There the matter rested.

A good many years have passed since this study was released but the situation remains uncertain. Resorts have come and gone during the century that has elapsed since the lake's historic high. Garfield Beach (which took its name from the steamer *General Garfield* then moored at hand), once most resplendent with its great pavilion and clean sandy shore, flourished from 1887 until 1904 when it burned. Saltair comprised an ornate Moorish dance hall with swimming pool 4,000 feet out in the lake, served by its own train. It lasted from 1893 until 1925 when it, too, was destroyed by fire. The building was promptly replaced, but Great Salt Lake began sharply declining, so that by 1934 Saltair was high and dry. Black Rock and Sunset Beaches came into being about this time but World War ii put a crimp in their activities and they are now defunct. Various yacht clubs and boat harbors have come and gone as enthusiasm for boating flared and waned. Sailing and rowing have enjoyed periods of high popularity but boats have always had to contend with serious problems like the heavy salt incrustation, the fickle winds and the shoal waters of this strange sea. Recently established facilities include Great Salt Lake Park (1969) and Silver Sand Beach, which has picnic and camping areas, a boat ramp and dock.

In the spring of 1974 a reversal of the drying trend became quite apparent when rising lake waters reached 4,201.4 feet above mean sea level on June 1. This was the highest in 45 years and had many repercussions. Caused primarily by climatic conditions, the rise of the lake resulted in damage to roadways and wildlife habitats through inundation, and in problems for the extractive industry because of dilution. But a revival of boating took place—more than 70 sailboats were counted at one time on the lake. The high water characterizes a 15 to 20 year elevation cycle expected to peak in the near future, after which a resumption of the general downtrend seems likely to set in.

Whatever the life expectancy of the human race may be, it seems most unlikely that our descendants (however remote) will see Lake Bonneville reconstituted, as it might be if in the progress of eternal time another Pluvial sequence should form. Relative to known geological ages, human existence has been only an episode—a few seconds at the end of the protracted evolutionary day. In contrast, the great swings of climatic alteration such as those that produced the ice ages and their intervening eras seem interminably prolonged.

Should such a pluvial stage materialize and these flats of northwestern Utah be overhwelmed again, we can forecast accurately the degree of flooding. If the Stansbury terrace were reached the sites of the principal cities and all the valley farmlands along the Jordan, Weber and Bear Rivers would be covered. At the Provo level almost all the presently inhabited land in the Utah portion of the Great Basin would become inundated. Otherwise, it might be observed that elsewhere in this province the lands that would be covered are relatively unoccupied and a full resurgence of lakes would affect only a few small towns such as Fallon, Lovelock, Lone Pine, Burns, etc. Many miles of railroads and highways would indeed be drowned but generally the lake basins other than Bonneville's are far from any centers of human activity. In any event there would be plenty of warning.

We might also inquire: what chance is there that Great Salt Lake, the remnant we know today, might dry up altogether? Based on known factors we can say that this is very improbable. Another Altithermal age would have to set in before it could happen; nor would Pyramid Lake—with its depth of 330 feet in contrast to Great Salt Lake's 30-foot maximum—be in danger of disappearing. There will be dry cycles and wet ones, varying widely in degree and duration, if the past is any indication of the future. Meanwhile, we continue to scrutinize the record, and in many disciplines we are finding out more and more of what the Great Basin was really like very long ago. How it differed in early times from today and from other provinces then and now are matters of increasing interest and study. We may worry too about its present condition and how human occupation has altered it, whether and how we can preserve its rare and elusive qualities in the face of threatening influences. We have here a debt and a duty to posterity.

THE NEW YORKER

SPECIAL CHRISTMAS RATES

First $32 ONLY $20 each additional
subscription one-year gift

Please send one year (52 issues) of THE NEW YORKER

TO
Gift Recipient's Name _____ (Please print)

MY NAME _____ (Please print)

Address _____ Apr. #   Address _____ Apr. #

City _____   City _____

State _____ Zip _____   State _____ Zip _____

Gift card to read "From _____ "

SPECIALLY DESIGNED GIFT CARDS
WILL BE SENT IN YOUR NAME.

To order more gifts, attach a separate sheet and mail in an envelope.

Additional postage: Canada $18 each subscription, other foreign
$24. (Please remit in U.S. funds)

☐ Enter or extend my own subscription
☐ Payment enclosed   ☐ Bill me later.
Charge my ☐ MasterCard ☐ Visa ☐ American Express

Account No. _____ Expire Date _____

Signature _____

4XRG7

CHAPTER XV

Some Conclusions

We have given an account here of the desert waters from the time they were plentiful everywhere in the Great Basin down through stages of dryness far more pronounced than what we now observe, through their first accommodation to the human race, and up to the present state of scarcity with intensive utilization. We have shown how they changed the landscapes, influenced the early culture and the patterns of settlement, and the manner in which they support the activities and social distribution today. It seems an irony of fate that when these waters were most abundant the human needs were minimal or non-existent, that now when these needs are acute and rapidly growing critical the resource is much attenuated.

The Great Basin and Alaska are the last sparsely inhabited parts of the United States into which any large migration can be expected normally to move. The pressures mount everywhere else, and the movement is taking place. Census figures for all of the eleven western states have risen sharply since the culmination of World War II and show that, for instance, Nevada's population has quadrupled in 25 years and its density has increased from about one person per square mile to almost five. Utah's growth, though not as spectacular, has been strong and the density for the state as a whole is now about 12 per square mile. The desert areas of Oregon and California within the Basin's boundary are still very thinly settled, as we have noted, yet undeniably they too have shared in the expansion.

Until recently most of this boom has occurred in urban areas, nearly all of which lie along the fringes of the province. All the potential ranchland has long been developed, and as farming methods improved fewer employees were required; so in time the rural areas could no longer support the people they produced. Gravitation to the cities followed. But population movements sometimes undergo quick change, and in the Great Basin such changes have come rapidly. A reversal of the nationwide surge to the cities seems to be taking place here, not just a flight to the suburbs but a spreading escape to the desert with its clean air and elbow room. Land developers have lately been very active, but in contrast to the wild schemes of the past, like the one that produced Metropolis, modern projects are likely to be based on sophisticated studies and elaborate planning.

Not far from the site of Metropolis, spreading southeast from the vicinity of Elko to the foothills of the Ruby Mountains, the Spring Creek "planned city" has been laid out. It involves over 20,000 acres of former rangeland which in 1971 was dedicated to the heterogenesis of a residential community. This most ambitious promotion, costing many millions, is by no measurement unique in either size or complexity and will be followed as it has been preceded by similar enterprises in these western states. The ultimate success of ventures such as this one will depend on the availability of land, energy and water in sufficient quantities and suitable quality—for these are critical.

In this relatively empty region a dearth of land might seem to be paradoxical, yet the scarcity exists. Seven-eighths of Nevada and about three-fourths of Utah lie in Federal or Indian ownership (title to Indian lands usually rests with the resident tribe). So it is safe to say that less than 20 per cent of the Great Basin is privately owned. Government land may be leased, harvested for timber, grazed under permit, prospected, located and mined; its use depends somewhat on the agency controlling it. But entry under the homestead laws or Desert Land Act is now virtually impossible and the public sale of tracts, subject to many obstacles, has been relatively limited. It is not altogether clear in what ways the region might absorb a massive influx other than by settlement on privately owned land (including that belonging to railroads, which is still fairly substantial[1]).

Providing energy in sufficient quantity conveniently may also become a problem in some isolated regions. At the present time there are transmission lines and interties across much of the Basin and pipelines carrying natural gas connect with a number of cities, but the growing national shortage of all forms of energy, especially natural gas, may eventually deprive areas like this one. Bottled gas is widely used and petroleum products are imported by rail,

---

[1] In the Humboldt River basin ownership of private land amounts to 3,620,000 acres, of which the Southern Pacific Land Co. has title to somewhat more than one-fifth (752,000). The original Federal land grants to the Central Pacific Railroad (1866 et seq.) totalled 5,086,603 acres (Ohrenschall, 1969).

truck or pipeline, but costs are high in the more remote sections and could become prohibitive for even light industry away from the main centers. The possibilities in geothermal development seem good, and exploration proceeds, for there are many indications of this energy source throughout the Basin. Energy needs will expand along with population and it remains to be seen how accurate the projections of future demand turn out to be.

The focus of this inquiry is water: the physical basis of all life processes. It is essential to the welfare and economy of a people, wherever they may live and however concentrated. One may ask in what ways new colonists of the Great Basin might be supplied. It is obvious that supplementary water will have to be developed in substantial quantities, either on site or through importation. Questions arise: if on site, how? and if imported, whence? Many possibilities have been deeply explored, pondered, advanced, argued and in some cases exploited. It is consistent with our interest to examine them here.

It would seem that existing supplies were utilized to the nth degree already, yet there are many ways in which these could be handled more efficiently. Conjunctive uses could be instituted to economize on water, such as the employment of treated sewage effluent in condenser cooling; two power stations, the Clark and Sunrise steam plants near Las Vegas, are already doing this. With water loss to evaporation running around 85 per cent in cooling tower operation and waste fluids being unacceptable for most other purposes, this is an excellent way to save.[2] The Fort Churchill generating station in Mason Valley has cooling ponds that extend the adjacent wildlife management area; migrating ducks and geese can alight upon the warm surface when other resting places are frozen. Such ponds are important, also, in preventing thermal pollution of streams and can serve as sports fisheries as well as waterfowl refuges.

Heavy losses accompanying agricultural use of water due to evaporation, transpiration and seepage indicate need for better controls, and extensive research has been devoted to finding new ways of cutting such waste. Many agents have been tested and

---

[2] Evaporative type cooling systems dissipate approximately 8 million gallons for every 10 kwh of electricity produced. At full load the Sierra Pacific Power Co.'s Fort Churchill station will evaporate 3,000 gallons a minute, a very large consumption. For the two steam stations in their system, Tracy and Fort Churchill, the 1971 power output has been estimated at 1.2 million kwh and a consequent loss to evaporation can therefore be assumed of 3,655 acre feet (data supplied by W. D. Montgomery, 25th Annual Nev. Water Conf., 1971).

proved as effective anti-evaporants and sealants. Some progress has been achieved with substances that spread on stored water surfaces to provide a "skin" through which losses to the atmosphere would be minimized. Bentonite, sodium clays and polymer chemicals are already being used to line canals, ditches and pond bottoms; asphalt-fibre glass, poly-vinyl, butyl-rubber and cement are more durable (and also more expensive) materials. Again, the difficulties are largely economic. Wild vegetation along streams and canals such as brush and thirsty cottonwoods that rob these conduits, transpiring their water content to the air, could be reduced or eliminated. Holding facilities at higher elevations where evaporation rates are lower due to cloudier and cooler conditions are costly but effective devices.

On-site development might also rely upon groundwater, for there are many aquifers distributed throughout the Great Basin containing very large (though certainly not unlimited) amounts of water. Some estimates of the total availables within reach of pumping in Nevada alone run to 250 million acre feet; a rule of thumb used in estimating these capacities is that, for the state as a whole, there are 2.5 million acre feet for every vertical foot of saturated soil or permeable rock. These aquifers, being almost loss-proof, are ideal containers—there is no evaporation from them and in most cases little or no subsurface outflow. Where basin interchanges do occur they are very gradual. These underground waters could be mined on a temporary basis to a heavy extent if full replenishment were assured, such as a firm prospect of massive water imports. At present the annual recharge is relatively small and large-scale pumping tends to lower water tables, rob the prevailing surface flows and impair existing water rights. This source has palpable economic as well as legal limitations, moreover.

Weather modification must still be regarded as a science in its infancy. Today's techniques are largely experimental and results are spotty. Cloud seeding with silver iodide crystals scattered from airplanes or released from generators on the ground have in some instances produced quite evident increases in precipitation but many unanswered questions remain. There are legal and political obstacles as yet not fully explored—perhaps not even identified—and in any case situations where these methods might be applied with some promise are not common. Interference with rainfall patterns could constitute a basis for court action, especially if it were shown that areas down-wind from cloud seeding activity had received diminished rainfall over several seasons or if flooding should follow such efforts.[3]

The field of water importation is a very broad one and the possibilities are enormous. So are the problems. When nuclear energy was first applied to power production in the mid-century it appeared that this might prove to be a panacea with special application to water problems: sea water would be distilled and pumped to desert areas at moderate cost from an infinite supply. But the economic hurdles involved are not easily jumped, and the desert is still waiting.

We might first consider these facts: some water is already being imported (from the Colorado River basin to the Imperial Valley) and, rather outrageously, water is being *exported* from this desiccated province in very large quantities (almost the entire Owens River increment passing to Los Angeles). A beginning might be made by way of producing new sources for southern California independent of the Great Basin's natural supply, thus releasing the discharge of the southern Sierra's eastern slope for use in the redevelopment of Owens Valley. Here would be a logical place to start the nuclear-powered process of converting and pumping sea water. We shall have something to say about desalting further along in this chapter.

It is appropriate to ask where large-scale imports to the Great Basin might come from. Three different sources immediately suggest themselves: the wasting northern rivers, the ocean, and the atmosphere. Consideration of the Colorado River and any streams in California as sources may be omitted since they are put to use elsewhere; but other rivers are not, and to varying extent their substance is dissipated in the Pacific Ocean.

The northern rivers include the Columbia-Snake system, the several Canadian networks, and the Yukon-Tanana drainage. Clearly the problems of utilizing the Columbia-Snake are large but they are dwarfed by those that surround the importation of Canadian and Alaskan water. These are not just of a technical or economic nature but also involve deep-seated parochial atttitudes and political taboos. Reluctance to share a constantly renewing resource for

---

[3] One form of weather modification seldom discussed, and perhaps no more than a theory, is "natural recycling." The concept is one of greater precipitation resulting from greater use: evaporated and transpired water, accumulating in the atmosphere and condensing, may bring increased rainfall. Many authorities discount this recycling potential, but possibilities seem more promising in the Great Basin than elsewhere for testing such a process, and additional studies would seem to be warranted (Laycock, 1970).

which there is no full or compelling present need may seem indefensible, yet it exists and would have to be overcome, and the only way we might hope to accomplish this would be by purchase. Were the price sufficiently attractive, a sale might reasonably follow.

A number of major diversion schemes have been seriously proposed, including the one known as the North American Water and Power Alliance, referred to in Chapter vi, the most publicized and certainly the most grandiose. It would transfer 100 million acre feet a year all the way from Alaska and northwestern Canada to the drier parts of Canada, the United States and Mexico. Other proposals involve tapping the Mackenzie, Liard, Peace and Athabaska Rivers. Laycock (1970) has made the flat statement that "very few professional water resource people in the United States or Canada believe any of the spectacular, large-scale diversion schemes are or will soon be feasible, even if technical, legal, administrative and other problems can be resolved." He said further that there have been no international agreements or even official discussions concerning such water transfers and he thinks any need for them would be at least 50 years hence. Laycock offers some interesting data: British Columbia alone has as large a streamflow as the western two-thirds of the United States, and export of a small part of it would provide very large long-term revenues without impairing any environments. Also, if Canada were to make two per cent of its supply available for sale, that would amount to four times the entire flow of the Colorado River. In discussion of unit costs he thought a figure of $40 per acre foot might be realistic. Carrying charges would be something else again.

One feature that might make the schemes more palatable to Canadians and at the same time lower costs is dual use of pipelines carrying water. Goods might be transported in solution or suspension, or perhaps in plastic pellets; both the products and the water would be sold, and at least the carrying charges would be defrayed. Agricultural, forest and mineral products handled in this way would greatly benefit the Canadian economy.

Short-range imports from the north seem more likely even though interstate rivalries and dog-in-the-manger attitudes will persist. It could be (and surely will be) argued that all the waters over the Columbia-Snake drainage are vital to the welfare of its originating states: Wyoming, Idaho, Washington and Oregon. Here again, though, some purchasing agreements might be arranged and were southern California or Arizona to become a party to them the water might well be routed through the Great Basin where rights of way would be easier to obtain; some small tribute in acre feet could then be exacted as a transit fee. Local supplies would be augmented in this way and groundwater recharged. The ideal solution would be an integrated regional grid similar to those used for sharing electrical energy. Bringing about any of these enterprises might require more political muscle than the Great Basin's voters would alone possess, for their cities and industries are relatively small and scattered; their best hopes would lie in forming limited partnerships with more powerful entities.

Now a look at the ocean: if an unlimited resource exists anywhere on earth it must lie here. Mankind should have the intelligence to convert this plenitude, to make it potable for living forms and industry and bring it to points of use, and to do all this economically. A great deal of thought has gone toward solving the problems of desalinization. Currently, four processes that work have been devised. The oldest is distillation—boiling the water and then condensing the steam—which produces a very high purity product. Of the capacity now operating, 90 per cent or more involves this method. Another is freezing, which is practical only for small-scale purification. Electro-dialysis uses an ion selective membrane influenced by an electric field. And finally, in reverse osmosis, the mineralized water is forced through a membrane.

There have been important advances in the technology of desalinization since 1952 when a research program at the Federal level was instituted, and the Office of Saline Water, created that year, has meanwhile spent about $200 million. All processes involve serious problems such as the difficulty of brine effluent disposal, finding skilled operators, obtaining electric power in remote locations, and the basic expense underlying any of these processes (O.S.W. Report, 1970).

Sen. Alan Bible of Nevada shed some light on this last element when he testified before the Interior Committee of the U.S. Senate in April 1971. He stated that the cost of converting sea water had been reduced from $4 a thousand gallons in 1952 to 65¢, as of then, and that there was real hope of a further reduction to 50¢ "in the relatively near future." He described the objective as "production on a large enough scale and at low enough cost so that our cities could be supplied and farmlands irrigated." The target seems remote: a single acre foot of water is the equivalent of 325,900 gallons and Nevada agriculture alone requires 1,550,000 acre feet per year (Raymond M. Pallesen, USDA, personal contact). At 50¢ a thousand gallons for desalted ocean water it would cost more than $250 million annually, plus pipeline and pumping expense, to irrigate Nevada's croplands in this manner. Pending some technological breakthrough the prospect seems unattainable.

So much for the northern rivers and the sea as points of origin for water imports to the Great Basin. There remains the atmosphere. We have discussed weather modification as an on-site process, yet in reality it is a form of water importation. Air masses pass over all regions of the world continually and these masses may be saturated or almost destitute of water. We see condensations of airborne water in the forms of clouds yet water vapor itself is invisible until condensed and is everpresent to some degree around us. Dr. Frits Went has pointed out that sagebrush and extreme desert plants can sharply cut their water loss by transpiration and their low water requirements under drought conditions can be met by internal dew formed down in the soil. He adds that the search goes on for plants which can utilize water vapor directly from the air, that this is almost inexhaustible (Proceedings, 24th Annual Nev. Water Conf., 1970), and we are still hopeful of achievement along this line. Apart from inducing precipitation, if we could extract water from the atmosphere directly and economically we would acquire a source of supply to answer every human need.

Municipal and industrial requirements vary considerably throughout the United States. The rate of consumption in some eastern cities runs as low as 150 gallons per person per day but rises to over 750 gallons in some parts of the arid West, at least in the hot summer months. Thus far, we have discussed supply options but we might now examine demand options too, for the way to make do with what we have is to curtail the drawdown. For instance, in the larger cities of Nevada water meters have been prohibited by a statute forbidding the use of "any measuring device." The intent when this legislation was enacted was to encourage water use, especially for trees, shrubs, lawns and gardens in order that the cities might be made more attractive. The results, however, have entailed considerable wasting even though some of the water inevitably spilling in the streets returns in due course to the river system. In times of drought only voluntary restraint is possible and heavy burdens are placed on the distributive agencies. Pumping from wells must be instituted, expenses rise, industry is deprived and water pressure drops everywhere.

Water quality is also a variable attribute. Time was when the natural source proved adequate to serve the small American city or town; simple filters and settling ponds were about all that was really needed. Then protective treatments came into play as various sorts of pollution, actual or threatened, grew. Today water treatment, to make it safe and palatable, can include not only settling and filtration but disinfection through the use of chlorine, aeration (spraying) to remove odors and CO_2, addition of copper sulphate to inhibit algae formation, fluoridation, and other chemical additives to remove salts. Fluoridation, a most divisive political issue, has been widely advocated as beneficial for the teeth of children but has been sparingly installed. Four main characteristics of water that can be measured by means of sophisticated electronic devices are conductivity, pH, dissolved oxygen and oxygen reduction potential. These indicators taken together furnish a reliable pollution index and they can be easily monitored and continuously recorded. Lately, preoccupation with environmental conditions has involved wide public interest and people have become concerned for the state of the human habitat, but there is nothing very new in the pollution threat since it has always been with us to a degree. Presumably early man, at some stage or other, realized he shouldn't wash his feet in his drinking water.

We have here a fragile environment served by a water supply we are outgrowing and moreover are finding vulnerable to many kinds of damage through misuse. The various ecological, industrial and recreational resources of the desert lands are in real and immediate danger from speculative mining, off-road vehicles, substandard construction and widespread littering. Many sections are pockmarked by prospectors' test pits that have no serious purpose, crisscrossed by highways, roads and trails not dictated by convenience or necessity, infested with shanties and disfigured by trash, from a scattering of beer cans or candy wrappers to junk car graveyards and full-scale public dumping. Atmospheric pollution and indiscriminate noise-making lead further to environmental destruction. Now legislation is pending in Congress which would designate National Desert Conservation Areas and provide funds for maintaining and protecting them.

The massive invasions of off-road machines capable of traveling almost anywhere are especially alarming. One annual event that has grown like a carcinoma involves thousands of motorcycles in point-to-point racing that has destroyed great stretches of desert. Hill climbing competitions for cycles and dune buggies should be confined to special locations along with cross-country and snowmobile racing. Sand boats, strange vehicles with sails instead of

engines, now in unrestricted use should be limited; and the prohibi-
tions applying to four-wheel drive vehicles which the U.S. Forest
Service enforces should be extended to cover the desert regions
under B.L.M. jurisdiction.

On the positive side, appropriate areas must be dedicated for
special uses: riding trails and parks where the ORV's would operate
year-round or share seasonally with snowmobiles. The increasing
designation of bicycle paths, though by no means as common
here as in most European countries, seems a portent and a
good one. The B.L.M. has set up an Off-road Vehicle Advisory
Committee to study the situation and make recommendations aimed
at reducing the impact of these exotic conveyances upon the vulnerable desert ambience.[4]

There are no national parks in the Great Basin (as of 1975) and
no prospect of establishing any seems clear. Two large national
monuments (Joshua Tree and Death Valley) and three smaller ones
(Cedar Breaks, Lehman Caves and Timpanogos Cave) are managed
by the N.P.S., who also maintain the Golden Spike National Historic
Site. Seven national parks lie contiguous to or just outside the Great
Basin boundary but none is within it, nor is any national recreation
area. State parks are few and far between, practically nonexistent
in the Basin's desert reaches except for some roadside rest areas
on major highways.

Population control may be the only answer to the challenging
need for preservation of the desert. The rate of increase here seems
to be dropping along with a somewhat lower birth rate but those
who already inhabit this region, growing in affluence, leisure time
and restlessness, constitute a formidable threat. For they are not
wholly wise or well-behaved, and the desert—once a forbidding and
unfamiliar territory—has become a most enticing arena in which
to pursue a variety of interests. Its effect on the individual is of
course entirely subjective, and it is only a wasteland if the beholder
feels repelled. Conan Doyle, in his first work of fiction (A Study
in Scarlet) called it "arid and repulsive . . . a region of desolation
and silence" but that was a long time ago and written for a very

---

[4] We tend to think of "the desert" in terms of great heat as well as dryness, but there
are very cold deserts, too. Antarctica, for instance, is undoubtedly the coldest, bleakest
area on earth and in every essential represents a desert, which by definition is simply a
region rendered barren by environmental extremes, especially by low rainfall. There are
vast expanses of tundra that qualify as such. We think of the Sahara, which is the largest
hot desert, as typical; in its class are also: the desert of central and western Australia,
2nd largest; the Gobi, which is the highest; and the Kalahari of southern Africa. There
is much desert in western South America, too, and the only continent without a true desert
is Europe.

distant audience. Observers today are more sophisticated and readers more discerning and knowledgeable. Gone is the cartoonist's cliche with its property saguaro, buffalo skull and mirage (though careless people still die of thirst or sunstroke in sandy places).

Joseph Wood Krutch, a scholarly and sensitive aficionado, made the following evaluation in his book, *The Voice of the Desert* (1954):

> In desert country everything from the color of a mouse or the shape of a leaf up to the largest features of the mountains themselves is more likely than not to have the same explanation: dryness. So far as living things go, all this adds up to what even an ecologist may so far forget himself as to call "an unfavorable environment." But like all such pronouncements this one doesn't mean much unless we ask "unfavorable for what and for whom?" For many plants, for many animals, and for some men it is very favorable indeed.

It seems probable that no one can be indifferent to the desert, for either they are enamored of it or they hate it. Even those who have the condition thrust upon them willy-nilly must come to an armed truce or be moved to an abiding love. For there is something absolute about the uncluttered space, the subtle colors, the truly deep and latent power of a vast and visible landscape. Should this macrocosm seem overwhelming—as indeed it does to some—there are always the miniatures at hand, the small living things to contemplate with their signs upon the carpet of sand, the minerals identifying a single rock, or the scent and habit of one persisting desert plant. For these forms the warm days and chilling nights are exactly what Nature has ordered and even man, when he is willing to adjust, can make this habitat his familiar home. Therein lies the opportunity for a most beguiling experience. For some it can be a complete fulfilment.

Energy Sources

The sun is considered the source of all energy, kinetic and potential, on and within the earth. In modern usage these forms are referred to as current and stored energy. Solar radiation, water power, storms and tides are examples of current energy; whereas the earth's contained heat, its fossil fuels—coal, petroleum, natural gas—and radioactive substances are stored forms. We have exploited the fossil fuels thoroughly but they are non-renewable and, at least oil and gas, will soon be exhausted.[1]

One educated estimate of the situation has been given by Lawrence Howles, senior projects engineer at British Nuclear Design & Construction, Ltd., writing in *New Scientist* (August 5, 1971). He asserts that between now and the year 2000 mankind will burn two-thirds of the earth's oil reserves and over one-fourth of its natural gas. We will hardly touch the great stocks of coal, he says, and the high cost of mining and transporting it will lead many countries to dependence upon thorium, uranium and its by-product, plutonium. He presents a diagram giving predicted world energy consumption, with oil, gas and nuclear sources rising in popularity while coal and hydro (not a large factor) are shown remaining steady. Nuclear power, now furnishing about 1 per cent of the world's needs, will rise to 24 per cent by 2000 A.D., he prophesies.

Winds, tides and solar radiation will continue as energy resources, wholly renewable, essentially forever. Potential utilization of the first two seems very limited, however, being subject to great technical difficulty: neither winds nor tides appear to be very promising availables for meeting any significant portion of the constantly multiplying demand. But solar heat seems the brightest long-range prospect in the frantic search for new and universal sources of energy. A huge amount reaches the earth's atmosphere: two watts per square centimeter per second! This is enough in 15 minutes to have provided for all the 1970 needs of the entire human race.[2] Much of it is dissipated or reflected and never penetrates to the surface of the earth; but an ample amount does and we may suppose that a technology will in the course of time be developed to convert it in substantial quantity. The oceans store an immense amount of solar heat and as a result of natural circulation fairly steep thermal gradients exist in many areas; a

---

[1] M. King Hubbert, "Energy Resources of the Earth," in *Scientific American*, Vol. 224, no. 3, Sept. 1971. An issue devoted entirely to "Energy and Power," with eleven authoritative articles.

[2] Holdren and Herrera, 1971.

most convenient one lies in the Gulf Stream off the coast of Florida. But power derived from temperature differences found in the sea appears at this stage to be somewhat utopian in concept, and the development of more practical techniques to utilize solar energy may be anticipated. It has been said, in illustration of the enormous power reaching the earth from the sun, that a single well-developed hurricane will expend as much energy as 1,000 Hiroshima-type atom bombs.

The Great Basin is assuredly among the most favorable areas where conversion of solar energy might be developed, with its relative freedom from cloud cover for long periods at a time, especially in its southern regions and during the summertime when insolation is strong and prolonged. Observations taken in southern Nevada over a 17-year period show an average of 210 clear days per year, with a percentage of possible sunshine during the months of May through October of almost 90 per cent.[3] The average given for the full year is 83 per cent, indicating great promise for both research and actual conversion.

The main thrust of the search for more energy has been directed toward development of coal, shale oil and tar sands previously considered out of economic reach or off-limits due to environmental hazard. Inflation in the price of the product has changed the picture, however, and costs of production including extras for environmental protection are now more in line with projected returns.

In the Great Basin the hunting continues for oil, natural gas, coal, uranium and geothermal heat, though for some of these the main prospects seem to lie outside. Tar sands, for instance, are mostly in Canada and the accessible oil shale appears confined to the Utah-Colorado plateau. The great coal deposits are also exterior to the Basin, as are most known occurrences of uranium. But drilling for oil and gas continues actively, and interest in geothermal heat is widespread—the u.s.g.s. lists about 400 Great Basin locations.[4]

Thermonuclear power production is based on heat resulting from controlled reaction in fissionable materials—heavy elements such as uranium and plutonium; the heat is converted to electricity. But there are great hazards inherent in this process and the adequacy of protective measures now being used has been called into question. Among them are the possibility of rupture and resulting cataclysm due to earthquake or nuclear accident and exposure of the dangerous but extremely valuable elements to theft and international blackmail. These hazards are not just science fiction.

Meanwhile research continues under forced draft to develop greater efficiencies and better processes: fuel cells, solar cells, fast-breeder reactors, plasma containment and nuclear fusion. The latter has been called by some visionaries the hope of the distant future[5] though it has serious

[3] U.S. Weather Bureau, *Climatology of the United States*, No. 62–42, 1960.
[4] Waring, 1965.
[5] Richard Wilson, "Nuclear Fusion: Our Best Energy Bet for the Future?" in *Harvard Magazine*, Vol. 76, no. 3, Nov. 1973.

technical problems and the best estimates indicate that fusion stations will certainly not be supplying any large portion of our energy needs before the year 2050. In fusion, two light elements are joined; deuterium and tritium are the ones most central to current research. Deuterium is plentiful in the ocean but tritium is very rare in nature. However, it can be obtained by bombardment of lithium, and here the deposits of the Great Basin come into play (Chapter XII, this text). The mining at Silverpeak, Nevada, may one day assume a vital importance in the energy picture.

Energy production and consumption alternatives need to be spelled out within the framework of a National Energy Policy, something we have yet to develop fully for the United States. Besides stimulating research and offering production incentives the government must further regulate or curb the appetites of both the industrial and domestic sectors. Already this country, with 6 per cent of the world's population, uses 35 per cent of its energy. Power rationing seems inevitable, bringing limitations on such luxuries as labor-saving refinements in factory and home, on elaborate and non-essential appliances, and on the unbridled independence of the individual to move at will, and extravagantly, in power-wasting vehicles. Some day the nature of our economy may become based on truly economical values.

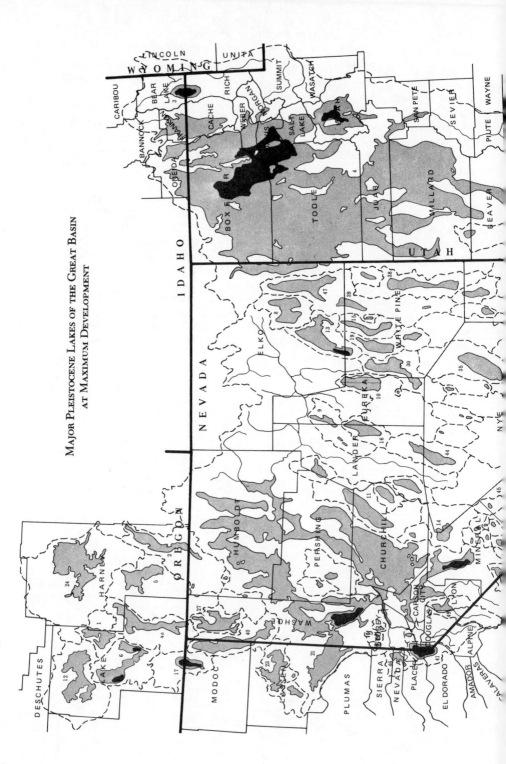

Major Pleistocene Lakes of the Great Basin at Maximum Development

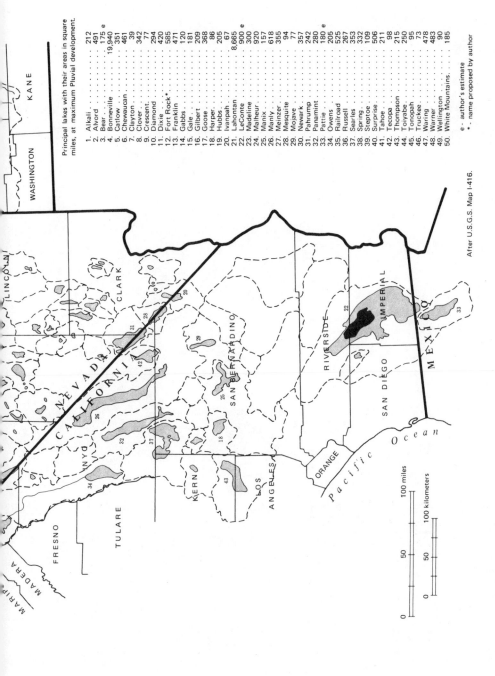

Principal lakes with their areas in square miles, at maximum Pluvial development.

1.	Alkali	212
2.	Alvord	491
3.	Bear	175 e
4.	Bonneville	19,940
5.	Catlow	351
6.	Chewaucan	461
7.	Clayton	39
8.	Clover	342
9.	Crescent	77
10.	Diamond	294
11.	Dixie	420
12.	Fort Rock*	585
13.	Franklin	471
14.	Gabbs	120
15.	Gale	181
16.	Gilbert	209
17.	Goose	368
18.	Harper	86
19.	Hubbs	205
20.	Ivanpah	67
21.	Lahontan	8,665
22.	LeConte	900 e
23.	Madeline	300
24.	Malheur	920
25.	Manix	157
26.	Manly	618
27.	Meinzer	355
28.	Mesquite	94
29.	Mojave	77
30.	Newark	357
31.	Pahrump	242
32.	Panamint	280
33.	Pattie	180 e
34.	Owens	205
35.	Railroad	525
36.	Russell	267
37.	Searles	353
38.	Spring	332
39.	Steptoe	109
40.	Surprise	506
41.	Tahoe	211
42.	Tecopa	98
43.	Thompson	215
44.	Toiyabe	250
45.	Tonopah	95
46.	Truckee	73
47.	Waring	478
48.	Warner	483
49.	Wellington	90
50.	White Mountains	185

e - author's estimate
* - name proposed by author

After U.S.G.S. Map I-416.

100 miles

100 kilometers

sln

Glossary

Aggradation—Modification of the earth's surface in the direction of uniformity of grade or slope, by deposition, as in a river bed.

Alluvium—Sand, gravel or soil deposited by running water on flood plains of valley floors.

Altithermal—A period when it was much warmer than now: ca. 7000-4500 BP.

Anathermal—The period preceding the Altithermal: Early Holocene to ca. 7000 BP.

Aquifer—A water-bearing rock formation, or group of formations.

Artifact—Any object made by human hands.

Assemblage—A cluster of associated physical objects.

Atlatl—A board or stick 20 to 24 inches long used in throwing a dart or lance.

Bajada—(Spanish) A descent or slope.

Basketry Terms—(see: coiling, twilling, twining, wicker).

Bolson—An undrained basin (from Spanish bolsa, a purse).

Bone Tube—A short, hollow bone supposedly used by shamans in curing ceremonies.

Burin—A flake or blade with chisel edge or point used in sculpturing or engraving.

Carbon dating—Dating an object by analyzing its radioactive carbon content.

Charmstone—An object believed by the owner to bring good luck.

Coiling—A pottery- or basket-making technique using a spirally coiled foundation, smoothed inside and out (pottery) or sewn and looped with an overcast stitch (basketry).

Complex—A cluster of highly similar specimens from a small area.

Coprolite—Fecal material of animal or human origin.

Culture—A recurrent assemblage of artifact types found over a wide region, implying the existence of a widespread lifeway; a group of specific named units about whose time and space existence definite data exist; a pattern of habits, skills, notions and tastes of a people (see: stage, horizon).

Dendrochronology—Dating an object by means of tree rings.

Diastrophic—Pertaining to processes by which the earth's crust is deformed, producing continents, oceans, basins, mountains, etc. (see also: orogenic, tectonic).

Forb—Any herbaceous plant other than a grass, especially one growing in a field or meadow.

Fossil—Any evidence of former life.

Geosol—A stratigraphic unit of distinctive material, laterally traceable.

Glacioeustacy—Changes in sea level due to storage or release of water on land as snow and glacier ice.

Graben—A block of terrain that has dropped down between two faults.

Halophyte—A salt-loving plant.

High Plains—The belt along the eastern Rocky Mountain base lying in Wyoming, Colorado and New Mexico.

Holocene—The present epoch, about 10,000 years old.

Horizon—A level, either in a site, or of a cultural development.

In situ—Refers to an artifact found in its original, undisturbed position.

Interstadial—Long intervals of desiccation occurring between Pluvial episodes.

Isobar—A line drawn on a map connecting points of equal barometric pressure.

Isohyet—A line drawn on a map connecting points receiving equal rainfall.

Isotherm—A line drawn on a map connecting points having identical temperature.

Mano—A handstone used for grinding, moved only back and forth on a *metate*.

Marl—A mixture of clays, carbonates of calcium and magnesium, and remnants of shells, forming a loam useful as a fertilizer.

Medithermal—The period following the Altithermal: ca. 4500 BP to the present.

Metate—The lower part of a stone grinding mill used for corn or other grain.

Midden—Accumulated refuse near a dwelling or inhabited site.

Milling stone—The lower part of a grinding mill used for seeds or nuts.

Moraine—Material eroded and deposited by glacial action.

Nothrotherium—The Shasta ground sloth found in Gypsum Cave.

Numic—A linguistic definition, specifically a northern branch of the Uto-Aztecan, prevalent throughout most of the Great Basin.

Olivella—A marine univalve; its shell was used for money and ornaments.

Orogenic—Pertaining to the process of mountain-building, especially by folding of the earth's crust.

pH—(potential of Hydrogen) A measure of the acidity or alkalinity of a solution, varying from 1 (extremely acid) to 14 (extremely alkaline).

Paleopedology—The study of fossil soils.

Partida—(Spanish) A party of soldiers.

Pedology—The scientific study of soils, their origins, characteristics and uses.

Petroglyph—A design incised on a rock or a cliff.

Phreatophyte—(Greek: *phreear*, a well) A well plant that habitually obtains its water supply from the zone of saturation (O. E. Meinzer).

Pictograph—A colored drawing or painting on a rock or cliff.

Playa—An arid basin sometimes covered with shallow water.

Pleistocene—The Ice Age, immediately preceding the Holocene; of about two million years' duration; derived from the Greek *pleistos* (most) and *kainos* (recent).

Pliocene—The epoch immediately preceding the Pleistocene; of about ten million years' duration.

Pluvial—The two or more Wisconsin stages, of late Pleistocene age, when the western basins were filled with lakes. *Early Pluvial:* periods of high humidity so remote as to have left no clear-cut shore features. *Postpluvial:* the period of desiccation following the last high lake stage.

Provenience—The position of an artifact in relation to its surrounding material.

Quaternary—The last million years or so of earth history; it includes the Pleistocene and the Holocene epochs.

Quid—A piece of vegetal matter that was chewed and then spat out.

Shaman—A medicine man, one who used supernatural powers to cure or to interpret, or (rarely) to inflict harm.

Sherd—A broken piece of pottery.

Site—A location showing signs of human occupancy.

Stage—A level in the sequence or ranking of cultures; it lacks the time-space connotation.

Tectonic—Pertaining to or designating structures resulting from deformation of the earth's crust, especially faulting.

Tephra—Volcanic material: ash-fall.

Terrace—An ancient shoreline, usually of a lake.

Tradition—The cultural continuity of a trait.

Trait—A diagnostic artifact or characteristic element of a culture.

Transfer—The export of water from one drainage basin to another by natural process or artificial means.

Twilling—A weaving technique in which each row is offset one strand, resembling steps or stairs.

Twining—A weaving technique with alternating strands; a strong, smooth weave.

Uto-Aztecan—A large family of languages and dialects, prevalent over a wide area of North and Central America.

Varve—A regular, annual layer of silt or clay deposited in a glacier-fed lake within one year's time.

Wicker—A type of weaving, the most elementary of the common techniques.

Xerophyte—(Greek: *xeros,* dry) A plant with spreading roots to catch surface moisture.

Zone—An area characterized by distinct physical conditions and populated by communities of specific organisms.

Bibliography

MAPS

FETH, J. H.   A new map of western coterminous United States showing the maximum known or inferred extent of Pleistocene lakes. *U.S.G.S. Professional Paper* 424-B, Art. 47.   1961.

GREER, DEON C.   Great Salt Lake, Utah: Map Supplement No. 14. *Annals of Assn. of Amer. Geographers*, Mar. 1971.

JONES, DAVID T. Lake Bonneville Maps. Ann Arbor, Mich: Edwards Bros., 1940.

MEINZER, OSCAR E.   Map of the Pleistocene Lakes of the Basin and Range Province and its Significance. *Geol. Soc. of Amer. Bulletin*, Vol. 33, no. 9, pp. 541–552.   1922.

NEVADA BUREAU OF MINES.   Metal Mining Districts of Nevada: Map 24.   Reno: Univ. of Nev., 1964.

NEVADA DIVISION OF WATER RESOURCES.   Water for Nevada—Hydrologic Atlas. A series of 22 maps consisting of 13 statewide maps showing precipitation, storage, flow, etc., and 9 maps of lakes and reservoirs.   Carson City: State Engineer's Office, June 1972.

RIDD, MERRILL K.   Landform Map of Utah: Map Supplement No. 3. *Annals of Assn. of Amer. Geographers*, Vol. 53, no. 4, Dec. 1963.

SNYDER, C. T., GEORGE HARDMAN, and F. F. ZDENEK.   Pleistocene Lakes in the Great Basin, *U.S.G.S. Map* I-416.   Wash., D.C: 1964.

WHITEBREAD, D. H., A. B. GRIGGS, W. B. ROGERS, and J. W. MYTTON.   Preliminary Geologic Map and Sections of the Wheeler Peak Quadrangle, White Pine County, Nevada. *U.S.G.S. Map* MF-244.   Wash., D.C: 1962.

GUIDEBOOKS, AND WORKS OF HISTORICAL AND SPECIAL INTEREST

ABELOE, WILLIAM N.   *Historic Spots in California.*   3rd edn., Stanford Univ. Press, 1966.

ARRINGTON, LEONARD J.   *Great Basin Kingdom: An Economic History of the Latter-Day Saints, 1830–1900.* Harvard Univ. Press, 1958; Bison Books edn., Univ. of Nebr. Press, 1966.

ASHBAUGH, DON.   *Nevada's Turbulent Yesterday . . . a Study in Ghost Towns.* Los Angeles: Westernlore Press, 1963.

AUSTIN, MARY H.   *Land of Little Rain* (1903); reprint, N.Y: Ballantine Books, 1971.

BANCROFT, H. H. *History of Utah.* San Francisco: History Co., 1889.

BANDI, HANS-GEORG. *Prehistory and History in Alaska.* Berne: Kümmerly & Frey (in U.S., Rand McNally), 1970.

BEAL, MERRILL. *Intermountain Railroads.* Caldwell, Id: Caxton, 1962.

BILLINGS, W. D. *Nevada Trees.* 2nd edn., Reno: Univ. of Nev. Agric. Exten. Svc., 1954.

BONNER, T. D. (ed.). *Life and Adventures of James P. Beckwourth.* N.Y: Harper, 1856; edn. with notes by Bernard DeVoto, N.Y: Knopf, 1931.

BONNEY, ORIN H. and LORRAINE. *Guide to the Wyoming Mountains.* Denver: Sage, 1960.

BROOKS, JUANITA. *John Doyle Lee: Zealot, Pioneer Builder, Scapegoat.* Glendale, Ca: Clark Co., 1961.

———. *The Mountain Meadows Massacre.* Norman: Univ. of Okla. Press, 1962.

BRUFF, J. GOLDSBOROUGH. *Gold Rush: Journals, Drawings, and other Papers,* ed. by Georgia W. Read and Ruth Gaines. N.Y: Columbia Univ. Press, 1949.

CAMP, CHARLES L. *Earth Song—A Prologue to History.* Palo Alto: Amer. West Publg. Co., 1970.

CHURCH, JAMES E., JR. "Snow and Life," in *Explorer's Journal,* Dec. 1960.

CLEMENTS, THOMAS. *Geological Story of Death Valley.* Death Valley '49ers, 1958.

CLINE , GLORIA GRIFFEN. *Exploring the Great Basin.* Norman: Univ. of Okla. Press, 1963.

COLLINGWOOD, G. H., and W. D. BRUSH. *Knowing Your Trees.* Rev. & enlarged by Devereux Butcher. Wash., D.C: Amer. For. Assn., 1972/ 1947.

CRAGEN, DOROTHY. (in Schumacher, *Deepest Valley,* 1962).

DALE, HARRISON C. *The Ashley-Smith Explorations and the Discovery of a Central Route to the Pacific, 1822–1829.* Revised edn., Glendale, Ca: Clark Co., 1941.

DEDECKER, MARY. (in Schumacher, *Deepest Valley,* 1962).

DEVOTO, BERNARD. *Mark Twain's America.* Boston: Little, Brown, 1932.

———. *The Year of Decision.* Boston: Little, Brown, 1943.

———. *Across the Wide Missouri.* Boston: Houghton Mifflin, 1947.

———. *The Course of Empire.* Boston: Houghton Mifflin, 1952.

ELLIOTT, RUSSELL R. *Nevada's Twentiety-Century Mining Boom.* Reno: Univ. of Nev. Press, 1966.

———. *History of Nevada.* Lincoln: Univ. of Nebr. Press, 1973.

ELLSWORTH, S. GEORGE. *Utah's Heritage.* Santa Barbara: Peregrine Smith, 1972.

FARQUHAR, FRANCIS P. *History of the Sierra Nevada.* Berkeley: Univ. of Calif. Press, with Sierra Club, 1966.

FENNEMAN, NEVIN M. *Physiography of the Western United States.* N.Y: McGraw-Hill, 1931.

FENTON, C. L. and M. A. *The Fossil Book.* N.Y: Doubleday, 1958.

FISHER, JAMES, and H.R.H. PRINCE PHILIP. *Wildlife Crisis*. N.Y: Cowles, 1970.

FORBES, JACK D. *Nevada Indians Speak*. Reno: Univ. of Nev. Press, 1967.

FRÉMONT, JOHN CHARLES. *Report of the Exploring Expedition to the Rocky Mountains, 1842, and to Oregon and North California, 1843–44*. Wash., D.C: Gales & Seaton, 1845.

——. *Narrative of Exploration and Adventure*, ed. by Allan Nevins. N.Y: Longmans, Green, 1956.

FRYXELL, FRITIOF (ed.). *François Matthes and the Marks of Time*. San Francisco: Sierra Club, 1962.

GIANELLA, VINCENT P. "Where Frémont Crossed the Sierra Nevada in 1844," in *Sierra Club Bulletin*, Oct. 1959.

GOETZMANN, WILLIAM H. *Army Exploration in the American West, 1803–1863*. Yale Univ. Press, 1959.

——. *Exploration and Empire*, N.Y: Knopf, 1966.

GOLDSWORTHY, MYRON. "Pershing County Water Conservation District Report," in *Nevada State Journal*, Dec. 24, 1969.

HAFEN, LeRoy R. and ANN W. *The Old Spanish Trail*. Glendale, Ca: Clark Co., 1954.

HANSEN, ALBERT A. *Dodder* (U.S.D.A. *Farmers' Bulletin* 1161). Wash., D.C: 1923.

HAZELTINE, BEN, CHARLES SAULISBERRY, and HARRY TAYLOR. *A Range History of Nevada*. Typed monograph reproduced by the authors, 1960.

HEALD, WELDON F. (in Peattie, *The Sierra Nevada*, 1947).

HELFRICH, DEVERE. *The Applegate Trail*. Klamath Falls, Or: Klamath County Hist. Soc., 1971.

HICKSON, JANE GREEN. *Dat So La Lee, Queen of the Washo Basketmakers*. Carson City: Nev. State Mus., 1967.

HOCK, RAYMOND. (in Schumacher, *Deepest Valley*, 1962).

HOLDREN, JOHN, and PHILIP HERRERA. *Energy: A Crisis in Power*. San Francisco: Sierra Club, 1971.

HOSMER, HELEN. (in T. H. Watkins et al., *The Grand Colorado*. Palo Alto: Amer. West Publg. Co., 1969).

HUDSON, W. H. *The Famous Missions of California*. N.Y: Dodge, 1901.

HULSE, JAMES W. *The Nevada Adventure: A History*. Reno: Univ. of Nev. Press, 1965.

HUNT, CYNTHIA A., and ROBERT M. GARRELS. *Water: The Web of Life*. N.Y: Norton, 1972.

IRVING, WASHINGTON. *Adventures of Captain Bonneville, U.S.A., in the Rocky Mountains and the Far West*. N.Y: Putnam, 1868.

JACKSON, BENJAMIN D. *A Glossary of Botanic Terms, with their Derivation and Accent*. Phila: Lippincott, 1928.

JACKSON, DONALD, and MARY LEE SPENCE (eds.). *The Expeditions of John Charles Frémont*. Urbana: Univ. of Ill. Press, 1970.

JAMES, G. W. *Lake Tahoe, the Lake of the Sky*. Chicago: Powner, 1956.

JOHNSTON, VERNA R. *Sierra Nevada* (Vol. 2 of *The Naturalist's America*). Boston: Houghton, Mifflin, 1970.

KERSTEN, E. W., JR. "The Early Settlement of Aurora, Nevada, and Nearby Mining Camps, in *Annals of Assn. of Amer. Geographers*, Vol. 54, no. 4, Dec. 1964.

KIRK, RUTH. *Exploring Death Valley*. Stanford Univ. Press, 1965.

KRUTCH, JOSEPH WOOD. *The Voice of the Desert*. N.Y: Sloane, 1954.

Lake Tahoe: Report of the Joint Study Commission, Richard Graves, Chrmn. 1967.

LARSON, GUSTIVE O. *Outline History of Utah and the Mormons*. Salt Lake City: Deseret Book Co., 1965.

LEADABRAND, RUSS. *A Guide to the Mojave Desert of California*. Los Angeles: Ward Ritchie Press, 1966.

LECONTE, JOSEPH. *Journal of Ramblings through the High Sierra of California* (1875); reprints: Sierra Club, 1960; Ballantine Books, 1971.

LEONARD, ZENAS. *Narrative*, ed. by W. F. Wagner. Cleveland: Burrows Bros., 1904.

LILLARD, RICHARD G. *Desert Challenge: An Interpretation of Nevada*. N.Y: Knopf, 1942.

MACK, EFFIE M., and B. W. SAWYER. *Here is Nevada: A History of the State*. Sparks, Nev: Western Pntg. & Publg. Co., 1965.

MATTHES, F. E. (in Peattie, *The Sierra Nevada*, 1947).

MILLER, DAVID E. "Great Salt Lake: An Historical Sketch," in *Guidebook to the Geology of Utah*, No. 20. Salt Lake City: Utah Geol. Soc., 1966.

MORGAN, DALE L. *The Humboldt: Highroad of the West*. N.Y: Farrar & Rinehart, 1943.

——. *The Great Salt Lake*. Indianapolis: Bobbs-Merrill, 1947; reprint Albuquerque: Univ. of New Mex. Press, 1973.

——. *Jedediah Smith and the Opening of the West*. Bobbs-Merrill, 1953.

MURRAY, KEITH A. *The Modocs and their War*. Norman: Univ. of Okla. Press, 1959.

MYRICK, DAVID F. *Railroads of Nevada and Eastern California*. 2 vols., Berkeley: Howell-North Books, 1962–1963.

NATIONAL PARKS SERVICE, REGION 3. *Great Salt Lake—A Preliminary Survey of the Park and Recreational Potential*. Wash., D.C: U.S. Dept. Inter., 1960.

Nevada, A Guide to the Silver State. Amer. Guide Ser. Portland: Binfords & Mort, 1940.

NEVADA BUREAU OF MINES. *The Story of Nevada Mining*. Pamphlet, 1969.

NEVADA FISH AND GAME COMMISSION. "Range and Habitat History," in *Nevada Wildlife, Centennial Issue*, Jan. 1965.

NEVINS, ALLAN. *Frémont, the West's Greatest Adventurer*. N.Y: Harper, 1928.

——. *Frémont, Pathmarker of the West*. N.Y: Longmans, Green, 1955.

OGDEN, PETER SKENE. *Snake Country Journals 1824–25 and 1825–26*, ed. by E. E. Rich and A. M. Johnson, intro. by Burt B. Barker. London: Hudson's Bay Record Soc., Pubns., Vol. 13, 1950; *Same for 1826–27*, ed. by K. G. Davies and Johnson. H.B.R.S., Pubns., Vol. 23, 1961; *Same for 1827–29;* H.B.R.S., Pubns., Vol. 28, 1971.

PAHER, STANLEY W. *Nevada Ghost Towns and Mining Camps.* Berkeley: Howell-North Books, 1970.

PEATTIE, DONALD CULROSS. *A Natural History of Western Trees.* Boston: Houghton Mifflin, 1953.

PEATTIE, RODERICK (ed.). *The Sierra Nevada.* N.Y: Vanguard Press, 1947.

PEIRSON, ERMA. *The Mojave River and its Valley.* Glendale, Ca: Clark Co., 1970.

PETERSON, ROGER TORY, and JAMES FISHER. *Wild America.* Boston: Houghton Mifflin, 1955.

POURADE, RICHARD F. *Anza Conquers the Desert . . . Expeditions from Mexico to California . . . 1774–76.* San Diego: Copley Press, 1971.

PREUSS, CHARLES. *Exploring with Frémont: The Private Diaries of Preuss,* trans. and ed. by Erwin G. and Elizabeth K. Gudde. Norman: Univ. of Okla. Press, 1958.

ROYLANCE, WARD J. *Utah, the Incredible Land: A Guide to the Beehive State.* Salt Lake City: Utah Trails Co., 1965.

SCHUMACHER, GENNY (ed.). *Deepest Valley.* San Francisco: Sierra Club, 1962.

——. *The Mammoth Lakes Sierra.* San Francisco: Sierra Club, 1959.

SCOTT, E. B. *The Saga of Lake Tahoe.* Crystal Bay, Nev: Sierra-Tahoe Publg. Co., 1964.

SCRUGHAM, JAMES G. *Nevada: A Narrative of the Conquest of a Frontier Land.* 3 vols., Chicago & N.Y: Amer. Hist. Soc., 1935.

SMITH, JEDEDIAH S. *The Travels of,* ed. by Maurice S. Sullivan. Santa Ana, Ca: Fine Arts Press, 1934.

STEGNER, WALLACE. *Mormon Country.* N.Y: Duell, Sloan & Pearce, 1942.

——. *The Sound of Mountain Water.* N.Y: Doubleday, 1969.

STEWART, GEORGE R. *The California Trail.* N.Y: McGraw-Hill, 1962.

——. *Names on the Land.* N.Y: Random House, 1945.

——. *Ordeal by Hunger.* Boston: Houghton Mifflin, 1960.

——. *Sheep Rock.* 1951; reprint N.Y: Ballantine Books, 1971.

——. *U. S. 40.* Boston: Houghton Mifflin, 1953.

STOKES, WILLIAM (ed.). *Guidebook to the Geology of Utah: No. 20, The Great Salt Lake.* Salt Lake City: Utah Geol. Soc., 1966.

STONE, IRVING. *Men to Match My Mountains: The Opening of the Far West, 1840–1900.* N.Y: Doubleday, 1956.

STRONG, EMORY. *Stone Age in the Great Basin.* Portland, Or: Binfords & Mort, 1969.

SULLIVAN, MAURICE S. *Jedediah Smith, Trader and Trail Breaker.* N.Y: Press of the Pioneers, 1936.

SUNSET MAGAZINE EDITORS. *Sunset Travel Guide to Nevada.* Menlo Park: Lane, 1971.

——. *Sunset Travel Guide to Utah.* Menlo Park: Lane, 1971.

THOMPSON & WEST (pubrs.). *History of Nevada,* ed. by Myron Angel. 1881; reproduced Berkeley: Howell-North, 1958.

Tuohy, Donald R.   *Nevada's Prehistoric Heritage.* Carson City: Nev. State Mus., 1965.

Vallentine, H. R.   *Water in the Service of Man.* Baltimore: Penguin Books, 1967.

Vanderberg, W. O.   "Placer Mining in Nevada," *Univ. of Nevada Bulletin,* Vol. XXX, no. 4, May 1964.

Wheat, Margaret M.   *Survival Arts of the Primitive Paiutes.* Reno: Univ. of Nev. Press, 1967.

Wheeler, Sessions S.   *The Desert Lake.* Caldwell, Id: Caxton, 1967.

——.   *The Nevada Desert.* Caldwell, Id: Caxton, 1971.

Whipple, Maurine.   *This is the Place: Utah.* N.Y: Knopf, 1945.

Wood, Harry O., M. W. Allen, and N. Y. Heck.   *Earthquake History of the United States: Part II, California and Western Nevada.* Pamphlet, U.S. Coast & Geodetic Survey, Serial no. 609. Wash., D.C: 1939.

PROFESSIONAL PAPERS

Aikens, C. Melvin, 1966.   "Fremont-Promontory-Plains Relationships," *Univ. of Utah Anthropological Papers,* No. 82.

——, 1967.   "Plains Relationships of the Fremont Culture: A Hypothesis," in *American Antiquity* (Wash., D.C.), Vol. 32, no. 2.

——, 1967.   "Excavations at Snake Rock Village and Bear River No. 2 Site," *Univ. of Utah Anthropological Papers,* No. 87.

——, 1970.   "Hogup Cave," *Univ. of Utah Anthropological Papers,* No. 93.

——, Kimball T. Harper, and Gary F. Fry, 1968.   *Hogup Mountain Cave: Interim Report.* Presented at annual meeting, Soc. for Amer. Archaeol., Santa Fe.

Antevs, Ernst, 1948.   "Climatic Changes and Pre-White Man," in "The Great Basin, with Emphasis on Glacial and Postglacial Times," *Bulletin of Univ. of Utah,* Vol. 38, no. 20, *Biological Ser.,* Vol. 10, no. 7, pp. 168–191.

——, 1955.   "Geologic-Climatic Dating in the West," in *American Antiquity* (Wash., D.C.), Vol. 20, no. 4, pp. 317–335.

Aschmann, Homer H., 1958.   "Great Basin Climates in Relation to Human Occupance," in "Current Views on Great Basin Archaeology," *Reports of Univ. of Calif. Archaeological Survey,* No. 42, pp. 23–40.

Bailey, G. E., 1902.   "The Saline Deposits of California," *Calif. State Mining Bureau Bulletin,* 24.

Bedwell, Stephen F., 1973.   "Fort Rock Basin—Prehistory and Environment." Eugene: Univ. of Oreg. Books.

Blackwelder, Eliot, 1948.   "The Geological Background," in "The Great Basin: With Emphasis on Glacial and Postglacial Times," *Univ. of Utah Bulletin,* Vol. 38, no. 20.

Blackwelder, Eliot, and E. W. Ellsworth, 1936.   "Pleistocene Lakes of the Afton Basin, California," in *Amer. Jour. of Science,* Vol. 31, no. 186.

BRYAN, ALAN L., 1972. "Summary of the Archaeology of Smith Creek and Council Hall Caves, White Pine County, Nevada," in *Nev. Archaeol. Survey Reporter* (Reno: Univ. of Nev.), Vol. 6, no. 1.

BUDGE, SETH ELLIOTT, 1950. "The Geography of Bear Lake Valley," Master's Thesis, Univ. of Utah.

CASJENS, LAUREL, 1973. "The Prehistoric Cultural Ecology of Southern Ruby Valley (Preliminary Report of Field Work, 1972)," in *Nev. Archaeol. Survey Reporter* (Reno: Univ. of Nev.), Vol. 7, no. 1.

COHENOUR, R. E. and K. C. THOMPSON, 1966. "Geologic Setting of Great Salt Lake," in *Guidebook to the Geology of Utah*, No. 20. Salt Lake City: Utah Geol. Soc.

CRESSMAN, LUTHER S., 1942. "Archaeological Researches in the Northern Great Basin," *Carnegie Institution of Washington, Publication* 538.

——, 1956. "Additional Radiocarbon Dates, Lovelock Cave, Nevada," in *American Antiquity*, Vol. 21, no. 3.

——, 1966. "Comments on Prehistory," in *The Current Status of Anthropological Research in the Great Basin: 1964*. Reno: Desert Res. Inst.

CRITTENDEN, M. D., JR., 1961. "Isostatic Deformation of Lake Bonneville Shorelines," prepr., Friends of the Pleistocene, 7th Annual Field Trip.

——, 1963. "New Data on the Isostatic Deformation of Lake Bonneville," *U.S.G.S. Professional Paper* 454-E. Wash., D.C.

——, 1967. "Viscosity and Finite Strength of the Mantle as Determined from Water and Ice Loads," *Geophys. J.R. Soc.* 14, pp. 261–279.

DAVIS, WILBUR A., 1966. "Theoretical Problems in Western Prehistory," in *The Current Status of Anthropological Research in the Great Basin: 1964*. Reno: Desert Research Institute.

EARDLEY, A. J., 1938. "Sediments of Great Salt Lake, Utah," *Bulletin of Amer. Assn. of Petrol. Geol.*, 22, pp. 1305–1411.

——, V. GVOSDETSKY, and R. E. MARSELL, 1957. "Hydrology of Lake Bonneville and Sediments and Soils of its Basin," in *Geol. Soc. of Amer. Bulletin*, Vol. 68, pp. 1141–1201.

EKHOLM, GORDON F., 1964. "Transpacific Contacts," in *Prehistoric Man in the New World*, ed. by Jesse D. Jennings and Edward Norbeck. Univ. of Chicago Press.

ELSASSER, ALBERT B., and ROBERT F. HEIZER, 1966. "Excavations of Two Northwestern California Coastal Sites," *Reports of Univ. of Calif. Archaeol. Survey*, No. 67.

FAGAN, JOHN LEE, 1974. "Altithermal Occupation of Spring Sites in the Northern Great Basin." Eugene: *Univ. of Oreg. Anthropological Papers*, no. 6.

FASSIG, OLIVER L., 1932. "Climatic Data to 1930, Nevada," in *A Climatic Study of the United States, Section 19*. Wash., D.C: G.P.O.

FAUL, HENRY, and G. A. WAGNER, 1971. "Fission Track Dating," in H. N. Michael and E. K. Ralph (eds.), *Dating Techniques for the Archaeologist*. Mass. Inst. of Tech. Press.

FOWLER, D. D., 1968. *Archaeological Survey in Eastern Nevada, 1966*. Reno: Desert Research Institute.

FOWLER, D. D., 1968. *The Archaeology of Newark Cave, White Pine County, Nevada.* Reno: Desert Research Institute.

——, 1973. "Dated Split-twig Figurine from Etna Cave, Nevada," in *Plateau,* Vol. 46, no. 2, pp. 54–63.

——, DAVID B. MADSEN, and EUGENE M. HATTORI, 1973. *Prehistory of Southeastern Nevada.* Desert Research Institute, *Pubns. in Social Sciences, No. 7.*

GALE, H. S., 1915. "Salines in the Owens, Searles and Panamint Basins, Southeastern California," *U.S.G.S. Bulletin* 580. Wash., D.C.

GILBERT, GROVE KARL, 1890. *Lake Bonneville.* U.S.G.S. *Monograph No. 1.*

GVOSDETSKY, V., and H. B. HAWKES, 1953. "Reappraisal of the History of Lake Bonneville," *Univ. of Utah Bulletin,* Vol. 43, no. 5.

HARDMAN, GEORGE, 1960. "Humboldt River Research Project," Paper presented at 14th Annual Nevada Water Conference, Carson City.

——, and CRUZ VENSTROM, 1941. "A One-Hundred-Year Record of Truckee River Runoff, Estimated from Changes in Levels and Volumes of Pyramid and Winnemucca Lakes," in *Amer. Geophysical Union, Trans.*

HARRINGTON, MARK R., 1957. "A Pinto Site at Little Lake, California," *Southwest Museum Papers,* No. 17. Los Angeles.

——, 1933. "Gypsum Cave, Nevada," *Southwest Museum Papers,* No. 8. Los Angeles.

HARRINGTON, MARK R., and RUTH D. SIMPSON, 1961. "Tule Springs, Nevada, with Other Evidences of Pleistocene Man in North America," *Southwest Museum Papers,* No. 18. Los Angeles.

HEIZER, ROBERT F., 1964. "The Western Coast of North America," in Jesse D. Jennings and Edward Norbeck (eds.), *Prehistoric Man in the New World,* pp. 117–148. Chicago: Univ. of Chicago Press.

——, and MARTIN A. BAUMHOFF, 1962. *Prehistoric Rock Art of Nevada and Eastern California.* Berkeley: Univ. of Calif. Press.

——, BAUMHOFF, and C. W. CLEWLOW, JR., 1968. "Archaeology of South Fork Shelter (NV-EL-11), Elko County, Nevada," in *Reports of Univ. of Calif. Archaeological Survey,* No. 71, pp. 1–58.

——, and ALEX. D. KRIEGER, 1956. "The Archaeology of Humboldt Cave, Churchill County, Nevada," *Univ. of Calif. Pubns. in Amer. Archaeol. and Ethnol.,* Vol. 47, no. 1, pp. 1–190.

HUBBS, CARL L., 1957. "Recent Climatic History in California and Adjacent Areas," in *Proceedings, Conference on Recent Research in Climatology at Scripps Institution of Oceanography, Mar. 25–27, 1957.* La Jolla, Calif.

——, 1959. "Recent Climatic History in California," in *Minutes of Semiannual Convention, Irrigation Districts Assn. of Calif.,* Santa Barbara, Dec. 10–12, 1958.

——, and ROBERT R. MILLER, 1948. "The Zoological Evidence," in "The

Great Basin: With Emphasis on Glacial and Postglacial Times," *Univ. of Utah Bulletin,* Vol. 38, no. 20.

——, MILLER, and LAURA C. HUBBS, 1974. "Hydrographic History and Relict Fishes of the North-Central Great Basin," *Memoirs of Calif. Acad. of Sciences,* Vol. VII. San Francisco: Feb. 8, 1974.

HUNT, CHARLES B., 1967. *Physiography of the United States.* San Francisco: W. H. Freeman & Co.

JACOBSEN, WILLIAM H., JR., 1966. "Washo Linguistic Studies," in *The Current Status of Anthropological Research in the Great Basin: 1964.* Reno: Desert Research Institute.

JENNINGS, JESSE D., 1957. "Danger Cave," *Univ. of Utah Anthropological Papers,* No. 27. (Also published in *American Antiquity,* Vol. 23, no. 2, pt. 2; and *Memoirs of Soc. for Amer. Archaeol.,* No. 14.)

——, 1964. "The Desert West," in Jennings et al., *Prehistoric Man in the New World,* pp. 149–174 (see below).

——, 1968. *Prehistory of North America.* Second edn., N.Y.: McGraw-Hill, 1974.

——, and EDWARD NORBECK (eds.), 1964. *Prehistoric Man in the New World.* Chicago: Univ. of Chicago Press *(Rice Univ. Semicentennial Pubns.).*

KING, CLARENCE, 1870. "Geological Exploration of the 40th Parallel," *U.S. Army Engineers Professional Papers,* No. 18. Wash., D.C: G.P.O.

—— (ed.)., 1877–80. *Report of the Geological Exploration of the 40th Parallel.* 7 vols., Wash., D.C: G.P.O.

KRIEGER, ALEX D., 1964. "Early Man in the New World," in Jennings et al., *Prehistoric Man in the New World,* pp. 23–81 (see above).

LARIVERS, IRA, 1962. *Fish and Fisheries of Nevada.* Carson City: Nev. State Fish and Game Commis.

LAYCOCK, ARLEIGH, 1970. "Canadian Water for Nevada?" in *Proceed. of 24th Annual Nevada Water Conference.* Carson City: Div. of Water Resources.

LINDGREN, WALDEMAR, 1898. "Description of the Truckee Quadrangle (California)," *U.S.G.S. Folios of Geologic Atlas,* No. 39. Wash., D.C.

MALDE, H. E., 1960. "Evidence in the Snake River Plain, Idaho, of a Catastrophic Flood from Pleistocene Lake Bonneville," *U.S.G.S. Professional Paper* 400-B. Wash., D.C.

——, and D. E. TRIMBLE, 1965. "Malad Springs to Pocatello," *Internat. Assn. for Quaternary Research (INQUA) 7th Congress (1965) Guidebook,* Field Conference E.

MALOUF, CARLING, 1966. "Ethnohistory in the Great Basin," in *The Current Status of Anthropological Research in the Great Basin: 1964.* Reno: Desert Research Institute.

MANSFIELD, GEORGE R., 1927. "Geography, Geology and Mineral Resources of Part of Southeastern Idaho," *U.S.G.S. Professional Paper* 152. Wash., D.C.

MARTIN, R. J., and E. CORBIN (eds.), 1936. *Climatic Summary of the U.S., Section 20, Western Utah.* Wash., D.C: U.S. Weather Bureau.

MAYO, E. B., 1934. "The Pleistocene Long Valley Lake in Eastern California," in *Science* (Wash., D.C.), Vol. 80, no. 2065, pp. 95–96.

MEHRINGER, PETER J., JR., 1967. "Pleistocene Studies in Southern Nevada," *Nevada State Museum Anthropological Paper,* No. 13. Carson City.

MICHAEL, H. N., and E. K. RALPH (eds.), 1971. *Dating Techniques for the Archaeologist.* Cambridge, Mass: Mass. Inst. of Tech. Press.

MIFFLIN, MARTIN D., 1968. *Delineation of Ground-Water Flow Systems in Nevada.* Reno: Desert Research Institute.

MORRISON, ROGER B., 1952. "Late Quaternary Climatic History of the Northern Great Basin," in *Geological Soc. of Amer. Bulletin,* Vol. 63, p. 1367 (May 8). New York.

——, 1963. "Geology of the Southern Carson Desert, Nevada," *U.S.G.S. Professional Paper* 401. Wash., D.C.

——, 1964. "Soil Stratigraphy: Principles, Applications to Differentiation and Correlation of Quaternary Deposits and Landforms, and Applications to Soil Science." Ph.D. dissertation No. 186, Univ. of Nevada, Reno.

——, 1966. "Predecessors of Great Salt Lake," in W. L. Stokes (ed.), *Guidebook to the Geology of Utah,* No. 20. Salt Lake City: Utah Geol. Soc.

——, 1968. "Means of Time-Stratigraphic Division and Long-Distance Correlation of Quaternary Successions," (in Morrison and Wright, 1968, see below).

——, and J. C. FRYE, 1965. "Correlation of the Middle and Late Quaternary Successions of the Lake Lahontan, Lake Bonneville, Rocky Mountain (Wasatch Range), Southern Great Plains, and Eastern Midwest Areas," *Nevada Bureau of Mines Report* 9. Reno: Univ. of Nev.

——, and HERBERT E. WRIGHT, JR. (eds.), 1968. "Means of Correlation of Quaternary Successions," in *Proceed., 7th Congress of Internat. Assn. for Quaternary Research (INQUA 1965).* Salt Lake City: Univ. of Utah Press.

NEVADA DIVISION OF WATER RESOURCES, 1971. *Water for Nevada, Planning Report,* in 3 parts: No. 1, *Guidelines for Nevada Water Planning;* No. 2, *Estimated Water Use in Nevada;* No. 3, *Nevada's Water Resources.* Carson City.

——, 1973a. *A Brief Water Resources Appraisal of the Truckee River Basin, Western Nevada,* by A. S. Van Denburgh, R. D. Lamke, and J. L. Hughes, *Report 57,* prepared cooperatively by the U.S.G.S. Carson City.

——, 1973b. "The Future Role of Desalting Nevada."

——, 1973c. "Water-related Recreation in Nevada—Present and Future." *Report,* 7.

OHRENSCHALL, JOHN C., 1969. "Legal Aspects of the Nevada Water

Plan—A Case Study of Law in Action," reprinted from *Natural Resources Lawyer*, Vol. 11, no. 3, July 1969.

ORR, PHIL C., 1952. "Preliminary Excavations of Pershing County Caves," *Nev. State Mus., Dept. of Archeol. Bulletin*, No. 1. Carson City.

——, 1956. "Pleistocene Man in Fishbone Cave, Pershing County, Nevada," *Nev. State Mus., Dept. of Archeol. Bulletin*, No. 2. Carson City.

PECK, E. L. and E. A. RICHARDSON, 1966. "Hydrology and Climatology of Great Salt Lake," in W. L. Stokes (ed.), *Guidebook to the Geology of Utah*, No. 20. Salt Lake City: Utah Geol. Soc.

RENFREW, COLIN, 1971. "Carbon 14 and the Prehistory of Europe," in *Scientific American*, Oct. 1971.

RINEHART, C. D., and N. K. HUBER, 1965. "The Inyo Crater Lakes," in *Mineral Information Service*, Vol. 18, no. 9 (Sept.), Calif. Div. of Mines and Geol. San Francisco.

ROZAIRE, CHARLES E., 1969. "Chronology of the Woven Materials from the Caves at Falcon Hill, Nevada," in *Anthropological Papers*, No. 14, Nev. State Mus., Carson City.

RUSCO, MARY, 1973. "Types of Anthropomorphic Figures in Great Basin Art," *Nev. Archaeol. Survey Reporter* (Reno: Univ. of Nev.), Vol. 7, no. 12.

RUSSELL, I. C., 1881–82. "Sketch of the Geological History of Lake Lahontan," in *U.S.G.S., 3rd Ann. Rept.* Wash., D.C.

——, 1884. "A Geological Reconnaissance of Southern Oregon," in *U.S.G.S. 4th Ann. Rept.* Wash., D.C.

——, 1885. *The Geological History of Lake Lahontan, a Quarternary Lake of Northwestern Nevada*. Wash., D.C: *U.S.G.S. Monograph 11*.

——, 1886-7. "Quaternary History of Mono Valley, California," in *USGS 8th Ann. Rept.* Wash., D.C.

RUSSELL, R. J., 1927. "The Landforms of Surprise Valley, Northwestern Great Basin," in *Univ. of Calif. Pubns. in Geology*, Vol. 2, pp. 231–254.

SCHAAFSMA, POLLY, 1971. "The Rock Art of Utah," *Papers of Peabody Mus. of Archaeol. and Ethnol.*, Vol. 65. Cambridge: Harvard Univ.

SHAMBERGER, HUGH A., 1972. "The Story of the Water Supply for the Comstock," *U.S.G.S. Professional Paper* 779; prepared in cooperation with Nev. State Dept. of Conservation and Natural Resources. Wash., D.C.

SIMPSON, JAMES H., 1876. *Report of Explorations across the Great Basin of the Territory of Utah for a Direct Wagon-Route from Camp Floyd to Genoa in Carson Valley, in 1859.* Wash., D.C: G.P.O.

SMITH, ALFRED MERRITT, 1940. *Common Methods of Measuring Water as Practiced in Western States.* Carson City: Nev. State Engineer's Office.

SMITH, GERALD A., 1957. *Newberry Cave, California.* Santa Barbara County Museum, *Scientific Ser.*, No. 1.

SNYDER, C. T., 1962. "A Hydrologic Classification of Valleys in the Great Basin . . . ," *Internat. Assn. of Scientific Hydrology, 7th Year,* Pubn. No. 3.

——, and W. B. LANGBEIN, 1962. "The Pleistocene Lake in Spring Valley, Nevada, and its Climatic Implications," in *Jour. of Geophys. Research,* Vol. 67, no. 6, pp. 2385-95 (June).

STANSBURY, HOWARD, 1852. *Exploration and Survey of the Valley of the Great Salt Lake of Utah.* Phila: Lippincott, Grambo.

STEWARD, JULIAN H., 1937. "Ancient Caves of the Great Salt Lake Region," *Bur. of Amer. Ethnol. Bulletin,* No. 116. Wash., D.C.

STEWART, OMER C., 1966. "Tribal Distributions and Boundaries," in *The Current Status of Anthropological Research in the Great Basin: 1964.* Reno: Desert Research Institute.

THOMAS, H. E., 1964. "Mineral and Water Resources of Nevada," in *U.S.G.S. Report.* Wash., D.C.

THOMPSON, D. G., 1929. "The Mojave Desert Region, California, a Geographic, Geologic and Hydrologic Reconnaissance," *U.S.G.S. Water-Supply Paper,* 578.

TUOHY, DONALD R., 1969. "The Test Excavations of Hanging Rock Cave, Churchill County, Nevada," in *Anthropological Papers,* No. 14. Carson City: Nev. St. Mus.

WARING, GERALD A., 1965. "Thermal Springs of the United States and Other Countries of the World—A Summary," *U.S.G.S. Professional Paper* 492.

WARREN, CLAUDE N., 1967. "The San Dieguito Complex: A Review and Hypothesis," in *American Antiquity,* Vol. 32, no. 2, pp. 168-185.

——, and ANTHONY J. RANERE, 1968. "Outside Danger Cave: A View of Early Man in the Great Basin," in "Early Man in North America: Symposium of the Southwestern Anthropological Association, San Diego, 1968." *Portales: Eastern New Mexico Contributions in Anthropology,* Vol. 1, no. 4, pp. 6-18.

——, and D. L. TRUE, 1961. "The San Dieguito Complex and its Place in California Prehistory," in *Archaeological Survey Report, 1960-61,* pp. 246-337. Los Angeles: Dept. of Anthropol., Univ. of Calif.

WHEELER, GEORGE M., 1879. *Beyond the 100th Meridian.* Wash., D.C: G.P.O., U.S. Geographical Surveys West of the 100th Meridian.

WHEELER, S. M., 1973. *The Archaeology of Etna Cave, Lincoln County, Nevada.* Reno: Desert Research Institute, *Pubns. in Social Sciences,* No. 7.

——, and GEORGIA N., 1969. "Cave Burials near Fallon, Churchill County, Nevada," in *Anthropological Papers,* No. 14. Carson City: Nev. St. Mus.

WOODBURY, W. V., 1966. "The History and Present Status of the Biota of Anaho Island, Pyramid Lake, Nevada." Master's thesis, Univ. of Nev., Reno.

Index